Michael Janczyk, Dirk von Suchodoletz, Bernd Wiebelt
and Martin Frank (Ed.)

Proceedings of the 10th bwHPC Symposium

High-Performance and Data-Intensive Computing in Baden-Württemberg

Freiburg – September 2024

Proceedings of the 10th bwHPC Symposium

High-Performance and Data-Intensive Computing in Baden-Württemberg

Freiburg – September 2024

by
Michael Janczyk, Dirk von Suchodoletz, Bernd Wiebelt
and Martin Frank (Ed.)

KIT Scientific Publishing

Impressum

KIT Scientific Publishing

Karlsruher Institut für Technologie (KIT)
KIT Scientific Publishing
Straße am Forum 2
D-76131 Karlsruhe

KIT Scientific Publishing is a registered trademark
of Karlsruhe Institute of Technology.
Reprint using the book cover is not allowed.

www.bibliothek.kit.edu/ksp.php | E-Mail: info@ksp.kit.edu | Shop: www.ksp.kit.edu

Print on Demand 2026 – Gedruckt auf FSC-zertifiziertem Papier

ISBN 978-3-7315-1401-5
DOI 10.5445/KSP/1000169488

Preface

The *bwHPC Symposium*, one of the central events for High Performance Computing (HPC) in the German federal state of Baden-Württemberg, celebrated its tenth edition in September 2024. Over the years, it has grown into a widely recognized exchange platform that brings together researchers from diverse disciplines with operators of large-scale federated research infrastructures. This event bridges the gap between discipline-specific conferences and infrastructure-focused workshops, serving as an interface for dialogue on strategic and societally relevant topics such as energy and resource efficiency.

The development of an open IT ecosystem for both research and infrastructure operations benefits enormously from in-person meetings, where new ideas and best practices can be shared. The symposium offered a rich mix of formats for engagement: panel discussions, scientific presentations, poster sessions, and lightning talks provided opportunities to present new concepts and to foster collaboration. Social and ceremonial events – including an evening lecture and the inauguration of the new NEMO2 cluster – created space for networking and informal exchange. Tutorials and courses, particularly geared towards early-career researchers, rounded off the program.

A central mission of the symposium series has been to support a cultural shift in academia; one that gives appropriate recognition to methods, optimization strategies, and software development as core elements of scientific careers. The present proceedings affirm this mission by compiling peer-reviewed contributions that reflect the breadth and depth of these developments.

Given the critical role of digital technologies in research, independent operation of HPC clusters, AI compute nodes, and cloud infrastructures at institutions across the state forms a cornerstone of the digital sovereignty and independence of science. The work presented here is underpinned by the long-term commitment of the Ministry of Science, Research and Arts Baden-Württemberg. This includes funding for system procurement and renewal, as well as support for the *bwHPC-S5* coordination projects. Moreover, the support structures developed – especially in the realm of research data management – are beginning to resonate within the NFDI. Operating the various infrastructures for scientific computing, artificial intelligence, and research data management requires substantial resources and expertise. To meet these diverse demands, cooperative approaches – such as those institutionalized in the *bwHPC* initiative, *bwCloud-OS*, and federated storage efforts – have proven successful.

Science, as a fundamental pillar of modern society, must not only strive for insight but increasingly justify its resource usage. Hence, this symposium placed special focus on **energy efficiency**. It is the responsibility of researchers, infrastructure operators, and funding bodies to seek new solutions and evolve the federated infrastructures in service of society as a whole. The state's concepts for High Performance Computing, Data Intensive Computing, and Cloud Computing[1] address a wide spectrum of scientific disciplines, each with unique algorithms, software stacks, and workflows. Optimization strategies for energy consumption must therefore remain open to diverse and multidisciplinary approaches.

The tenth bwHPC Symposium placed special emphasis on sustainability and resource-conscious computing. The program was expanded to introduce a new level of engagement between researchers, system operators, and domain-specific support experts. Key focus areas included:

- Optimization of job execution workflows, especially for complex tasks (e.g., data staging, intelligent job scheduling, minimizing idle node time, avoiding resource blocking)
- Scientific code optimization for performance and efficiency
- Porting scientific codes to modern CPUs, accelerators, and programming environments
- Energy-aware cluster operation strategies, such as idle shutdown or adaptation to variable energy pricing
- Enhanced user feedback, including increased transparency on energy consumption per computation step
- Formation of cross-disciplinary *tiger teams*, a proven support format, to advance energy efficiency goals

[1] This book contains an abridged version of the concept.

A long-term goal is to institutionalize sustainability and energy efficiency as recurring themes in future symposium programs.

The symposium built bridges between disciplines, methodologies, and the technical-operational underpinnings of digital research. HPC, cloud computing, AI hardware platforms, and research data storage together constitute the foundational infrastructure that enables scientific discovery. As research becomes increasingly reliant on digital workflows and scalable infrastructure, new challenges arise from the growing volumes of data processed and retained through high-performance and high-throughput computing. These demand significant long-term resource commitments, especially in terms of energy and storage.

The expanded thematic scope of this year's symposium, reflected in the conference program and this volume, includes a growing attention to cloud computing, workflows, data management, software strategies, and energy optimization. Foundational infrastructures like *bwHPC* and *bwCloud-OS*, together with research data storage, form the backbone of an ecosystem of services being developed within the National Research Data Infrastructure (NFDI). This holistic perspective considers not only the researchers and technical systems, but also the national strategies, with the developments in Baden-Württemberg potentially serving as a blueprint for similar efforts across Germany.

This volume of proceedings is structured into four thematic chapters: The first, *Scientific Computing and AI Applications*, features peer-reviewed contributions that connect research questions with computations performed on *bwHPC* systems and other federated infrastructures – spanning topics from climate modeling and biologically inspired learning to adversarial attacks and quantum computing benchmarks. The second, *HPC Operations and Resource Management*, addresses the operational side of large-scale computing, including resource accounting, scheduling strategies, and remote desktop access. The third chapter, *Green IT and Energy Efficiency*, reflects one of the central themes of this symposium, bringing together contributions on sustainability transparency, cooperative green IT strategies, and energy-efficient scientific computing. Finally, the fourth chapter, *Infrastructure and Data Management*, presents conceptual and project-based contributions on federated storage, automated provisioning, and the strategic framework for HPC and data-intensive computing in Baden-Württemberg.

The broader scope of this symposium and its stronger emphasis on sustainable computing have been fruitful. Energy and efficiency discussions permeated many talks, presentations, and panel discussions, echoing the growing need for code, workflow, and resource optimization in light of increasing AI demands. Moving forward, the task lies in the operationalization and dissemination of these best practices. Incentivization and stronger community integration are vital next steps. The symposium has already laid the foundation for these efforts in several areas.

The Editors

Freiburg, September 2024

Welcome Address from the Ministry of Science, Research and Arts Baden-Württemberg

Baden-Württemberg is renowned for its innovative strength. This was recently confirmed by a study of the German Economic Institute, which ranks our state third among the most innovative regions worldwide – directly behind Massachusetts and California.[1] A key driver of this top position is High Performance Computing (HPC). Without high-performance computers, it would not be possible to conduct complex scientific simulations or apply artificial intelligence (AI) efficiently. HPC enables solutions to pressing societal challenges in fields such as medicine and climate research.

Our state strategy for HPC is a prime example of long-term planning. As early as the 1980s, Baden-Württemberg installed its first HPC systems. With our 2008 strategy, we laid the foundation for the cooperative use of computing clusters. Since then, we have continuously expanded our digital research infrastructure.

In June 2024, the state government decided to extend the HPC strategy until 2032 in order to remain internationally competitive in supercomputing. In doing so, we will incorporate national and European strategies and make a significant contribution to the implementation of HPC and AI strategies at both the federal and EU levels. New focal points of our strategy include energy efficiency and research software. Across the state, infrastructures are evolving into energy-efficient hybrid platforms that support both compute-intensive simulations and AI applications.

In Baden-Württemberg, the scientific computing centers work in close cooperation to cover all performance levels of HPC. The High-Performance Computing Center Stuttgart

---

[1] Transatlantic Subnational Innovation Competitiveness Index 2.0, Viktor Lazar et al., 2023: https://www.iwkoeln.de/fileadmin/user_upload/Studien/Externe_Studien/2023/Transatlantic_Subnational_Innovation_Competitiveness_Index_2.0.pdf.

(HLRS), the National High Performance Computing Center at KIT, as well as universities and universities of applied sciences with their partners, ensure a statewide supply of computing power. This coordinated approach is a unique feature in Germany and secures the leading position of Baden-Württemberg as a location for research. Our state HPC strategy is a prime example of consistently developed and expanded excellence.

This success is based on precise and forward-looking strategic priorities as well as a strong culture of collaboration. Our excellent research infrastructure is not only a technological foundation, but also the result of the dedication and creativity of many bright minds in Baden-Württemberg. Together, we develop solutions to the major tasks and challenges of our time. Baden-Württemberg is a hub of innovation, home to inventors and pioneers, and we take pride in our innovative excellence.

Our achievements are the result of collective effort. I therefore extend my sincere thanks to all those who are committed to science and, through it, to the common good – for their support and valuable engagement.

Dr. Hans J. Reiter
Ministerial Director
Ministry of Science, Research and Arts Baden-Württemberg

Contents

I Scientific Computing and AI Applications

The role of orbital parameters on the simulated sea surface temperature of the Earth-like aquaplanet

Olga Erokhina[*], Kira Rehfeld[†]

[*]Institute of Environmental Physics, Heidelberg University, Heidelberg
[†]Tübingen University, Tübingen

Abstract

We evaluate a role of independent orbital parameters, namely, eccentricity, obliquity, and longitude of perihelion, on the simulated Earth-like aquaplanet sea surface temperature. We choose the parameters to be in the range that Earth underwent during last 150000 years and will undergo within next 150000 years. Our results reveal that the sea surface temperature variability within this time span does not increase 0.3 K and that the main parameter that defines the amount of incoming solar radiation that reaches the aquaplanet surface and causes its warming or cooling is the obliquity.

1 Introduction

Aquaplanet experiments (APE) simulate a planet that is different from our current Earth by the absence of orography and constant bathymetry, therefore, fully covered by water. This setup allows to unravel complex relationship between numbers of processes which define Earth climate. Initially APEs were used to study different atmospheric phenomena and lately were proposed as a tool to compare different Atmospheric General Circulation Models (AGCM) and possible sources of differences between them (Neale et al.,

2000). APEs are performed using different AGCMs typically of intermediate complexity in a configuration that often includes sea ice component. Some experiments were also performed with coupled Atmosphere-Ocean General Circulation models (AOGCMs).

Previous studies evaluated the role of different model parameters on the aquaplanet climate. Thus, the role of eccentricity, obliquity, insolation, CO_2 concentration, gravity, rotational rate, planet radius was studied (e.g., Chavas et al., 2019; Hertwig et al., 2015, 2016; Kilic et al., 2017a; Kilic et al., 2017b; Linsenmeier et al., 2015; Salameh et al., 2018). Kilic et al. (2017a) investigated the role of insolation in the coupled AGCM – sea ice model and found that the value of solar irradiance determines weather the planet is covered by ice or water. The contribution of different topographical barriers that is important for the circulation was also investigated (e.g., Enderton et al., 2009; Hertwig et al., 2016; Marshall et al., 2007). Both, parameters and topography sensitivity APEs can be very useful sources not only for evaluating the model itself but also for understanding past and future climate variability of Earth.

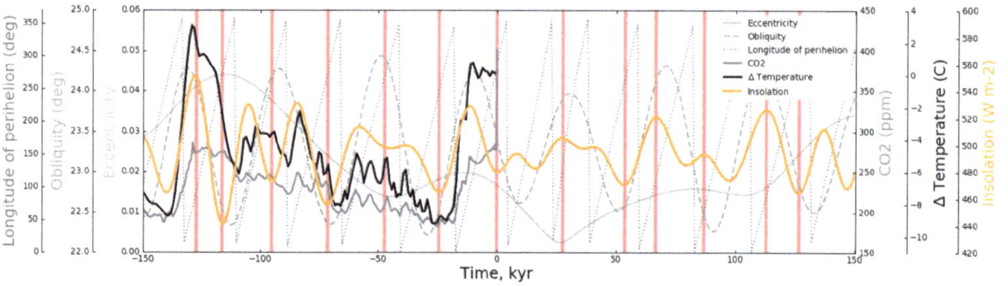

Figure 1: Timeseries of Earth's orbital parameters (eccentricity (grey solid line), obliquity (deg, grey dashed line), and longitude of perihelion (deg, grey dotted line)) and July insolation at 65 °N (W m^{-2}, orange line) from Laskar et al. (2004) from -150000 to 150000 yr; reconstructed pCO2 (ppm, Köhler et al., 2017b, dark grey solid line) and temperature change (°C, Snyder, 2016, black solid line) from -150000 to 150000 yr. Red solid vertical lines denotes time slices chosen for sensitivity experiments.

Several studies have already been done aiming at understanding important climatic transition in the past, like e.g. glacial-interglacial inception (e.g., Hertwig et al., 2016; Williams et al., 2006) and the aquaplanet's climate variability on long time scales (e.g., Hertwig et al., 2015; Marshall et al., 2007, 1000 – 20000 yrs). So far none of above-mentioned studies has focused on studying Earth-like orbital configuration that Earth experienced in the past or will undergo in the future. Understanding the role of orbital configuration is important as it can be one of the possible driving force of sea surface temperature (SST) variability as the position of the planet on its orbit defines how much of incoming solar radiation will reach the surface and will cause temperature changes. Here we aim at understanding how different orbital configurations which correspond to extreme values of incoming Earth insolation over the last and the future 150000 yrs affect the aquaplanet climate (Figure 1; Table 1).

2 Model description and experiment setups

2.1 Model overview and spin-up setup

In this study we use the Planet Simulator[1] that is a climate model of intermediate complexity for Earth, Mars and other planets (PlaSim, Fraedrich et al., 2005) coupled to the Large Scale Ocean circulation model (LSG, Maier-Reimer et al., 1992) in an aquaplanet setup. The model is designed to be applicable for long transient simulations that can be executed locally or on the cluster.

We run AGCM PlaSim in T21 resolution with 10 layers coupled to LSG with a 22 unevenly distributed layers on a 72 $\times$ 72 grid points in the aquaplanet setup. The aquaplanet setup does not have any orography and have constant bathimetry and, therefore the planet is uniformly covered by ocean of constant depth (5500 m). The spin-up is started with the uniform atmosphere and ocean and forced with the prescribed SST as *CONTROL* in Neale et al. (2000). As a reference state, we use an aquaplanet with a present-day orbital configuration. To avoid model drift, the control setup was run for 10000 years, the mean state of the last 3000 year is used as a spin-up for sensitivity experiments.

2.2 Experiment setups

Sensitivity experiments are started from the present-day aquaplanet spin-up (see Subsection 2.1). Each of sensitivity experiment requires about 3000 years to reach steady state. Experiment setups are only different in orbital parameters. The choice of combination of orbital parameters follows from evaluating the reconstructed and projected values of incoming solar radiation (Laskar et al., 2004, orange line on Figure 1). For the

[1] University of Hamburg version, https://www.mi.uni-hamburg.de/en/arbeitsgruppen/theoretische-meteorologie/modelle/plasim.html.

sensitivity experiments we choose several orbital parameter configurations that corresponds to maximal and minimal values of insolation. All values are listed in Table 1. Reconstructed and projected Earth eccentricity, obliquity and longitude of perihelion are taken from Laskar et al. (2004). We also show corresponding reconstructed Earth temperature change and $pCO2$ from Snyder (2016) and Köhler et al. (2017a), correspondingly, to show Earth response to changing parameters. For the analysis, we use last 500 years of experiments.

Table 1: Orbital parameters (eccentricity, obliquity (°), longitude of perihelion (°)) and insolation at 65 °N (W m^{-2}) for aquaplanet sensitivity experiments. Experiment notations are $apeYYYx$ where ape stands for aquaplanet experiment, YYY corresponds to the year in 1000 yrs, and x can be either p (past) or f (future), PD indicates present day conditions.

Experiment name	Year (1000 yrs)	Eccentricity	Obliquity (°)	Longitude of Perihelion (°)	Insolation (W m^{-2})
ape127p	−127	0.0409858	24.091012	92.652534	550.446721
ape116p	−116	0.0438771	22.536149	272.200712	440.544154
ape095p	−95	0.0375395	24.180502	258.793245	472.482840
ape071p	−71	0.0237902	22.355996	276.010688	455.285984
ape047p	−47	0.0139868	24.406398	268.076328	497.862550
ape024p	−24	0.0180946	22.523017	246.195660	464.353415
apePD	0	0.0167024	23.439291	282.917945	479.341411
ape028f	28	0.0024328	23.909274	141.060909	504.668666
ape054f	54	0.0115398	22.592563	267.082372	470.047561
ape067f	67	0.0141457	24.131225	113.919739	520.403862
ape087f	87	0.0156819	22.458305	65.490020	492.748533
ape113f	113	0.0161970	24.244703	84.203219	525.812953
ape127f	127	0.0243437	22.818313	293.460092	463.808014

3 Results and Discussion

3.1 Control aquaplanet experiment

The mean simulated SST in the control experiment is 295.28 K (Figure 2, black line). The pattern of the incoming solar radiation (Figure 3) shows clear seasonality with a maximum insolation in high latitude during respective to the hemisphere summer month and minimum during winter. The maximal value of insolation occurs in subtropics during summer month, whereas minimal insolation reaches the top of the atmosphere in the respective winter. The insolation seasonality in its turn causes SST variation during the year. Thus, tropics and subtropics has almost the same temperature during the year with a slight seasonality. The SST from equator to approximately 30 °N and 30 °S varies within nearly 9 K from 305.5 K. The seasonality is much more pronounced in the poles where SST lowers down to 278.5 K during respective winter month (Figure 3).

3.2 Sensitivity experiments

Figure 2 shows simulated mean SSTs in all sensitivity experiments for the past (left) and the future (right) orbital parameters configuration. The results clearly split into two main group with regard to the control experiment, namely, warm and cold cases. Both these cases occur in the past and in the future, the difference with regard to the control experiment does not exceed 0.3 K. To understand what causes warming or cooling we consider one cold (ape071p) and one warm (ape047p) cases.

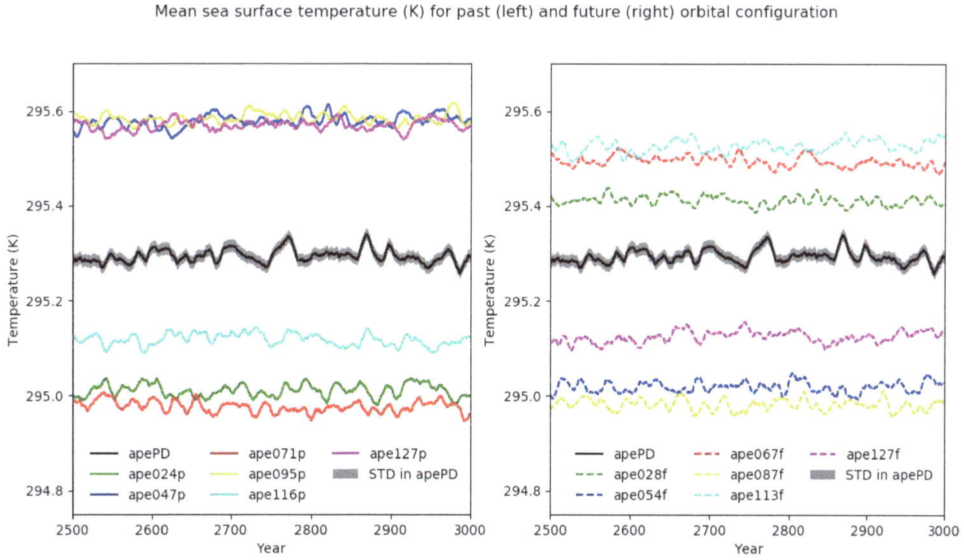

Figure 2: Simulated aquaplanet SST (K) in sensitivity experiments for past (left) and future (right) Earth-like orbital parameters. Grey shaded area is standard deviation (STD) in the control experiment. Experiments and abbreviations are listed in Table 1.

Figure 3 depict Hövmüller diagram for incoming solar radiation and simulated SSTs in the atmosphere for the control experiment apePD and its difference with warm and cold cases. Thus, for the cold case, less solar radiation reaches high latitudes with highest values on both poles due to corresponding summer period. Slightly more radiation with a maximal difference in subtropics reaches during respective winter in the corresponding hemisphere. These changes induce much colder polar SSTs (up to 1 K) and almost an order of magnitude smaller warming in tropics (up to 0.1 K). The warm case is almost an opposite. There is more incoming solar radiation in high latitudes with a maximum on the poles during corresponding summer periods and less with a maximal difference in subtropics reaches during respective winter. This causes up to 1 K warming with a maximum in the poles and a minor tropical cooling that does not exceed 0.1 K.

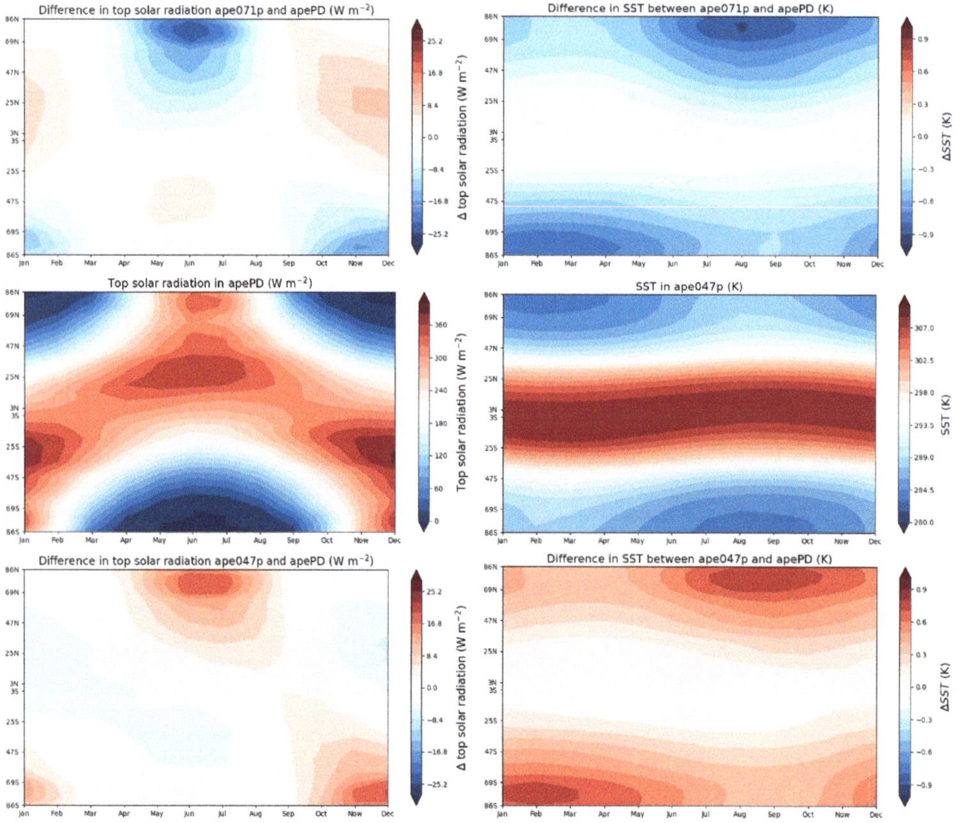

Figure 3: Hövmüller diagram of the incoming solar radiation (left middle, Wm^{-2}) and simulated SSTs (right middle, K) in the control experiment apePD. Top and bottom panel depict differences between control apePD and cold ape071p (top) and control and warm ape047p (bottom) experiments. Left top and bottom panels show difference in incoming solar radiation (Wm^{-2}). Right top and bottom depicts difference in simulated SSTs (K).

3.3 The role of orbital parameters

Figure 4 summarizes results of sensitivity experiments where the horizontal axis is the obliquity, vertical is longitude of perihelion, splines on the figure depict possible values of the eccentricity over the chosen time interval of 300000 years, bubbles reflect the values of eccentricity for the single experiment, and the color is the mean simulated SST. Negative values in the bubble correspond to the past and positive is to the future time.

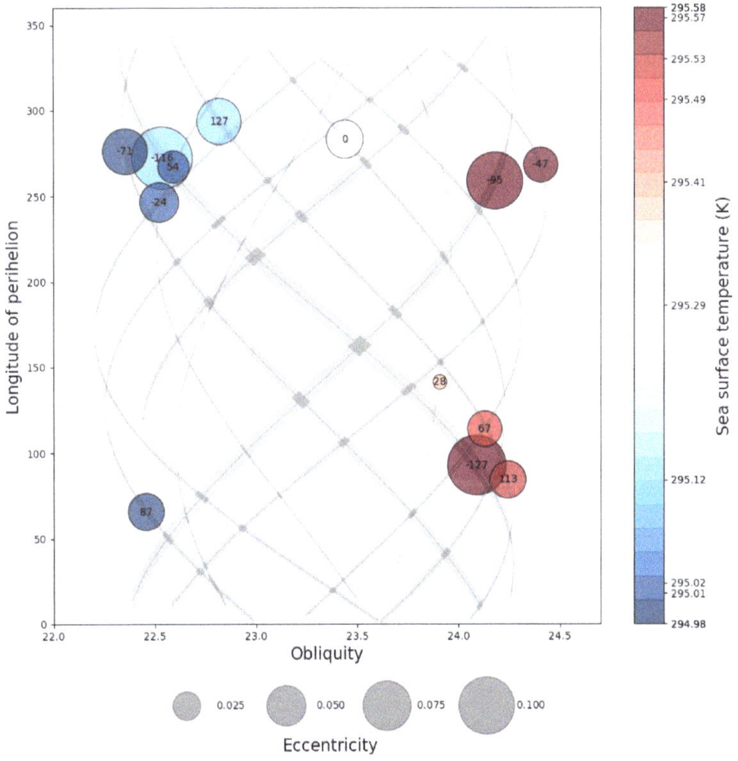

Figure 4: The plot depicts obliquity (°) versus longitude of perihelion (°). Splines depict all possible eccentricity values over the past 150000 and future 150000 years. The width of the line corresponds to the value of eccentricity (thin lines are for small values, thick lines are for big values). Bubbles represent eccentricity for the chosen experiment. The color stands for the mean simulated SST (K). Numbers in bubbles correspond to the first three digit if the experiment, negative values are for past times.

The control aquaplanet experiment with present-day Earth-like orbital parameters reveals not to cold and not too warm temperatures that also agrees with the incoming solar radiation in Figure 1. Other values clusters in two areas where the main difference is the value of obliquity that as it was shown earlier defines the amount, the time and the location of the incoming solar radiation that causes surface warming or cooling. The eccentricity value does not explicitly affect the simulated SSTs as in both clusters the whole possible range of eccentricities is presented. There is also a clusterization around longitude of perihelion, nearly 275 ° for cold and 100 ° for warm cases.

4 Summary and conclusions

In this study we evaluate the role of different orbital parameters on the simulated climate of the Earth-like aquaplanet. Our sensitivity experiments reveals that the key parameter that defines SST variability is the obliquity or the planet axis tilt with regard to the orbital plane. We evaluated the simulated mean SST between different aquaplanet configurations and compared it with the setup corresponding to the present-day Earth-like aquaplanet value. The difference in SST does not exceed 0.3 K which when extrapolating to the Earth climate (SST variability is nearly 8 K; Figure 1) indicates that other component (e.g., greenhouse gases) have more important role in changing climate.

Acknowledgements

This work was performed on the computational resource bwUniCluster funded by the Ministry of Science, Research and Arts Baden-Württemberg and the Universities of the State of Baden-Württemberg, Germany, within the framework program bwHPC.

Data availability

For this study we use University of Hamburg PlaSim version available via https://www.mi.uni-hamburg.de/en/arbeitsgruppen/theoretische-meteorologie/modelle/plasim.html. Experiment set ups, plotting scripts and data used for producing figure are available at https://github.com/paleovar/erokhina_rehfeld_aquaplanet_2024.

Corresponding Author

Olga Erokhina: olga.erokhina@uni-heidelberg.de
Astronomisches Rechen-Institut, Heidelberg University
Mönchhofstraße 12-14, 69120 Heidelberg

ORCID

Olga Erokhina https://orcid.org/0000-0002-2207-7979
Kira Rehfeld https://orcid.org/0000-0002-9442-5362

References

Chavas, D. R. and K. A. Reed (2019). »Dynamical Aquaplanet Experiments with Uniform Thermal Forcing: System Dynamics and Implications for Tropical Cyclone Genesis and Size«. In: *Journal of the Atmospheric Sciences* 76.8, pp. 2257–2274. DOI: 10.1175/JAS-D-19.

Enderton, D. and J. Marshall (2009). »Explorations of atmosphere-ocean-ice climates on an aquaplanet and their meridional energy transports«. In: *Journal of the Atmospheric Sciences* 66 (6), pp. 1593–1611. ISSN: 0022-4928. DOI: 10.1175/2008JAS2680.1.

Fraedrich, K., H. Jansen, E. Kirk, U. Luksch and F. Lunkeit (2005). »The Planet Simulator: Towards a user friendly model«. In: *Meteorologische Zeitschrift* 14.3, pp. 299–304.

Hertwig, E., F. Lunkeit and K. Fraedrich (2015). »Low-frequency climate variability of an aquaplanet«. In: *Theoretical and Applied Climatology* 121 (3-4), pp. 459–478. ISSN: 1434-4483. DOI: 10.1007/s00704-014-1226-8.

– (2016). »The role of atmospheric greenhouse gases, orbital parameters, and southern ocean gateways: an idealized model study«. In: DOI: 10.48550/arxiv.1602.01259. arXiv: 1602.01259.

Kilic, C., C. C. Raible and T. F. Stocker (2017a). »Multiple Climate States of Habitable Exoplanets: The Role of Obliquity and Irradiance«. In: *The Astrophysical Journal* 844 (2), p. 147. ISSN: 0004-637X. DOI: 10.3847/1538-4357/aa7a03.

Kilic, C., C. C. Raible, T. F. Stocker and E. Kirk (2017b). »Impact of variations of gravitational acceleration on the general circulation of the planetary atmosphere«. In: *Planetary and Space Science* 135, pp. 1–16. ISSN: 0032-0633. DOI: 10.1016/j.pss.2016.11.001.

Köhler, P., C. Nehrbass-Ahles, J. Schmitt, T. F. Stocker and H. Fischer (2017a). »A 156 kyr smoothed history of the atmospheric greenhouse gases CO2, CH4, and N2O and their radiative forcing«. In: *Earth System Science Data* 9.1, pp. 363–387.

Köhler, P., C. Nehrbass-Ahles, J. Schmitt, T. F. Stocker and H. Fischer (2017b). »Continuous record of the atmospheric greenhouse gas carbon dioxide (CO2), final spline-smoothed data of calculated radiative forcing (Version 1)«. In: In supplement to: Köhler, P et al. (2017): A 156 kyr smoothed history of the atmospheric greenhouse gases CO2, CH4, and N2O and their radiative forcing. Earth System Science Data, 9(1), 363-387, PANGAEA. DOI: 10.1594/PANGAEA.871271.

Laskar, J. et al. (2004). »A long-term numerical solution for the insolation quantities of the Earth«. In: *Astronomy & Astrophysics* 428.1, pp. 261–285.

Linsenmeier, M., S. Pascale and V. Lucarini (2015). »Climate of Earth-like planets with high obliquity and eccentric orbits: Implications for habitability conditions«. In: *Planetary and Space Science* 105, pp. 43–59. ISSN: 0032-0633. DOI: 10.1016/j.pss.2014.11.003.

Maier-Reimer, E. and U. Mikolajewicz (1992). *The Hamburg large scale geostrophic ocean general circulation model, cycle 1*. DKRZ.

Marshall, J., D. Ferreira, J. M. Campin and D. Enderton (2007). »Mean climate and variability of the atmosphere and ocean on an aquaplanet«. In: *Journal of the Atmospheric Sciences* 64 (12), pp. 4270–4286. ISSN: 0022-4928. DOI: 10.1175/2007JAS2226.1.

Neale, R. B. and B. J. Hoskins (2000). »A standard test for AGCMs including their physical parametrizations: I: The proposal«. In: *Atmospheric Science Letters* 1 (2), pp. 101–107. ISSN: 1530-261X. DOI: 10.1006/asle.2000.0019.

Salameh, J., M. Popp and J. Marotzke (2018). »The role of sea-ice albedo in the climate of slowly rotating aquaplanets«. In: *Climate Dynamics* 50 (7-8), pp. 2395–2410. ISSN: 1432-0894. DOI: 10.1007/s00382-017-3548-6.

Snyder, C. W. (2016). »Evolution of global temperature over the past two million years«. In: *Nature* 538.7624, pp. 226–228.

Williams, G. P. and K. Bryan (2006). »Ice age winds: An aquaplanet model«. In: *Journal of climate* 19.9, pp. 1706–1715.

Energy-Efficient Information Representation in MNIST Classification Using Biologically Inspired Learning

Patrick Stricker[*†‡], Florian Röhrbein[†], Andreas Knoblauch[*]

[*]KEIM Institute, Albstadt-Sigmaringen University, Germany
[†]Department of Computer Science, Chemnitz University of Technology, Germany
[‡]Data Science & Data Engineering, Infraserv GmbH & Co. Höchst KG, Germany

Abstract

Efficient representation learning is essential for optimal information storage and classification. However, it is frequently overlooked in artificial neural networks (ANNs). This neglect results in networks that can become overparameterized by factors of up to 13, increasing redundancy and energy consumption. As the demand for large language models (LLMs) and their scale increase, these issues are further highlighted, raising significant ethical and environmental concerns. We analyze our previously developed biologically inspired learning rule using information-theoretic concepts, evaluating its efficiency on the MNIST classification task. The proposed rule, which emulates the brain's structural plasticity, naturally prevents overparameterization by optimizing synaptic usage and retaining only the essential number of synapses. Furthermore, it outperforms backpropagation (BP) in terms of efficiency and storage capacity. The approach eliminates the need for pre-optimization of network architecture, offering dynamic adaptability during training. Additionally, it mirrors the brain's ability to reserve memory space for new experiences, a feature that enhances its ability to learn and adapt over time. This positions our learning rule as a promising framework for developing brain-inspired models that optimize resource allocation and adaptability.

1 Introduction

Deep neural networks (DNNs) have revolutionized fields such as computer vision, natural language processing, and speech recognition with their impressive performance in supervised learning tasks (Alam et al., 2020; He et al., 2015; LeCun et al., 2015; Shwartz-Ziv et al., 2023). Nevertheless, DNNs frequently encounter difficulties associated with overparameterization, largely due to the use of backpropagation (BP). The intrinsic characteristics of gradient-based optimization inevitably lead to the storage of redundant information and potential noise, assigning nonzero weights to each synapse regardless of network size. Although DNNs are inspired by the human brain, current models are unable to fully replicate the brain's efficient generalization and learning capabilities by focusing on the synaptic weight plasticity as the sole mechanism (Stricker et al., 2024). In contrast, the human brain demonstrates efficient information processing through sparse neural connections, driven by both spatial and energy constraints (Knoblauch et al., 2016; Tiddia et al., 2024). Sparse connectivity enhances generalization by reducing the storage of noise and redundant information. Based on Alemi et al. (2017)'s discovery that compression correlates with improved generalization, we suggest that this might explain the brain's superior generalization ability.

While methods such as dropout layers and skip connections can mitigate some effects of overparameterization, it should be noted that these techniques serve to mask the drawbacks of increased model size. Han et al. (2015) demonstrated, that a significant proportion of large architectures contain considerable redundancy, with sizes far exceeding what is necessary for optimal performance. This overparameterization results in inflated computational resource demands and increased carbon emissions, exacerbating environmental and ethical concerns, particularly given the rapid growth of generative AI. Recent studies on models like Llama and Minitron (Sreenivas et al., 2024) have highlighted the severity of this issue, showing that pruned Large Language Models (LLMs) can achieve comparable or superior performance while using 40-150 times fewer training tokens. The short lifespan of many LLM deployments, combined with their substantial resource consumption, intensifies the need for more efficient and sustainable approaches. Thus, there is a critical need for algorithms that deliver high performance without unnecessary complexity. Our proposed framework addresses this by focusing on efficient information representation, emulating the brain's ability to achieve efficient performance with sparse connectivity. This approach reduces model size and resource usage, providing a solution to the issues of overparameterization and excessive resource consumption.

In our previous work (Stricker et al., 2024), we introduced a biologically inspired learning framework that not only achieves performance comparable to that of BP but also offers substantial benefits in energy-efficient information representation. The framework retains only those synapses, that are essential for the classification task, thereby emulating the efficiency observed in the brain. The selective retention of synapses, a process known as structural plasticity (Janzakova et al., 2023; Knoblauch et al., 2016; Rosa et al., 2020; Tiddia et al., 2024), reflects the brain's capacity to optimally and efficiently store information. This contrasts with BP, which scales by utilising all available synapses.

This paper extends our earlier research (Stricker et al., 2024) by focusing specifically on the efficiency of information representation in the MNIST classification task. We frame our learning framework as a neural associative network, which frequently serves as a computational model of brain functions (Knoblauch et al., 2009). Using this framework, we reinterpret the MNIST classification task as a heteroassociative memory problem, where patterns are linked and retrieved through sparse synaptic connections. This approach enables the quantification of information storage and compression. Our approach is predicated on the assumption that the neural network forms a Markov chain, following the insights of Tishby and Zaslavsky (Shwartz-Ziv et al., 2017; Tishby et al., 2015), and integrates a Variational Information Bottleneck (VIB) layer (Hoffmann et al., 2022). The stochastic encoding layer learns the distribution of hidden layer activations, pretrained with our approach or the benchmark. This allows for a more precise calculation of mutual information, allowing for a deeper analysis of information representation.

The results are benchmarked against a range of methods, including the method proposed by Chorowski et al. (2015), which applies nonnegativity and sparsity constraints to BP, as well as standard BP. While Chorowski's methods demonstrate superior accuracy, our approach is shown to outperform both in terms of storage efficiency and classification performance relative to the number of nonsilent synapses used.

The application of biologically inspired learning rules has the potential to lead to the development of more sustainable models. Thus, drawing inspiration from these biologically inspired rules could assist in addressing the growing need for energy efficiency in AI. We provide evidence that our framework maintains comparable classification performance, significantly improves storage efficiency, and reduces network size.

2 Modeling

2.1 The Memory Task

Memories are commonly identified with patterns of neural activity that can be revisited, evoked, or stabilized by appropriately modified synaptic connections (Knoblauch et al., 2016). In the simplest case, such a memory corresponds to a group of neurons that fire at the same time and, according to the Hebbian hypothesis that »what fires together wires together« (Hebb, 1949), develop strong mutual synaptic connections (Caporale et al., 2008; Clopath et al., 2010; Knoblauch et al., 2012, 2016). These groups of strongly connected neurons, known as cell assemblies (Hebb, 1949; Knoblauch et al., 2016; Palm et al., 2014), are closely related to associative networks and play an important role in neuroscience as models of neural computation for various brain structures.

Formally, networks of cell assemblies can be modeled as associative networks, which are essentially single-layer neural networks employing Hebbian learning Knoblauch et al. (2016). The concept, first introduced by Steinbuch in 1961, featured a single-layer network where neurons receive inputs from an address pattern and establish associations directly using binary neurons and synapses (Steinbuch, 1961). The model can be extended to a two-layer architecture, thereby enabling the processing of more complex patterns. In this setup, an address pattern u is mapped to a hidden layer that extracts intermediate representations, which are then projected to a content pattern v. The synaptic matrix A is updated locally according to Hebbian learning principles.

In our study, MNIST classification is framed as a heteroassociative memory task using a two-layer network. The first layer captures intermediate representations of image patterns u, while the second layer maps these representations to the final labels v. Heteroassociation in this context involves learning and storing classification patterns in synaptic weight matrices, which serve as the memory matrix A, with negative weights clipped to zero to ensure nonnegativity (Knoblauch et al., 2009; Kohonen, 1977). This method effectively emulates associative memory processes, reflecting how neural networks perform pattern recognition and information retrieval (Knoblauch et al., 2009).

Recent research utilizing FashionMNIST has demonstrated the effectiveness of heteroassociative learning rules for pattern denoising, showing how associative memory principles can be applied in classification tasks (Kymn et al., 2024). The study revealed that models leveraging associative memory could effectively denoise structured patterns, emphasizing the relevance of such methods for classification tasks. This research supports the applicability of MNIST datasets for similar tasks, as MNIST and FashionMNIST exhibit comparable structural and complexity characteristics.

2.2 Competitive Hebbian Plasticity and Weight Perturbation

To address the heteroassociative memory problem in MNIST classification, we use our previously developed biologically inspired learning framework (Stricker et al., 2024). This framework integrates multiple plasticity rules, including competitive excitatory Hebbian plasticity (Chorowski et al., 2015), nonnegativity constraints, and weight perturbation (WP) (Cauwenberghs, 1993; Dembo et al., 1990; Nambusubramaniyan et al., 2022; Stricker et al., 2024; Züge et al., 2023). These mechanisms ensure that learning is both efficient and biologically plausible, promoting sparsity in hidden layers and maintaining nonnegativity across synaptic weights. The classification layer further employs homeostatic plasticity through bias neurons, where the bias values act as thresholds to enhance class discrimination while ensuring stable convergence (Chorowski et al., 2015; Stricker et al., 2024).

The modification of synaptic weights w_{ij} between a neuron i and a neuron j in the layer above in the hidden layer is given by:

$$\Delta w_{ij} = \eta z_j \cdot (x_i - \sum_{k \neq j} z_k w_{ik}), \tag{1}$$

where x_i represents the input from neuron i, η denotes the learning rate, and $z_j = \sum_{u=1} x_u w_{uj}$ refers to the resulting activity of neuron j.

The classification layer is updated via the following equation:

$$\Delta w_{ki} = \eta\alpha \cdot \Delta w_{ki}^{hebbian} + \eta\beta \cdot \Delta w_{ki}^{WP}, \tag{2}$$

where the parameters α and β denote the contribution of the corresponding plasticity mechanism. The WP component, Δw_{ki}^{WP}, is calculated using the following update rule:

$$\Delta w_{ij}^{\mathrm{WP}} = -\frac{\eta}{\sigma^2}(E^{pert} - E)\xi_{ij}, \tag{3}$$

where E^{pert} refers to the error of the perturbed trial, E denotes the error of the unperturbed trial, ξ_{ij} represents the perturbation term, and σ^2 reflects the strength of the perturbation. In this approach, weights are adjusted based on performance changes from perturbations, where improvements lead to updates in the direction of perturbations, and degradations result in opposite adjustments (Züge et al., 2023).

The bias weights are updated according to the following equation:

$$\Delta b_k = \eta\gamma \left(\frac{1}{K} \cdot \sum_{k=1}^{K} z_{kt} - \frac{1}{N} \cdot \sum_{t=1}^{N} z_{kt} \right), \tag{4}$$

where the first term denotes the mean activation of the layer, the second term represents the mean activation of the current minibatch, and γ controls the contribution of this learning rule (Hoffmann et al., 2022). As this work focuses on classification tasks, training batches with equally distributed labels are assumed. This simplifies the mean target activation to $\frac{1}{K}$ (Stricker et al., 2024).

2.3 Information Theory for Deep Associative Neural Networks

To quantify the mutual information within a multilayer network, we adopt an information-theoretic perspective inspired by Tishby and Zaslavsky (Shwartz-Ziv et al., 2017; Tishby et al., 2015). They show that neural networks form a Markov chain of successive representations, where each layer T can be treated as a random variable with its encoder $P(T \mid X)$ and decoder $P(Y \mid T)$. This clarifies the flow of information across network layers and aligns inherently with our approach. The Markov chain model's assumption that each layer's state depends only on the immediately preceding layer is naturally satisfied by our Hebbian learning rule, which updates weights based on local activity.

Traditional methods for estimating mutual information, such as bin discretization, can be biased and sensitive to bin size (Hoffmann et al., 2022; Poole et al., 2019). To address these issues, we opted to obtain variational approximations of mutual information using a Variational Autoencoder (VAE)-based approach (Hoffmann et al., 2022).

In this study, we depart from the conventional methodology by incorporating a deterministic bottleneck in the form of a pretrained hidden layer preceding the variational encoder, while setting the β parameter to zero. This adjustment removes the typical information bottleneck, ensuring that compression is solely induced by the frozen hidden representations while still allowing for accurate mutual information estimation.

In order to calculate and compare the information representation and compression induced by different learning rules, it is first necessary to extract a deterministic hidden representation, designated as H, from a neural network which has been pretrained using either our approach, BP, or constrained BP. We then use a stochastic encoding layer to model $p(Z \mid H)$, where Z is the latent variable. This encoding layer is parameterized by $2K$ parameters, where K is the size of the layer. Specifically, the layer outputs means μ and variances σ (after applying a softplus transformation) for Z, approximating its distribution as $\mathcal{N}(Z \mid \mu, \sigma)$ (Alemi et al., 2017). This setup ensures that the encoder effectively captures the distribution of Z. We then estimate the mutual information $I(X; Z)$ using the Kullback–Leibler divergence $D_{KL}[p(Z \mid X) \| p(Z)]$, following the approach described in (Alemi et al., 2017; Hoffmann et al., 2022; Shwartz-Ziv et al., 2017; Tishby et al., 2015).

2.4 Performance Measures for Associative Memory

Biological neural networks achieve efficient memory storage through sparse connectivity, which is driven by both spatial and energy constraints. The energy cost associated with neural signaling is closely linked to the maintenance of nonsilent synapses, which are crucial for memory retention (Attwell et al., 2001; Knoblauch et al., 2016; Laughlin et al., 2003; Lennie, 2003). Inspired by these principles, we evaluate neural network performance in terms of associative memory capabilities using the synaptic capacity C^S metric introduced by Knoblauch et al. (2009, 2016). This metric quantifies memory efficiency by normalizing channel capacity against the number of nonsilent synapses. Synaptic capacity C^S is defined as:

$$C^S = \frac{I(Z; X)}{\text{Number of nonsilent synapses}} \text{ [bits/synapse]}, \tag{5}$$

where $I(Z; X)$ represents the mutual information between the latent variable Z and the input X. This measure reflects how effectively the network uses its connections for memory storage and retrieval while minimizing the number of nonsilent synapses. By adopting C^S, we align with the brain's approach of compressing information and reducing parameter count, thus providing insights into memory efficiency and network performance relative to synaptic resources.

3 Numerical Experiments and Results

3.1 Experimental Setup

This paper explores associative neural networks for MNIST classification, focusing on information representation through a heteroassociative memory approach. We employ a one-hidden-layer feedforward network where the hidden layer's weight matrix is updated using competitive Hebbian plasticity, as detailed in Subsection 2.2. The update rule for the hidden layer is given by (1), while the classification layer is trained with a combination of (1) and (3), resulting in (2). Bias weights are updated according to (4). Experiments were conducted using the Keras framework with TensorFlow as the backend.

A modified sigmoid activation function is used in the hidden layer, transforming outputs from $[0.5, 1.0]$ to $[0.0, 1.0]$ to align with the nonnegative values processed by the network. We use batch processing to extend trials over time with duration T, where each mini-batch consists of N_{batch} inputs indexed by $t = 1, ..., N_{batch}$.

For our experiments, we use a subset of the MNIST dataset[1] and apply Min-Max scaling to standardize pixel values between 0 and 1. Weight matrices are initialized with values drawn from a random uniform distribution between 0.01 and 0.1, and the cross-entropy loss function is employed for optimization (Stricker et al., 2024).

To assess storage and energy efficiency, we train networks using our approach, BP, or constrained BP. After training, we extract a deterministic hidden representation H from these networks and apply a stochastic encoding layer to model $p(Z \mid H)$. We set K for each network architecture according to $2K = M$, where M is the number of hidden units. Mutual information $I(X; Z)$ is then estimated from this stochastic encoding to evaluate information compression and synaptic capacity. We compare these results with

[1] The MNIST dataset comprises 70,000 grayscale images of handwritten digits (28 $\times$ 28 pixels), including 60,000 training and 10,000 test images (Hoffmann et al., 2022; LeCun et al., 2023). Our focus is on the digits 1, 2, and 6.

benchmarks and analyze synaptic capacity to identify optimal network architectures for both storage and energy efficiency.

3.2 Efficient Simulation Using BWHPC and Local Prototyping

Initial prototyping on a local NVIDIA RTX 4080 facilitated rapid development of smaller models with reduced batch sizes. However, larger batch sizes are essential for the effectiveness of our learning rule (Stricker et al., 2024). The RTX 4080 is capable of efficiently processing models with batch sizes up to 500. Beyond this threshold, its computational resources become inadequate, necessitating sequential processing of mini-batches, which significantly impedes training efficiency.

To address this limitation, final simulations were conducted on the bwUniCluster 2.0, utilizing GPUs such as the A100, H100, and Tesla P100. These GPUs provided the required scalability and performance to manage larger models and batch sizes. As shown in Table 1, the A100 and H100 exhibited performance comparable to the RTX 4080 for smaller models. However, they demonstrated enhanced scalability for increased batch sizes and model complexity, which allowed for the maintenance of efficient epoch times.

Table 1: Mean epoch times and standard deviations for different GPUs (in seconds per epoch), measured during benchmarking of smaller-scale experiments.

GPU	RTX 4080	H100	Tesla P100	A100
Time	2.255 ± 0.114	2.309 ± 0.0476	2.891 ± 0.235	2.307 ± 0.073

Computational workloads on the bwUniCluster required 5 to 15 GB of RAM, depending on model complexity and batch size. Despite these variations, the enhanced scalability of the A100 and H100 GPUs ensured the efficient processing of larger models, maintaining competitive runtime performance.

All experiments were executed using Keras and TensorFlow to ensure consistency across environments.

3.3 Analysis of Network Storage Capacity and Connectivity Through Mutual Information

Table 2 summarizes the results for various network topologies and training algorithms. As shown in our previous work (Stricker et al., 2024), increasing the number of hidden neurons M nearly eliminates the performance disparity between our learning rule and constrained BP. The remaining discrepancy is likely due to the precise gradient calculations and negative biases used by BP, which are not present in our framework.

Table 2: Performance of Different Algorithms with Various Hidden Units

Hidden Neurons	Algorithm	Test Accuracy	I(X,Z)	C^S
10	BP	**99.01%**	22.50 bits	2.87×10^{-3}
	Chorowski et al.	98.34%	16.10 bits	1.08×10^{-2}
	Authors	64.29%	**12.80 bits**	$\mathbf{1.63 \times 10^{-2}}$
30	BP	**99.17%**	127.62 bits	5.43×10^{-3}
	Chorowski et al.	99.01%	72.99 bits	2.22×10^{-2}
	Authors	86.21%	**52.18 bits**	$\mathbf{6.66 \times 10^{-2}}$
100	BP	**99.23%**	435.93 bits	5.56×10^{-3}
	Chorowski et al.	99.10%	217.43 bits	5.93×10^{-2}
	Authors	89.79%	**198.33 bits**	$\mathbf{2.53 \times 10^{-1}}$
200	BP	**99.17%**	518.79 bits	3.31×10^{-3}
	Chorowski et al.	99.10%	402.91 bits	1.31×10^{-1}
	Authors	95.55%	**372.66 bits**	$\mathbf{4.75 \times 10^{-1}}$

Performance metrics for our algorithm compared to two benchmark algorithms. Metrics include accuracy (as a percentage), mutual information $I(X, Z)$ in bits, and synaptic capacity in bits per nonsilent synapse. The best values in each category are highlighted in bold. Benchmarks were replicated to ensure comparability. Hyperparameters for our algorithm are: $\eta = 0.000158$, $\alpha = 0.1$, $\beta = 446.25$, $\gamma = 0.1$, $\sigma^2 = 0.0157$.

Notably, the improvement observed in the baseline scenario, compared to our prior work, is attributed to the use of a modified sigmoid activation function. This adjustment significantly enhanced performance and addressed issues where training a model with the baseline configuration was previously infeasible [2].

The mutual information $I(X, Z)$ increases with layer size across all approaches, which is consistent with the notion that a larger number of synapses enables the storage of more information. Our method achieves the most effective information compression

[2] For a detailed analysis of performance metrics and further insights, please refer to Stricker et al. (2024).

and consistently outperforms both Chorowski et al. (2015)'s approach and BP across all tested architectures. BP retains the most information overall by keeping all synaptic weights nonzero.

For sparse algorithms, such as constrained BP and our approach, synaptic capacity C^S increases with layer size due to its linear dependence on the amount of mutual information stored. BP, with all synapses being nonzero, exhibits the lowest synaptic capacity, indicating overparameterization and the retention of redundant and noisy information. In contrast, our method achieves the highest synaptic capacity efficiently retaining only essential synapses while storing fewer bits compared to other methods. This demonstrates that our method results in the most efficient information representation, with the fewest nonzero synapses and lowest stored information across all scenarios.

4 Discussion

We evaluated the effectiveness of our biologically inspired learning rule for associative neural networks by analyzing its impact on information representation and synaptic capacity across various network topologies and training algorithms. Our findings indicate that our method significantly improves synaptic capacity compared to both constrained and unconstrained BP, especially in larger architectures. Our approach maintains high classification accuracy while efficiently utilizing synaptic resources. Additionally, our method's ability to balance compression with synaptic capacity results in superior energy efficiency compared to methods that focus solely on minimizing mutual information.

In contrast to biologically implausible compression algorithms like constrained BP and VAE, which focus solely on minimizing mutual information, our approach adopts a dual strategy to maximize both compression and synaptic capacity. Inspired by neuroplasticity in the human brain, which balances spatial and energy constraints for efficient information processing (Knoblauch et al., 2016), our method prevents overparameterization while enhancing both efficiency and performance.

Our biologically inspired learning rule effectively models brain mechanics by optimizing synaptic capacity and achieving energy-efficient information representation. In contrast, methods like constrained BP often retain redundant information as network size exceeds the minimal number of hidden neurons necessary for satisfactory classification accuracy. Despite using nonnegativity constraints and activity regularization, these methods struggle with overparameterization. Our approach overcomes these limitations by using local competition and nonnegativity to ensure that weights converge to solutions primarily determined by the input data's covariance matrix (Zhou, 2022), thereby effectively learning the minimal sufficient statistics.

While traditional theories attribute adult learning and memory to Hebbian modification of synaptic weights, recent research suggests that structural plasticity, involving network rewiring and the generation or removal of synapses, also plays a crucial role in learning and memory (Bliss et al., 1993; Hebb, 1949; Knoblauch, 2017; Knoblauch et al., 2016; Navlakha et al., 2015; Paulsen et al., 2000; Song et al., 2000; Tiddia et al., 2024; Zito et al., 2002). In order to model these processes, researchers have developed mathematical frameworks that simulate network dynamics, to evaluate the impact of such structural changes on memory and performance. Knoblauch et al. (2016) employ a Markov approach to define synapses in three states: potential, instantiated but silent, and instantiated and stabilized. Structural plasticity in their model relates to transitions between these states (Knoblauch et al., 2016; Tiddia et al., 2024). Tiddia et al. (2024) approach structural plasticity through synaptic rewiring, where synapses below a predefined threshold are pruned and rewired at regular intervals.

Although these methodologies are based on biological principles, they do not fully capture the brain's adaptability. Once synapses are consolidated or stabilized in these models, they cannot be pruned or adjusted further. In contrast, the brain continuously rewires to accommodate new memories while maintaining synaptic density (Navlakha et al., 2015; Zito et al., 2002). Additionally, these methods require explicit modeling of synaptic retention rates and the optimization of network architecture before achieving optimal information representation.

In contrast, our method inherently promotes these properties through its plasticity mechanisms, integrating compression and capacity optimization without the need for additional constraints. By dynamically regulating retained parameters based on data and signal dynamics, our approach maintains efficiency while reflecting the brain's ability to reserve 'space' for new memories and preserve adaptability even in a stable state. This results in a more flexible and energy-efficient model, offering insights into the brain's resource allocation strategies. While our method achieves slightly inferior classification performance compared to BP, it closely mirrors the brain's adaptive learning processes. Thus, it presents a promising approach for emulating efficient associative memory and advancing our understanding of neural resource management. We are actively researching methods to close this performance gap and enhance the overall efficacy of our approach.

5 Conclusion

Our study investigates a biologically inspired learning rule that utilizes Competitive Hebbian plasticity principles to enhance energy-efficient information representation in DNNs. By optimizing synaptic capacity and managing redundancy, our approach mirrors the brain's strategy of maintaining sparse and effective neural connections. In contrast to traditional methods that struggle with overparameterization and redundant information, our method achieves significant advancements in storage efficiency, network size reduction, and energy consumption. This approach demonstrates the potential of biologically inspired learning rules to develop more sustainable and scalable AI models, meeting the growing demand for energy-efficient and ethical AI solutions.

Although our method exhibits slightly inferior classification performance compared to BP, it provides a promising approach for emulating efficient associative memory and advancing our understanding of neural resource management. By dynamically regulating retained parameters based on data and signal dynamics, our approach offers a potential explanation for how the brain optimally allocates neurons and synapses while avoiding overparameterization. This method also reserves capacity for future learning, reflecting the brain's adaptive processes. We are actively working to close the performance gap and further improve our approach.

Future research will address the performance limitations identified in this study by enhancing classification accuracy and computational efficiency, while maintaining the benefits of our approach. We will also investigate the model's ability to learn multiple tasks within a single network, emulate broader brain generalization capabilities, and assess its effectiveness on more complex architectures and deeper DNNs to evaluate scalability and performance under increased network complexity.

Corresponding Author

Patrick Stricker: strickerp@hs-albsig.de
KEIM Institute, Albstadt-Sigmaringen University,
Poststraße 6, 72458 Albstadt, Germany

ORCID

Patrick Stricker https://orcid.org/0009-0000-3632-4400
Florian Röhrbein https://orcid.org/0000-0002-4709-2673
Andreas Knoblauch https://orcid.org/0000-0002-2534-0250

References

Alam, M., M. D. Samad, L. Vidyaratne, A. Glandon and K. M. Iftekharuddin (2020). »Survey on Deep Neural Networks in Speech and Vision Systems«. In: *Neurocomputing* 417, pp. 302–321.

Alemi, A. A., I. Fischer, J. V. Dillon and K. Murphy (2017). »Deep Variational Information Bottleneck«. In: *Proc. Int. Conf. Learn. Representations (ICLR)*. Version v7, arXiv:1612.00410. DOI: 10.48550/arXiv.1612.00410.

Attwell, D. and S. Laughlin (2001). »An Energy Budget for Signaling in the Grey Matter of the Brain«. In: *J. Cereb. Blood Flow Metabol.* 21, pp. 1133–1145. DOI: 10.1097/00004647-200110000-00001.

Bliss, T. and G. Collingridge (1993). »A Synaptic Model of Memory: Long-Term Potentiation in the Hippocampus«. In: *Nature* 361, pp. 31–39.

Caporale, N. and Y. Dan (2008). »Spike Timing-Dependent Plasticity: A Hebbian Learning Rule«. In: *Ann. Rev. Neurosci.* 31, pp. 25–46. DOI: 10.1146/annurev.neuro.31.060407.125639.

Cauwenberghs, G. (1993). »A Fast Stochastic Error-Descent Algorithm for Supervised Learning and Optimization«. In: *Adv. Neural Inf. Process. Syst.* Vol. 5, pp. 244–251.

Chorowski, J. and J. M. Zurada (2015). »Learning Understandable Neural Networks With Nonnegative Weight Constraints«. In: *IEEE Trans. Neural Netw. Learn. Syst.* 26.1, pp. 62–69. DOI: 10.1109/TNNLS.2014.2310059.

Clopath, C., L. Büsing, E. Vasilaki and W. Gerstner (2010). »Connectivity Reflects Coding: A Model of Voltage-Based STDP with Homeostasis«. In: *Nat. Neurosci.* 13, pp. 344–352. DOI: 10.1038/nn.2479.

Dembo, A. and T. Kailath (1990). »Model-Free Distributed Learning«. In: *IEEE Trans. Neural Netw. Learn. Syst.* 1.1, pp. 58–70.

Han, S., J. Pool, J. Tran and W. Dally (2015). »Learning Both Weights and Connections for Efficient Neural Network«. In: *Adv. Neural Inf. Process. Syst.* Pp. 1135–1143.

He, K., X. Zhang, S. Ren and J. Sun (2015). »Deep Residual Learning for Image Recognition«. In: *CoRR* abs/1512.03385. DOI: 10.48550/arxiv.1512.03385. arXiv: 1512.03385.

Hebb, D. O. (1949). *The Organization of Behavior: A Neuropsychological Theory*. New York, NY: John Wiley and Sons.

Hoffmann, M. and P. Mäder (2022). »Synaptic Scaling – An Artificial Neural Network Regularization Inspired by Nature«. In: *IEEE Trans. Neural Netw. Learn. Syst.* 33.7, pp. 3094–3108.

Janzakova, K. et al. (2023). »Structural plasticity for neuromorphic networks with electropolymerized dendritic PEDOT connections«. In: *Nat. Commun.* 14.1, p. 8143. DOI: 10.1038/s41467-023-43887-8.

Knoblauch, A. (2017). »Impact of structural plasticity on memory formation and decline«. In: *Rewiring the Brain: A Computational Approach to Structural Plasticity in the Adult Brain*. Ed. by A. van Ooyen and M. Butz. Elsevier, pp. 361–386.

Knoblauch, A., F. Hauser, M.-O. Gewaltig, E. Körner and G. Palm (2012). »Does Spike-Timing-Dependent Synaptic Plasticity Couple or Decouple Neurons Firing in Synchrony?« In: *Front. Comput. Neurosci.* 6, p. 55. DOI: 10.3389/fncom.2012.00055.

Knoblauch, A., G. Palm and F. T. Sommer (2009). »Memory Capacities for Synaptic and Structural Plasticity«. In: *Neural Comput.* 22.2, pp. 289–341.

Knoblauch, A. and F. T. Sommer (2016). »Structural Plasticity, Effectual Connectivity, and Memory in Cortex«. In: *Front. Neuroanat.* 10.

Kohonen, T. (1977). *Associative Memory: A System Theoretic Approach*. Berlin: Springer.

Kymn, C. J., S. Mazelet, A. Thomas and B. A. Olshausen (2024). »Binding in Hippocampal-Entorhinal Circuits Enables Compositionality in Cognitive Maps«. In: *J. Neurosci.* License: CC BY-NC-SA 4.0.

Laughlin, S. and T. Sejnowski (2003). »Communication in Neuronal Networks«. In: *Science* 301, pp. 1870–1874. DOI: 10.1126/science.1089662.

LeCun, Y., Y. Bengio and G. Hinton (2015). »Deep Learning«. In: *Nature* 521, pp. 436–444.

LeCun, Y., C. Cortes and C. Burges (2023). *Mnist Handwritten Digit Database*. URL: http://yann.lecun.com/exdb/mnist.

Lennie, P. (2003). »The Cost of Cortical Computation«. In: *Curr. Biol.* 13, pp. 493–497. DOI: 10.1016/S0960-9822(03)00135-0.

Nambusubramaniyan, S., A. Knoblauch and F. Röhrbein (2022). »Scalable Layer-Parallel Readout Training Rule for Self-Organizing Recurrent Neural Networks«. In: *Proc. Bernstein Conf.* DOI: 10.12751/nncn.bc2022.165.

Navlakha, S., A. L. Barth and Z. Bar-Joseph (2015). »Decreasing-rate pruning optimizes the construction of efficient and robust distributed networks«. In: *PLOS Comput. Biol.* 11, pp. 1–23.

Palm, G., A. Knoblauch, F. Hauser and A. Schüz (2014). »Cell Assemblies in the Cerebral Cortex«. In: *Biol. Cybernet.* 108, pp. 559–572. DOI: 10.1007/s00422-014-0596-4.

Paulsen, O. and T. Sejnowski (2000). »Natural Patterns of Activity and Long-Term Synaptic Plasticity«. In: *Curr. Opin. Neurobiol.* 10, pp. 172–179. DOI: 10.1016/S0959-4388(00)00076-3.

Poole, B., S. Ozair, A. van den Oord, A. A. Alemi and G. Tucker (2019). »On Variational Bounds of Mutual Information«. In: *arXiv preprint*. DOI: 10.48550/arxiv.1905.06922. arXiv: 1905.06922.

Rosa, C. L., R. Parolisi and L. Bonfanti (2020). »Brain Structural Plasticity: From Adult Neurogenesis to Immature Neurons«. In: *Front. Neurosci.* 14, p. 75. ISSN: 1662-453X. DOI: 10.3389/fnins.2020.00075/full.

Shwartz-Ziv, R. and Y. LeCun (2023). »To Compress or Not to Compress–Self-Supervised Learning and Information Theory: A Review«. In: *arXiv Preprint*. DOI: 10.48550/arxiv.2304.09355. arXiv: 2304.09355.

Shwartz-Ziv, R. and N. Tishby (2017). »Opening the Black Box of Deep Neural Networks via Information«. In: *CoRR* abs/1703.00810. DOI: 10.48550/arxiv.1703.00810. arXiv: 1703.00810.

Song, S., K. Miller and L. Abbott (2000). »Competitive Hebbian Learning Through Spike-Timing-Dependent Synaptic Plasticity«. In: *Nat. Neurosci.* 3, pp. 919–926. DOI: 10.1038/78829.

Sreenivas, S. T. et al. (2024). »LLM Pruning and Distillation in Practice: The Minitron Approach«. In: *arXiv preprint arXiv:2408.11796*. DOI: 10.48550/arxiv.2408.11796. arXiv: 2408.11796.

Steinbuch, K. (1961). »Die Lernmatrix«. In: *Kybernetik* 1, pp. 36–45.

Stricker, P., F. Röhrbein and A. Knoblauch (2024). »Weight Perturbation and Competitive Hebbian Plasticity for Training Sparse Excitatory Neural Networks«. In: *Proc. Int. Joint Conf. Neural Networks (IJCNN)*. Yet to publish. Yokohama, Japan: IEEE.

Tiddia, G., L. Sergi and B. Golosio (2024). *A Theoretical Framework for Learning Through Structural Plasticity*. DOI: 10.48550/arxiv.2307.11735. arXiv: 2307.11735.

Tishby, N. and N. Zaslavsky (2015). »Deep Learning and the Information Bottleneck Principle«. In: *CoRR*. DOI: 10.48550/arxiv.1503.02406. arXiv: 1503.02406.

Zhou, H. (2022). »Activation Learning by Local Competitions«. In: *arXiv* 2209.13400v2.

Zito, K. and K. Svoboda (2002). »Activity-dependent synaptogenesis in the adult mammalian cortex«. In: *Neuron* 35, pp. 1015–1017.

Züge, P., C. Klos and R. M. Memmesheimer (2023). »Weight versus Node Perturbation Learning in Temporally Extended Tasks: Weight Perturbation Often Performs Similarly or Better«. In: *Phys. Rev.* 13.

Adversarial Evasion Attacks on Computer Vision using SHAP Values

Frank Mollard[*], Marcus Becker[‡], Florian Röhrbein[†]

[*]Business Intelligence & Data Science, Infraserv GmbH & Co. Höchst KG, Germany
[‡]International School of Management, Germany
[†]TU-Chemnitz, Germany

Abstract

The paper introduces a white-box attack on computer vision models using SHAP values. It demonstrates how adversarial evasion attacks can compromise the performance of deep learning models by reducing output confidence or inducing misclassifications. Such attacks are particularly insidious as they can deceive the perception of an algorithm while eluding human perception due to their imperceptibility to the human eye. The proposed attack leverages SHAP values to quantify the significance of individual inputs to the output at the inference stage. A comparison is drawn between the SHAP attack and the well-known Fast Gradient Sign Method. We find evidence that SHAP attacks are more robust in generating misclassifications particularly in gradient hiding scenarios.

1 Introduction

Adversarial attacks on deep learning models, such as Artificial Neural Networks (ANN), aim to undermine performance by reducing output confidence or inducing misclassifications (Zhou et al., 2022). These attacks pose a serious threat because they deceive the perception of the algorithm while being deliberately designed to avoid detection by human perception. There are various access paths for an attack, with either the training data (poisoning), the model itself, or the application data (evasion) being targeted. When attacking the training data, the attacker must have access to it. This involves either changing or adding data. Evasion attacks, on the other hand, refer to the input of the trained model in the inference phase. The input is only manipulated slightly by adding imperceptible perturbations so the viewer will barely notice any differences. This makes evasion attacks very attractive for attackers, as they can remain unnoticed. We make a distinction between white-box and black-box attacks. White-box attacks require knowledge of the model and access to it (Hitaj et al., 2017; Tramèr et al., 2016). Black-box attacks, on the other hand, do not require any knowledge of the model. However, it is important that the input and output of the model must at least be observable (Fredrikson et al., 2015; Moosavi-Dezfooli et al., 2016; Papernot et al., 2016a, 2017; Rosenberg et al., 2017; Shokri et al., 2017; Tramèr et al., 2016).

In the field of white-box attacks, there are several approaches, some of which differ significantly, reflecting the diversity of strategies explored in scientific research. One of the first papers dealing with white-box evasion attacks is by Szegedy et al. (2014), in which the authors ensured that the model would misclassify a so-called adversarial example by optimising its distance from the correctly classified original input. Moosavi-Dezfooli et al. (2016) proposes a method called DeepFool. Papernot et al. (2016b) developed an algorithm that only changed around 4 % of the input data to lead to miscalculation. Alaifari et al. (2019) added slight deformations to the input to keep the manipulation invisible, thereby inducing misclassifications. Probably the best-known method is called the Fast Gradient Sign Method (FGSM) by Goodfellow et al. (2015). The advantage of this method lies in its relative simplicity of implementation compared to the previously discussed approaches. It leverages the fact that the optimisation relies on gradient descent. For every classification with a non-perfect result, there will be a gradient that is not equal to zero. This allows the sign of the gradient to be added to any observation x, reversing the gradient descent.

$$x' = x + \varepsilon \cdot \text{sign}(\nabla_x L(x, t, \omega)) \tag{1}$$

The observations x, the target t and the model parameters ω are constant. As the gradient ∇ of the loss function L is close to zero in a good model, only the signs are used. The scalar ε represents the magnitude of the attack. For instance, if the slope of the loss function is negative, ε is subtracted from the pixel value x, vice versa. This causes a shift in the direction of increasing errors, resembling a reverse gradient descent process. Though, the ε is assumed to be equal for all weights, even though the gradients may be different, potentially leading to overly strong or weak adjustments for the non-linear loss function.

The FGSM prioritizes speed over efficiency (Carlini et al., 2017), which means that attacks often fail. Kurakin et al. (2017) enhance this method by incorporating an iterative approach, where the overall ε is broken down into smaller increments, and the gradient is recalculated at each step. This accounts for the non-linearity of the loss functions of ANN. The modification substantially boosts the strength of FGSM attacks while maintaining a relatively straightforward implementation – in comparison to the other methods discussed. However, this approach only alleviates the issue of excessively strong or weak steps.

Therefore, based on the FGSM, we propose a white-box attack with comparable implementation complexity that relies on **SH**apley **A**dditive ex**P**lanation (SHAP) values as introduced by Lundberg et al. (2016) and Lundberg et al. (2017) instead of gradients (see equation 5). SHAP values provide information about the extent to which individual inputs contribute to the output in the inference phase. In Section 2 we define SHAP values and also discuss the computational intensity to subsequently show in Section 3 why and how SHAP attacks work using four very different data sets and architectures. In Section 4 we compare FGSM from Kurakin et al. (2017) with SHAP attacks and in Section 5 we conclude.

It is crucial to publicly disclose the types of attacks in order to make the models resilient and to establish countermeasures. Without this transparency, attacks could be developed and deployed secretly, potentially harming models currently in use.

2 SHAP Values

Post-analytical methods such as **L**ocal **I**nterpretable **M**odel-agnostic **E**xplanations (LIME) by Ribeiro et al. (2016) or SHAP values are model-agnostic, meaning they explain the importance of input variables independently from the classifier. SHAP values offer several benefits compared to other post-analytical methods. Unlike LIME, SHAP values can be interpreted both locally and globally. Furthermore, they are additive, meaning that when all individual effects are summed, they precisely match the model's output.

To ensure the convergence of an additive feature attribution method to a unique solution when explaining model outputs, three properties are essential:

Note: Models for the post-analytical explanation of prediction outputs often use simplified inputs x' (Lundberg et al., 2016)

Local accuracy ensures that the post-hoc explanation model $g(x')$ for a simplified input x' matches the output of the original model $f(x)$, where x denotes the original input.

Missingness means that a missing input x is treated the same as an input with no effect.

Consistency addresses the issue of multicollinearity. In statistical explanatory models, such as the ordinary least squares method, linear dependence between predictors can be so significant that they change the signs of the coefficients. While this does not impact the prediction accuracy, it affects the interpretation of the model (Farrar et al., 1967). Therefore, in a consistent model, if the influence of x increases or remains unchanged, its attributed impact should not decrease.

Young (1985) demonstrated that Shapley values satisfy the three conditions above.

SHAP values quantify the impact of a variable *i* on a given task. Starting from the mean of the target variable as the baseline, one model is calculated for each possible subset S of variable combinations for N variables in total. A power set is used to calculate the total contribution ϕ of a variable i to the result. This approach involves weighting each individual (marginal) contribution obtained by adding a variable.

For instance, if variables A, B, and C are considered, the process of determining the contribution of A begins at a level without variables (just the average of the target variable) and progresses to a level where a model includes all three variables. Marginal contributions are assessed at each stage, moving from one level to the next. So, the model with only variable A is compared to the baseline (i.e., the average without any variables) and is weighted by one-third. For models with two variables, combinations such as AB and AC are evaluated, each weighted by one-sixth, which sums to one-third in total. The model including all variables is also weighted by one-third. Each marginal contribution of a variable results from the model output including the corresponding variable $f_x(S \vee i)$ and excluding $f_x(S)$.

$$\phi_i = \sum_{S \subseteq N_i} = \frac{(N - |S| - 1)!|S|!}{N!}[f_x(S \vee i) - f_x(S)] \tag{2}$$

The first factor $\frac{(N-|S|-1)!|S|!}{N!}$ is the weight, the second $[f_x(S \vee i) - f_x(S)]$ is the marginal contribution. This facilitates the determination of how variables contribute to a specific outcome for each observation. However, with N possible variables and k[1] variables included, the number of total possibilities (including the mean of the target) is calculated by

$$\sum_{k=0}^{N} \binom{N}{k} = 2^N \tag{3}$$

This may result in very high computational complexity. Therefore, in practical implementations, a dataset sampling method is employed wherein a constrained least squares problem is addressed using a feasible quantity of data points. However, despite this simplification, high computational costs remain, which is especially notable in the field of computer vision and requires processing with suitable high-performance architecture.

SHAP values are to be understood more as a framework as they use other methods in the background, such as LIME, DeepLift from Shrikumar et al. (2016), or layer-wise relevance propagation from Bach et al. (2015). Eventually, the key strengths of SHAP values stem from their use of the power set, leading to additive contributions, along with a well-defined mathematical foundation.

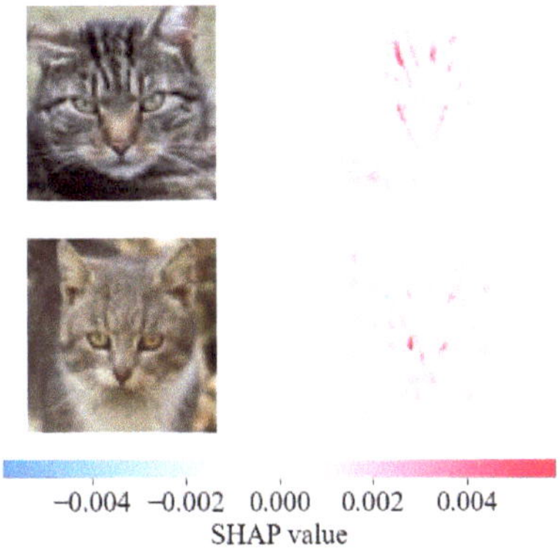

Figure 1: What makes a Cat a Cat?

In the case of images, each pixel at channel level (hereinafter referred to as a »pixel«) can be regarded as a variable x. This makes it possible to determine which areas in an

[1] k is not equalt to S. S contains a certain subset, whereas k is only the number of variables considered at a certain level.

image speak for and against the corresponding result in a classification task. Figure 1 illustrates the classification process for a dataset consisting of pixels of cats and dogs.

At the bottom, the intensity represents the influence of a specific region: Red shades indicate a higher likelihood of a cat, while the blue shades indicate a lower likelihood of a cat. Figure 1 demonstrates that SHAP values can identify which pixels contribute positively or negatively toward a specific class. This indicates that this calculation method could potentially be used to conduct adversarial attacks by modifying the corresponding regions. However, the image does not yet clarify the underlying rules governing this process.

3 SHAP Attack

Given that SHAP values identify the contributions and magnitudes of individual pixels to the model's output, it is plausible to utilise these values to counteract these influences, potentially inducing misclassifications. The strength over similar attacks, like gradient attacks, is that SHAP values take into account the magnitude of a pixel's influence on the outcome. In contrast, gradient attacks only multiply the sign of the remaining gradient by a scalar ε, ignoring the magnitude of the influence. This means that fewer pixels need to be manipulated, which makes the SHAP attack more subtle. Figure 2 illustrates the relationship between SHAP values and pixel values.

If a pixel exhibits an exceptionally high or low value, it can exert a considerable influence. In a sufficiently well-fitted classification model, a pixel with an intermediate magnitude tends to have a rather neutral effect. This means that pixels with a value in the middle of the range (between 0-1) are more likely to have a SHAP value close to zero (according to Figure 2 at a pixel value of approximately 0.50). Analysis of SHAP values across various datasets and architectures listed below confirm this assertion. Additionally, it is important to recognise that a pixel's value is not always positively correlated with its influence on the model output.

For the magnitude of a single pixel of an image, the relationship to ϕ_i often linearly increases or decreases, as depicted in Figure 2 (A Pixel, Another Pixel) for example. In other occasions the relationship might be convex (Yet Another Pixel Figure 2) or concave with either increasing or decreasing tendency. What they all have in common is that they intersect or approach the zero line at approximately the same point. If

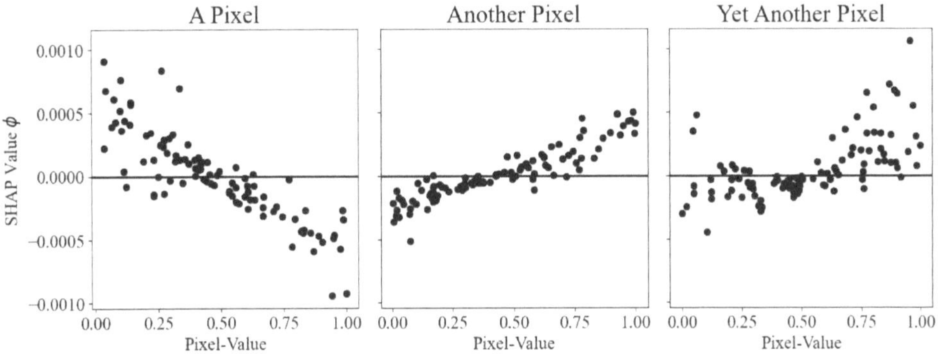

Figure 2: 100 Images, 3 different Pixels (SHAP Values vs. underlying Pixel magnitude) for the »Animal Faces« Dataset.

these relationships, meaning all the pixels from several images, are overlain, it becomes evident that the neutral area mentioned earlier appears somewhere in the centre of the range (in this case 0-1). The result is an almost butterfly pattern, as illustrated in Figure 3. In this case, the neutral area is around 0.4.

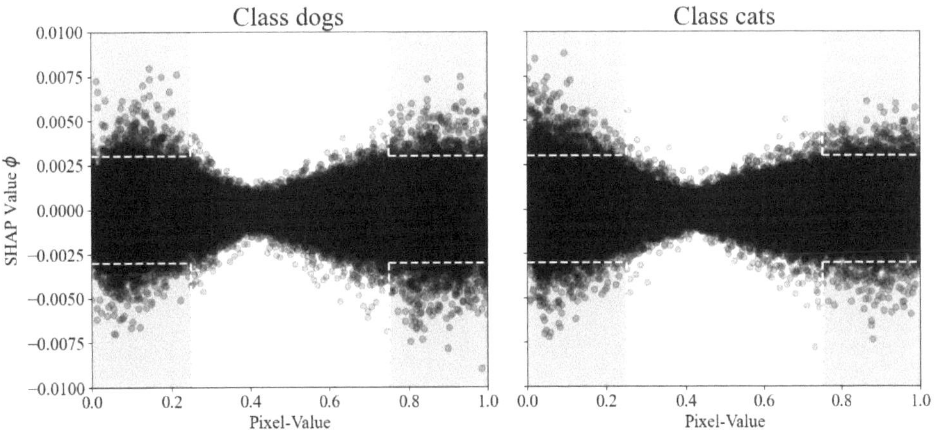

Figure 3: 500 Images x 64x64x3 Pixel (SHAP Values vs. underlying Value) for the »Animal Faces« Dataset.

The grey fields mark the pixel areas with the strongest positive or negative influence. As explained in detail below, the butterfly pattern can be exploited by shifting the pixels into the neutral area in such a way that everything that points positively or negatively to a certain class is neutralized, leading to an increase in uncertainty in the classification.

In order to exclude both architecture and dataset dependencies in the observed pattern, we use different architectures and datasets.

The **Animal Faces dataset** from Kaggle shows portrait photos of cats, dogs and wild animals in 512x512 and three colour channels. We reduce these to 64x64x3. The applied model has 3 convolutional layers and a total of around 76k parameters.

The the **Cats and Dogs Filtered dataset** from Google shows cats and dogs in the format 160x160x3. In contrast to the previous dataset, the dogs and cats are not displayed as portraits, but in different environments and poses, which increases the variance of the dataset in comparison. To examine how SHAP attacks behave with very deep networks, we perform a transfer learning with EfficientNetB7 from Tan et al. (2020) with more than 66 million parameters.

The **MNIST** data set shows handwritten digits from 0-9 in the format 28x28x1 (greyscale). This data set is completely different from all others. The applied classification model has two convolutional layers followed by a dense layer with a total of 450k parameters.

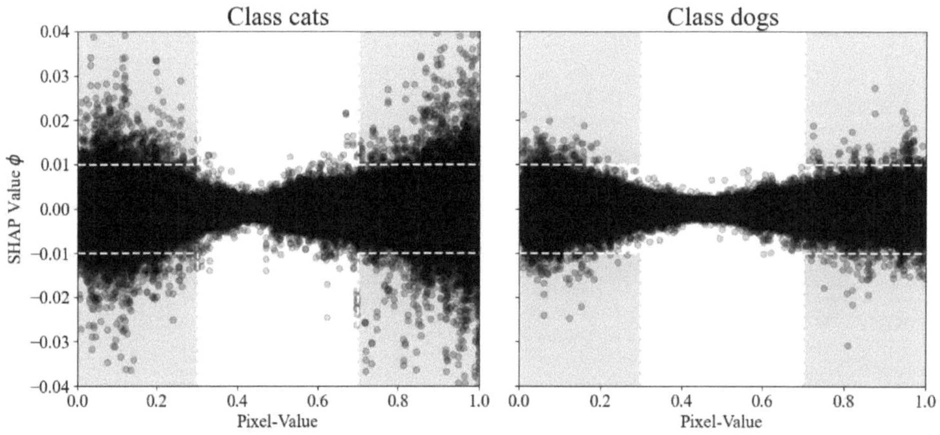

Figure 4: 500 Images x 160x160x3 Pixel (SHAP Values vs. underlying Value) of the »Cats and Dogs filtered« Dataset.

The **Woman and Man Faces** dataset from Kaggle contains portraits with male and female appearance in 64x64x3 format. Human faces are very different from animal faces in terms of statistical properties because humans do not have fur to hide skin aging and animals do not wear clothes. Therefore, increased variance is to be expected. The model applied has 3 convolutional layers and a total of around 76k parameters.

Figure 4 shows the correlation between SHAP values an pixel values for the Cats and Dogs Filtered dataset from Google using the very deep EfficientNetB7. When applied to the MNIST data set, the same pattern can be seen for each class.

It is noticeable in Figure 5 that the area with less influence on the model output is not close to 0.4 as in the two examples above, but rather lower, at around 0.3 or below. The same pattern can also be observed for human faces, as illustrated in Figure 6.

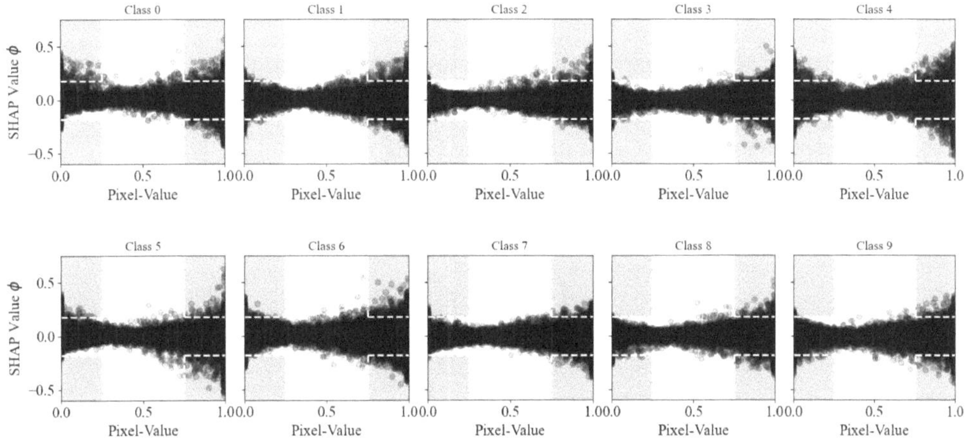

Figure 5: 500 Images x 28x28 Pixel (SHAP Values vs. underlying Value) »MNIST« Dataset.

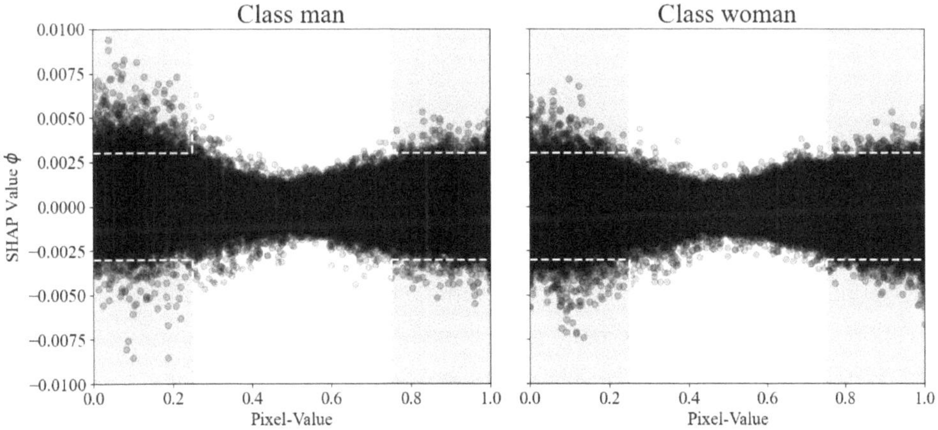

Figure 6: 500 Images x 160x160x3 Pixel (SHAP Values vs. underlying Value) of the »Woman and Man Faces« Dataset.

Initially, it might seem plausible to neutralise positive influences (ϕ) on the classification result. However, pixels generally exhibit correlations with one another. If only the positive components were removed, the information would still be available via a simple inverse conclusion. This means that the mere neutralisation of pixel values speaking for a certain class when applying a convolutional neural network does not necessarily lead to misclassification, since the pattern is still present but only other pixels justify it instead. This is similar to removing all the red areas from Figure 1 so the same pattern still remains between the blue areas. It is, therefore, also important to neutralise the regions that speak against the class in order to disrupt the confidence of the model. Consequently, moving away from the grey areas would lead to a reduction in the influence of the respective pixel. In light of this, the SHAP attack can be defined as

$$V = \phi \geq v \vee \phi \leq -v \tag{4}$$

$$x' = x + \varepsilon \cdot \begin{cases} -\phi, & \text{if } x \geq 1 - h \ \wedge \ V \\ \phi, & \text{if } x \leq h \ \wedge \ V \end{cases} \tag{5}$$

where $\varepsilon \in [0, \infty]$ stands for the intensity of the attack. In our investigations, $\varepsilon = \frac{1}{20\sigma_\phi}$, with σ_ϕ as the standard deviation of ϕ, proved to be a good starting point. SHAP Values are represented by ϕ. v is a real numbered vertical threshold to ensure that only strong influences are used for manipulation. We recommend $2\sigma_\phi$ for v as a first orientation. The parameter h ensures that only pixels with an increased absolute value are manipulated. Values between 0.2 and 0.3 are recommended.

4 Comparison between SHAP Attack and FGSM

Adversarial evasion attacks have two requirements. On the one hand, they should lead to misclassification; on the other hand, they should remain invisible to human and machine perception. In the following, a comparison is made between FGSM according to Kurakin et al. (2017) and SHAP attacks. The parameters ε are adjusted so the attacks remain barely subtle. For this purpose, a visual comparison is made to assess the performance of the two algorithms at the adjusted ε. In addition, a mass evaluation is performed on the data sets to determine the misclassification performance under the circumstances described above.

4.1 Visual Assessment

To gauge the degree of subliminality of the different attacks, the »Animal Faces« dataset is visualised first. The optimal ε, ensuring the attack is imperceptible, is simulated as 0.2 for FGSM and 50 for SHAP attacks. 52 % misclassifications occur with FGSM and 73 % misclassifications with SHAP attacks. The SHAP attacks have a more sustained effect than FGSM when ε is increasing.

Based on a cut-off of 50 %, there are fewer misclassifications using FGSM (see e.g. second image in Figure 7). FGSM does not generally lead to a reduction in the confidence for a specific class. SHAP attacks, however, consistently lead to a reduction in the probability of the attacked class – assuming that the classification model is sufficiently well-fitted.

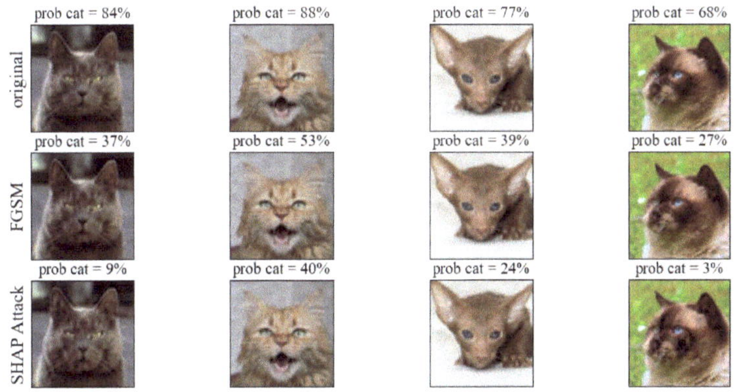

Figure 7: 3 Images x 64x64x3 Pixel Attack Comparison on the »Animal Faces« Dataset.

For human faces (»Woman and Man Faces« dataset from kaggle) similar relations are observed. Here ε is 60 for the SHAP attack and 0.2 for FGSM. The FGSM attack achieved a misclassification rate of 69 % and SHAP attacks of 98 %. Figure 8 provides a visual demonstration.

Concerning invisibility, it becomes evident (from Figures 7 and 8 respectively) that both attacks exhibit comparable effectiveness, though SHAP attacks demonstrate a stronger influence. The stronger misclassification by SHAP attacks in this case is caused by the difference in methodology. While FGSM merely multiplies the gradient sign by a constant, SHAP attacks tend to concentrate on particularly important areas in the image

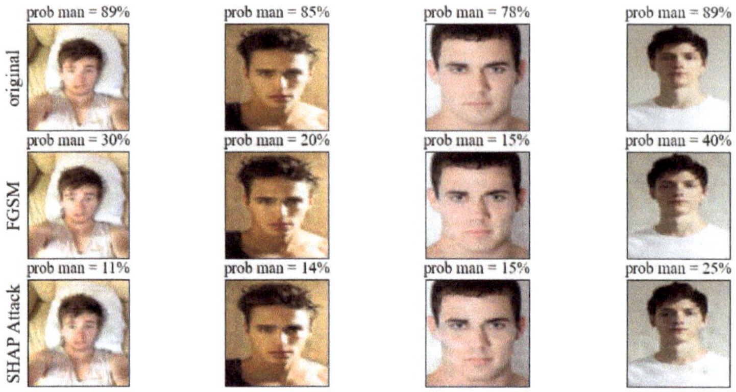

Figure 8: 3 Images x 64x64x3 Pixel Attack Comparison on the »Man and Woman Faces« Dataset.

and leave the unimportant areas untouched. Consequently, pixels with significant influence (ϕ) undergo more pronounced alterations under the SHAP attack methodology.

4.2 Mass Evaluations

Table 1 presents the rates of misclassification using FGSM by Kurakin et al. (2017) and SHAP Attacks. These rates occur at an attack intensity ε, where the manipulation remain imperceptible. With MNIST, imperceptibility is not possible because the manipulation cannot be concealed by the missing channels. Here, the attack was designed in such a way that the perceptibility was slight and comparable between the methods. The classes are balanced in all data sets used for comparison, to ensure that no minority class problem occurs.

Table 1: Misclassification Rate for Evasion Attack using FGSM by Kurakin et al. (2017) and SHAP Attack

Misclassification Rate

Dataset	FGSM		SHAP Attack		Model Accuracy
Animal Faces	52 %	$\varepsilon = 0.2$	73 %	$\varepsilon = 50$	99.5 %
Cats and Dogs Filtered	98 %	$\varepsilon = 0.01$	89 %	$\varepsilon = 80$	98 %
MNIST	34 %	$\varepsilon = 0.2$	60 %	$\varepsilon = 1.5$	99 %
Woman and Man Faces	69 %	$\varepsilon = 0.2$	98 %	$\varepsilon = 60$	97 %

The table illustrates that gradient-based attacks yield variable outcomes, occasionally surpassing expectations but often underperforming. In contrast, SHAP-based attacks consistently result in stable misclassification rates. The instability of gradient-based attacks can be attributed to the gradients becoming uninformative; a phenomenon known as »gradient masking«. This issue can arise due to stochastic, vanishing, exploding or scattered gradients (Gupta et al., 2021). Furthermore, if the loss function exhibits non-smooth behaviour at the approximated minimum, the residual gradient's direction may be incorrect for vanishing gradients, thus, potentially increasing classification confidence rather than decreasing it. This phenomenon has been shown in the mass evaluations. For some FGSM attacks, the classification confidence has increased instead of decreasing. SHAP attacks are independent of the loss function as they only represent the behaviour of the model-output in relation to certain variables (pixels), as seen in equation 2.

5 Conclusion

The study has demonstrated the successful use of SHAP values in conducting white-box adversarial attacks on computer vision models. By utilising the explainability of SHAP values to measure the influence of individual inputs, the proposed SHAP attack method is more robust in causing misclassifications than traditional FGSM attacks. These findings highlight the susceptibility of deep learning models to evasion attacks that subtly alter input data, underscoring the necessity for developing more resilient models to counter such adversarial threats. Additionally, the research reveals the dual potential of SHAP values as tools for both model explanation as well as for the identification and exploitation of model weaknesses.

Future research should focus on improving the defence mechanisms of computer vision models to mitigate the risks posed by these attacks. A development towards better generalized models would be desirable, where the influence of individual pixels is more balanced across the image and the classification relies less on individual pixels.

However, it should also be noted that SHAP attacks not only require access to the model but also the availability of sufficient inference data for the calculation of the SHAP values. Depending on the resolution of the images and the number of classes, high computing resources may also be required due to the high computational complexity. As a result, the practical application of a large number of very high-resolution images or even videos in combination with complex models may be limited or only manageable with very high computing resources.

Corresponding Author

Frank Mollard: f.mollard@aol.com
Business Intelligence & Data Science, Infraserv GmbH & Co. Höchst KG, Germany

ORCID

Frank Mollard https://orcid.org/0000-0002-6469-4764
Marcus Becker https://orcid.org/0000-0001-5801-3785
Florian Röhrbein https://orcid.org/0000-0002-4709-2673

References

Alaifari, R., G. S. Alberti and T. Gauksson (2019). *ADef: an Iterative Algorithm to Construct Adversarial Deformations*. DOI: 10.48550/arxiv.1804.07729. arXiv: 1804.07729 [cs.CV].

Bach, S. et al. (2015). »On pixel-wise explanations for non-linear classifier decisions by layer-wise relevance propagation«. In: *PloS One* 10.7, e0130140.

Carlini, N. and D. Wagner (2017). *Towards Evaluating the Robustness of Neural Networks*. DOI: 10.48550/arxiv.1608.04644. arXiv: 1608.04644 [cs.CR].

Farrar, D. E. and R. R. Glauber (1967). »Multicollinearity in Regression Analysis: The Problem Revisited«. In: *The Review of Economics and Statistics* 49.1, pp. 92–107. DOI: 10.2307/1937887.

Fredrikson, M., S. Jha and T. Ristenpart (2015). »Model inversion attacks that exploit confidence information and basic countermeasures«. In: *Proceedings of the 22nd ACM SIGSAC Conference on Computer and Communications Security*. ACM, pp. 1322–1333.

Goodfellow, I. J., J. Shlens and C. Szegedy (2015). *Explaining and Harnessing Adversarial Examples*. DOI: 10.48550/arxiv.1412.6572. arXiv: 1412.6572 [stat.ML].

Gupta, K. and T. Ajanthan (2021). *Improved Gradient based Adversarial Attacks for Quantized Networks*. DOI: 10.48550/arxiv.2003.13511. arXiv: 2003.13511 [cs.CV].

Hitaj, B., G. Ateniese and F. Perez-Cruz (2017). »Deep models under the GAN: Information leakage from collaborative deep learning«. In: *arXiv preprint arXiv:170207464*.

Kurakin, A., I. Goodfellow and S. Bengio (2017). *Adversarial examples in the physical world*. DOI: 10.48550/arxiv.1607.02533. arXiv: 1607.02533 [cs.CV].

Lundberg, S. and S.-I. Lee (2016). *An unexpected unity among methods for interpreting model predictions*. DOI: 10.48550/arxiv.1611.07478. arXiv: 1611.07478 [cs.AI].

– (2017). *A Unified Approach to Interpreting Model Predictions*. DOI: 10.48550/arxiv.1705.07874. arXiv: 1705.07874 [cs.AI].

Moosavi-Dezfooli, S. M., A. Fawzi and P. Frossard (2016). »Deepfool: a simple and accurate method to fool deep neural networks«. In: *Proceedings of the IEEE Conference on Computer Vision and Pattern Recognition*, pp. 2574–2582.

Papernot, N., P. McDaniel and I. Goodfellow (2016a). *Transferability in Machine Learning: from Phenomena to Black-Box Attacks using Adversarial Samples*. DOI: 10.48550/arxiv.1605.07277. arXiv: 1605.07277.

Papernot, N. et al. (2016b). »The Limitations of Deep Learning in Adversarial Settings«. In: *2016 IEEE European Symposium on Security and Privacy (EuroS&P)*, pp. 372–387. DOI: 10.1109/EuroSP.2016.36.

Papernot, N. et al. (2017). »Practical Black-Box Attacks against Machine Learning«. In: *Proceedings of the 2017 ACM on Asia Conference on Computer and Communications Security*. ASIA CCS '17. Abu Dhabi, United Arab Emirates: Association for Computing Machinery, pp. 506–519. ISBN: 9781450349444. DOI: 10.1145/3052973.3053009.

Ribeiro, M. T., S. Singh and C. Guestrin (2016). *"Why Should I Trust You?": Explaining the Predictions of Any Classifier*. DOI: 10.48550/arxiv.1602.04938. arXiv: 1602.04938 [cs.LG].

Rosenberg, I. et al. (2017). »Generic black-box end-to-end attack against RNNs and other API calls based malware classifiers«. In: *arXiv preprint arXiv:170705970*.

Shokri, R. et al. (2017). »Membership inference attacks against machine learning models«. In: *2017 IEEE Symposium on Security and Privacy (SP)*. IEEE, pp. 3–18.

Shrikumar, A., P. Greenside, A. Shcherbina and A. Kundaje (2016). »Not Just a Black Box: Learning Important Features Through Propagating Activation Differences«. In: *arXiv preprint arXiv: 1605.01713*.

Szegedy, C. et al. (2014). *Intriguing properties of neural networks*. DOI: 10.48550/arxiv.1312.6199. arXiv: 1312.6199 [cs.CV].

Tan, M. and Q. V. Le (2020). *EfficientNet: Rethinking Model Scaling for Convolutional Neural Networks*. DOI: 10.48550/arxiv.1905.11946. arXiv: 1905.11946 [cs.LG].

Tramèr, F. et al. (2016). »Stealing machine learning models via prediction APIs«. In: *USENIX Security Symposium*, pp. 601–618.

Young, H. P. (1985). »Monotonic solutions of cooperative games«. In: *International Journal of Game Theory* 14.2, pp. 65–72.

Zhou, S. et al. (2022). »Adversarial Attacks and Defenses in Deep Learning: From a Perspective of Cybersecurity«. In: *ACM Comput. Surv.* 55.8. ISSN: 0360-0300. DOI: 10.1145/3547330.

Benchmarking Quantum Red TEA on CPUs, GPUs, and TPUs

Daniel Jaschke[a,b,c], Marco Ballarin[b,c], Nora Reinić[b,c], Luka Pavešić[b,c], Simone Montangero[a,b,c]

[a]Institute for Complex Quantum Systems, Ulm University, Albert-Einstein-Allee 11, 89069 Ulm, Germany
[b]Dipartimento di Fisica e Astronomia »G. Galilei« & Padua Quantum Technologies Research Center, Università degli Studi di Padova, Italy I-35131, Padova, Italy
[c]INFN, Sezione di Padova, via Marzolo 8, I-35131, Padova, Italy

Abstract

We benchmark simulations of many-body quantum systems on heterogeneous hardware platforms using CPUs, GPUs, and TPUs. We compare different linear algebra backends, e.g., NumPy versus the PyTorch, JAX, or TensorFlow libraries, as well as a mixed-precision-inspired approach and optimizations for the target hardware. *Quantum Red TEA* out of the *Quantum TEA* library specifically addresses handling tensors with different libraries or hardware, where the tensors are the building blocks of tensor network algorithms. The benchmark problem is a variational search of a ground state in an interacting model. This is a ubiquitous problem in quantum many-body physics, which we solve using tensor network methods. This approximate state-of-the-art method compresses quantum correlations which is key to overcoming the exponential growth of the Hilbert space as a function of the number of particles. We present a way to obtain speedups of a factor of 34 when tuning parameters on the CPU, and an additional factor of 2.76 on top of the best CPU setup when migrating to GPUs.

1 Introduction

Tensor network (TN) methods used for the simulation of quantum many-body systems rely heavily on HPC resources. Carefully optimizing and benchmarking these algorithms can result in significant savings of resources. This is essential to emulate bigger systems, include more details in the description of the system, or increase precision. Today's heterogeneous computing platforms open even more possibilities for optimization and a combination of various approaches. We demonstrate where computational gains are possible. As using various hardware requires flexibility, we implement a software design with interchangeable numerical libraries.

Tensor network methods have long been established as a method for the simulation of many-body quantum systems, see Refs. (Bañuls, 2023; Orús, 2014; Schollwöck, 2011). Today, they are used to numerically solve problems in fields ranging from condensed matter physics and lattice gauge theories and quantum simulation, to quantum circuit design (Montangero, 2018). Quantum-inspired methods employ TNs to solve optimization problems, partial differential equations, or machine learning tasks (Gourianov et al., 2022; Lucas, 2014; Stoudenmire, 2018). The variety of applications and their computational cost make TN methods an excellent target for exploring optimizations and benchmarking.

We benchmark the *Quantum TEA* (Quantum Tensor network Emulator Applications) library (Bacilieri et al., 2024; Ballarin et al., 2024; Silvi et al., 2019) with a ground state search for a two-dimensional quantum Ising model (Sachdev, 2011). *Quantum TEA Leaves* implements various TN algorithms as a Python package. *Quantum Red TEA* enables additional tensor classes. We choose the groundstate search of the two-dimensional quantum Ising model on a 16×16 lattice as the benchmark problem, because of its relevance for the current research. The tensor contractions and linear algebra decompositions are either solved with NumPy/CuPy, PyTorch, JAX, or TensorFlow (Abadi et al., 2015; Ansel et al., 2024; Bradbury et al., 2018; Harris et al., 2020; Okuta et al., 2017). In total, we outline seven approaches where we expect a potential speedup. We successfully demonstrate how to leverage the different libraries, e.g., we gain a speedup factor of 34 in the CPU benchmark.

The manuscript is organized as follows. In Section 2, we introduce TN methods to the extent necessary to follow the benchmarks and describe the setup. In Section 3, we evaluate the benchmark results for CPUs, GPUs, and TPUs. We conclude in Section 4.

2 Methods and benchmark setup

The benchmark is set up around three main choices: (a) we choose a binary tree tensor network (TTN) representation for the wavefunction $|\psi\rangle$; (b) we consider a ground state search, i.e., minimizing the energy E of the wavefunction $|\psi\rangle$; (c) the underlying model is a two-dimensional quantum Ising model with nearest-neighbor interactions. We discuss the rationale behind and consequences of the choices below.

In short, TN methods are based on efficiently, but approximately, representing states of quantum systems, i.e., vectors living in a given Hilbert space, as products of a set of tensors. Didactically, the approach separates a large vector into a set of tensors with singular value decomposition, where only a set of states associated with the largest singular values is kept. Due to an intrinsic relation between entanglement, i.e., quantum correlation, and the distribution of the singular values, this is an optimal way to approximate quantum states. The number of kept singular values, i.e., the maximal size of a tensor's link, uniquely determines the accuracy of the approximation. The *maximal bond dimension* χ is thus a central parameter of TN algorithms.

We choose the TTN as it is particularly apt for representing quantum systems with long-range interactions. These long-range interactions arise in the 2D quantum Ising model when it is mapped into a 1D chain. The physical sites of the lattice are represented as the leaves of the tree, while the rest of the network is there to transfer entanglement between the distant sites. For a more detailed discussion of TN methods, we direct the reader to (Schollwöck, 2011), while specifics of TTNs are reviewed in (Silvi et al., 2019).

To find the ground state of a given model, we iterate, i.e., we *sweep*, through the network and locally optimize each tensor in a way that minimizes the energy. This procedure involves contracting the tensor with its environment, locally solving an eigenproblem to find the smallest eigenvalue, and performing decompositions to update the neighboring tensors afterwards. The ground state is reached by repeating this process multiple times, until convergence is reached. See Figure 1a) for a sketch of an 8-qubit TTN and its first two sweeps. The computational workload thus dominantly comes from a large number of linear algebra tasks and manipulations of the tensors: tensor contractions, sparse eigenproblems, as well as SVD, QR, and eigen-decompositions. Because the TTN uses rank-three tensors of dimensions up to $\chi \times \chi \times \chi$, the complexity of these operations scales as $\mathcal{O}(\chi^4)$. The simplified sketch of the library is shown in Figure 1b) with the two python modules, one abstract tensor class, five different tensor backends, i.e., implementations of the abstract tensor class, as well as the algorithms and simulations using the tensor classes.

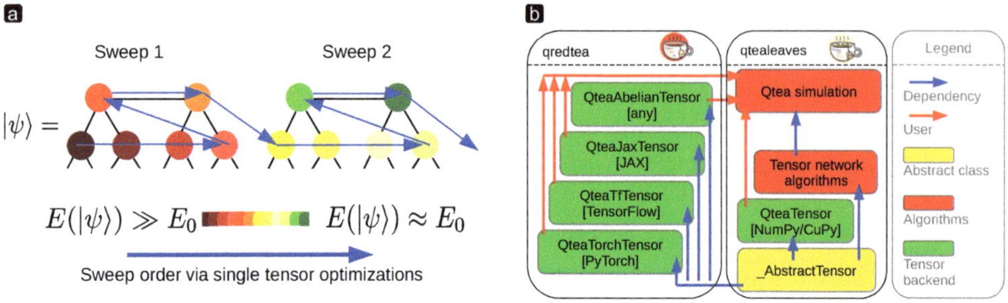

Figure 1: *Algorithm and simplified library setup.* **a** A binary tree tensor network represents the wavefunction $|\psi\rangle$ and the energy $E(|\psi\rangle)$ is minimized via a series of sweeps, where each sweep consists of local tensor optimizations. With each optimization, the wavefunction converges towards the ground state with its ground state energy E_0. **b** We consider two python packages from *Quantum TEA* for the ground state search. The Quantum TEA Leaves library comes with the tensor network algorithms as well as with an abstract class for tensors; moreover, the default tensors are implemented with NumPy/CuPy. Any implementation of the abstract tensor class is suitable for the algorithms. The Quantum Red TEA library leverages the abstract class to implement optional tensors using PyTorch, JAX, and TensorFlow. Moreover, Quantum Red TEA encodes block-sparse tensors with an Abelian symmetry.

We choose the ground state search as it is a ubiquitous problem in quantum physics, but also because it leads to an easily accessible interpretation of the benchmark. Because the ground state energy E_0 is a global minimum of energy, lower energies represent a better outcome of the algorithm. Comparison of computational time versus obtained energy is our main figure of merit.

The Hamiltonian H for the ground state search of the quantum Ising model in 2d is

$$H = -J \sum_{\langle i,j \rangle} \sigma_i^x \sigma_j^x - g \sum_i \sigma_i^z \, , \tag{1}$$

where sites are labeled with $i = (i_x, i_y)$ and j referring to positions in a 2d lattice and $\langle i,j \rangle$ contains all pairs of nearest-neighbors, The Pauli matrices σ^x and σ^z define the interactions with coupling $J = 1$ and the local field with coupling g. The linear system size is denoted by N, so that the total number of qubits is N^2, In the following, we set $N = 16$. The ratio g/J is set so that the system is close to the quantum critical point. In this point, the ground state is strongly correlated, which imposes sufficient computational challenges.

We anticipate the potential for optimization in the following choices:

i) *Picking linear algebra libraries:* NumPy is the defacto-standard for numerical computation in python and is therefore the standard backend in *Quantum TEA Leaves*. However, the alternatives to NumPy/CuPy provide all necessary interfaces in terms of tensor contractions and linear algebra decompositions to run the ground state search. Our implementation approach relies on an abstract tensor class, which allows us to easily run the same TN algorithm with NumPy/CuPy, PyTorch, JAX, and TensorFlow. We provide an initial comparison between these libraries for *Quantum TEA* and its TTN ground state search. Note that the different libraries introduce different dependencies for low-level linear algebra, i.e., BLAS/LAPACK versus Eigen or Arpack versus a custom Lanzos solver.

ii) *Exact renormalization group tensors (ERGT):* Each tensor in the lowest layer of the TTN contains two physical sites, which contain d degrees of freedom (in our case $d = 2$). These tensors thus have dimensions at most $d \times d \times d^2$, and can be represented exactly. Written as a matrix $(d \times d) \times (d^2)$, it is an exact unitary transformation with a complete set of orthonormal vectors. Depending on the maximum bond dimension, more ERGTs exist in lower layers. Any optimization on the ERGTs can be accounted for in their parent tensors as no relevant degree of freedom has been truncated yet. We explore if skipping the ERGTs leads to a speedup.

iii) *Mixed-precision tailored to TN methods:* the algorithm starts in a random guess state, which is far from optimum. Multiple iterations optimize the TN until it approximates the target state as good as possible with the given parameters of the algorithm. As arithmetic for single precision is faster than double precision, we exploit this by executing the first iterations in single-precision before moving the last sweeps to double-precision numbers.

iv) *Parallelization on CPUs:* We investigate the parallel speedup of one simulation on CPUs for the different backend libraries. Parallelization occurs at the level of the BLAS/LAPACK or Eigen library.

v) *GPUs-support:* The benefit of GPUs is well established and all four linear algebra libraries support GPUs. We benchmark simulations on CPU versus GPU.

vi) *Optimization of tensor dimensions:* GPUs reach peak performance at matrix dimensions which respect the underlying hardware, e.g., rows of a matrix being a multiple of 128 bytes. We study whether enforcing such a dimension benefits the execution time of the complete algorithm as it does for matrix-matrix multiplications (NVIDIAUsersGuide, 2023).

vii) *TPUs support for simulations:* TPUs are another class of accelerators with features such as just-in-time compilation of functions for the best performance. The first step towards profiting from the platform is the migration towards the hardware, which we achieve by leveraging our different backend libraries.

Together, the approaches encode the heterogeneous computing platforms from various aspects including hardware and precision. The benchmark executes on an *Intel Xeon Platinum 8480+* node or with a *NVIDIA A100-SXM-64GB* mounted on an *Intel Xeon Platinum 8358* on *leonardo* (CINECA). The TPU benchmark runs on Google's TPU v4-8.

3 Quantum Red TEA benchmark

The first part of the benchmark in Subsection 3.1 uses CPUs where we analyze higher-level optimization, like the mixed-precision approach tailored to the ground state search. Based on the results, we look into the speedup that can be gained for GPUs in Subsection 3.2. The number of simulation parameters is too large to consider all combinations, so we in general focus on one aspect of the simulation and pick one data point to compare with the next optimization.

3.1 CPU benchmark

In the following section, we establish the baseline for further optimization. We also use the opportunity to show the scaling of the simulation time with the bond dimension χ. The bond dimension χ directly influences the underlying matrix dimension for the linear algebra operations. The Hamiltonian of a quantum system can be complex in general, although many models, including the one in Eq. (1) can be represented with real-valued Hamiltonians. Typically, simulations run with double-complex by default to capture complex Hamiltonians; the mixed-precision implementation requires flexibility in the data types, i.e., single-real, double-real, single-complex, and double-complex are available, and we also have the opportunity to compare real versus complex arithmetic.

In Figure 2a), we address the effects of points *i)* and *ii)* for different bond dimensions; here, we start with a complex-valued ansatz. We compare the obtained energy with computation time. To enable log-log plots, we plot the energy relative to the lowest energy obtained across all simulations E_{min} and manually set the best simulation's error to the next smaller power of ten, here 10^{-4}. We expect simulations with higher bond dimensions to achieve better precision at the cost of a longer computation time; the diagonal trend in Figure 2a) reflects the improvement with bond dimension. We use $\chi \in \{16, 32, 64\}$, with the size of the marker corresponding to the bond dimension used. Surprisingly, we find a difference in runtime of a factor of two between libraries, e.g., PyTorch versus NumPy at $\chi = 64$. We find that the order from the fastest to slowest at $\chi = 64$ is: JAX, TensorFlow, PyTorch, and NumPy. Our results demonstrate the advantage of choosing the most suitable backend-library.

a

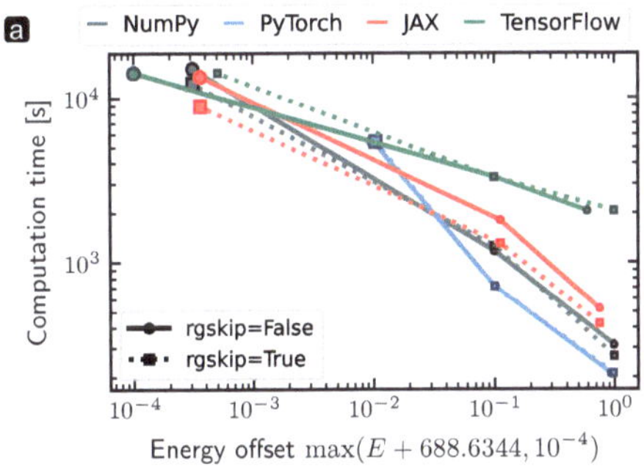

b

Sweeps	NumPy	PyTorch	JAX	TensorFlow
SSSSSS	t = 977s E = -688.62346	627s -688.62502	1365s -688.60703	1914s -688.59615
SSSSDD	t = 2249s E = -688.62380	976s -688.63446	2198s -688.63420	2721s -688.62307
SSSDDD	t = 3249s E = -688.62382	1515s -688.62908	2352s -688.63421	3101s -688.63315
DDDDDD	t = 5046s E = -688.63382	2031s -688.63394	3394s -688.62370	4050s -688.63370
ZZZZZZ	t = 12207s E = -688.63413	5379s -688.62395	8881s -688.63408	14233s -688.63394

Figure 2: *CPU benchmark: baseline and mixed-precision tailored to tensor networks.* a The baseline for the ground state search benchmark with no optimizations is given by the data with «rgskip=False». To allow for log-error plots, we plot $\max\left(E - \min_{\chi,\text{lib},\text{rgskip}}(E(\cdot)), \epsilon = 10^{-4}\right)$. The largest markers refer to the largest bond dimension out of $\chi \in \{16, 32, 64\}$ for each backend library, where the different backend libraries perform differently. Then, we tune our setting and skip small exact tensors in the optimization, see «rgskip=True», leading only to a speedup for JAX. b Mixed-precision allows to increase precision as we converge to the ground state in multiple sweeps. We perform six sweeps with single-real (S), double-real (D), and double-complex (Z) data types and show selected entries. Mixed-precision always leads to a speedup; note that precision decreases for NumPy and TensorFlow with more single-precision sweeps, while the precision fluctuates for PyTorch and JAX.

The speedup gained by skipping exactly represented tensors in optimization sweeps, see point *ii)*, is also shown in Figure 2a): the data set with squared markers and dashed lines skips small tensors. The impact depends on the choice of library and χ, from no clear impact for NumPy, PyTorch, and TensorFlow, to a slight improvement in runtime and precision for JAX.

In Figure 2b), we investigate the effect of mixed-precision by performing six sweeps while changing the precision. The label S denotes a sweep with single-real precision, and D with double-real precision. The final obtained energy total wall-time ought to be compared to six sweeps in double-complex, label «ZZZZZZ». The simulation time decreases for more single-precision sweeps; the speedup comes with losing the precision of the ground state energy for NumPy and TensorFlow. In contrast, the precision fluctuates for PyTorch and JAX and no clear dependency with the number of single-precision sweeps is visible. For example, we find that the NumPy backend loses one digit of precision for an SSSSDD pattern. These results show that it is possible to gain a speedup at a reasonable precision by choosing a suitable strategy for approach *iii)*.

a

Cores	NumPy	PyTorch	JAX	TensorFlow
1	t = 2249s E = -688.62380	976s -688.63446	2198s -688.63420	2721s -688.62307
4	t = 5424s E = -688.62424	443s -688.62393	1727s -688.63393	2619s -688.63421
14	t = 5486s E = -688.62397	1680s -688.62391	1426s -688.63393	2624s -688.62385
16	t = 6099s E = -688.62315	1523s -688.63022	1372s -688.63393	2281s -688.62376
112	t = 4475s E = -688.62380	2756s -688.62917	1081s -688.63393	2130s -688.62378

b

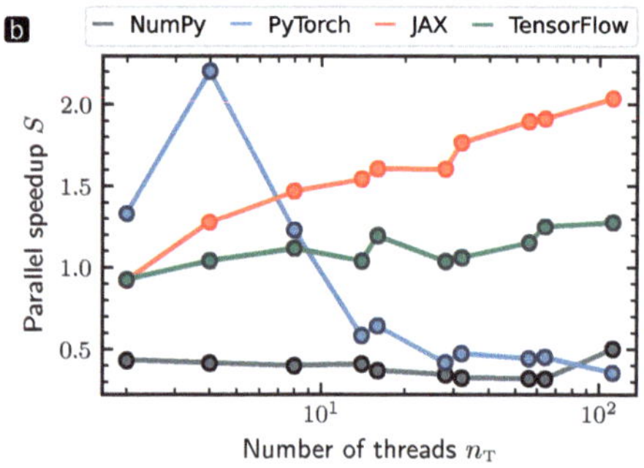

Figure 3: *Built-in CPU parallelization of tensor operations via the linear algebra libraries.* a The energies show no significant trend when changing the number of threads. The wall times can decrease moderately for PyTorch, JAX, and TensorFlow. In contrast, parallelization even slows down simulations with the NumPy-backend as well as for PyTorch with many cores. b The parallel speedup S over the number of threads n_T reflects the data of the table in a) with parallel speedup except for NumPy. The use of multiple CPU is not justified by the observed speedup for any backend, except for PyTorch with two and four cores.

As the last step for the CPU benchmark, we consider parallelization on a single node. Numerical libraries like openBLAS come with threading; therefore, we expect to observe a parallel speedup when increasing the number of threads. No additional parallelization in our TN algorithms, e.g., of sweeps, is required to profit from this parallelization. Figures 3a) and b) indicate a parallel speedup $S = T_{parallel}/T_{single}$ for the PyTorch, JAX and TensorFlow backend. PyTorch peaks at a speedup of about 2 for 4 cores; JAX and TensorFlow reach their maximum speedup at 112 cores. Potential explanations for the features in the speedup are optimizations for powers of 2 for PyTorch, see each local maxima at 8, 16, 32, and 64 threads, or the NUMA node size of 14 for JAX, see local maxima for 14 or 28 threads. The configuration of NumPy seems ill-configured for the profile on leonardo. Overall, the parallel speedup stays behind the number of cores and saturates for the given problem sizes below 3. Additional tuning is necessary to leverage the resources and identify bottlenecks.

To conclude, we find that optimizing approaches *i)* through *iv)* provides a potential speedup, but the improvement depends on picking the right library-backend in the first place. This applies to the question of parallelization in particular. The overall speedup we gain is significant, with a factor of 34 with the PyTorch-backend for the optimized setup (4 threads, SSSSDD sweep pattern, skip ERGT) in comparison to the original double-complex simulation with the NumPy-backend.

3.2 GPU benchmark

In the following, we first address the migration to the GPU, i.e., approach *v)*, and then look into fine-tuning the tensor dimensions as proposed in approach *vi)*. We compare a single CPU core to a single GPU. Executing the simulation on the GPU comes with some additional constraints and options. The main constraint of the GPU is the 64GB of memory, where we are not exceeding this 64GB for 256 sites and $\chi = 64$. Moreover, we tune the preference of the linear algebra algorithms according to our preliminary studies, e.g., solving SVDs via eigendecompositions. The settings of the algorithm require SVDs and truncated bond dimensions are possible.

Figure 4a) compares the energy obtained with different bond dimensions χ and different libraries on CPU and GPU. We use a sweep pattern of four single-precision plus two double-precision sweeps with a real-valued ansatz. We see that for both devices the PyTorch-backend is much faster while achieving equal or almost equal precision as other libraries. Note that the increase in computational time with increasing χ is much slower for the GPU than for the CPU. We find that the GPUs are slower for very small χ, but provide a sizeable speedup over CPU already for $\chi = 32$. As expected, approach *v)* is successful and leads to an additional speedup over the best CPU simulation of 2.76 times.

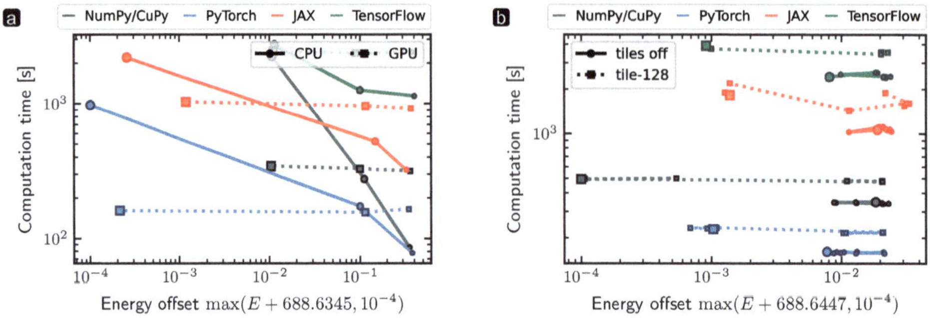

Figure 4: *GPU benchmark for mixed-precision and block-size optimization.* **a** We port the mixed-precision simulations to the GPU and compare their speedup to their corresponding CPU version. We iterate over the bond dimensions $\chi \in \{16, 32, 64\}$ where the largest bond dimension in each curve is indicated with the bigger markers. **b** Matrix-matrix multiplications are optimized in CUDA for the block-size of the memory, i.e., tiles are enforced internally. We can enforce our tensor shapes to be a multiple of this tile size and observe if there is additional speedup; but tiling leads to a slowdown for all backends. Each curve consists of bond dimension $\chi \in \{60, \ldots 68\}$ with the biggest bond dimension indicated by a bigger marker.

Now, we move to the tiling size, which potentially helps to improve performance as demonstrated in Ref. (NVIDIAUsersGuide, 2023). Figure 4b) shows two data sets for $\chi \in \{60, \ldots, 68\}$ without and with enforcing a tiling, solid versus dotted lines. If activated, we enforce a tiling of 128 bytes; note that $\chi = 64$ enforces only the maximal bond dimension, while tensors may have other bond dimensions due to the truncation of singular values. We expect a separation of the two data sets in case enforcing the tiling has an effect, but the data does not support the claim. In contrast, the runtime increases slightly when enforcing tiling on our side. Therefore, we conclude that *vi)* provides no benefit.

In summary, the migration to the GPU as approach *v)* is successful with a total speedup of 94 over the double-complex NumPy-backend baseline on CPUs. Further tuning as enforcing a tiling dimension does not lead to an additional speedup.

3.3 TPU benchmark

We move to the TPU benchmark, which has as an accelerator similar challenges for an implementation as GPUs, e.g., data transfer between host and device. PyTorch, TensorFlow, and JAX support TPUs. We focus on JAX after an initial assessment and considering previous studies on linear algebra with JAX (Lewis et al., 2022). JAX relies on just-in-time (jit) compilation of functions that are cached for each data type, shape, etc. The jit compiler opens up possibilities for optimization, e.g., avoiding unnecessary compilation.

We benchmark on Google's TPU v4-8 for three bond dimensions $\chi \in \{32, 64, 128\}$, six single-precision sweeps, and tiling on/off. The computation times of the TPU v4-8 cannot compete with GPUs and are closer to the ones of CPUs, see Figure 5a). At bond dimension $\chi = 64$, there is a speedup of the TPU over the CPU, albeit with a smaller precision. The difference in wall time when doubling the bond dimensions is less than 1.1 on the TPU, which is far below the expected scaling with $\mathcal{O}(\chi^4)$. This means that other contributions still present a significant contribution in comparison to the expensive linear algebra steps.

a

Bond dimension	CPU	XLA	XLA + tile=128
$\chi = 32$	t=1065s E=-**688.**51693	1131s -**687**.98895	n.a. n.a.
$\chi = 64$	t=1823s E=-**688.61092**	1180s -**687**.06878	1625s -**684**.32439
$\chi = 128$	t=4692s E=-**688.**57309	1244s -**686**.84771	1701s -**6**68.38448

b

XLA compile log	CPU	XLA	XLA + tile=128
Time ($\chi = 64$) Counter	41s 459	32s 459	48s 742
Time ($\chi = 128$) Counter	42s 459	56s 459	140s 1207

Figure 5: *TPU benchmark for single-precision and block-size optimization with JAX.* **a** We port the mixed-precision simulations to the TPU and compare different parameterizations. We observe approximately a factor 2 in difference in simulation time for doubling the bond dimension χ. The two data points per line refers to four versus six single-precision steps with the bigger marker for six single-precision sweeps. Finally, we check if tiling bond dimensions to 128 bytes has any effect, e.g., due to tiling or fewer jit-compiling efforts. **b** We extract the number of jit-compile events and their cumulated time. A change in data types leads to about 20 more calls to the compiler. Higher bond dimensions lead to more compilation time. Tiling does not overcome this problem as truncations do not lead to different dimensions in our example.

As each function has to be compiled for each set of parameters, approach *vi)* seems to fit into the beneficial optimization for TPUs: limiting the number of possible bond dimensions also limits the number of compile events. Surprisingly, it is not beneficial; computation time increases, and the compile time of the jit-compiler also increases, because the number of compile events increases. In Figure 5b), we extract the actual number of jit-compiler calls and the compile time to track the effects of bond dimension and tiling. The higher number of jit-compilations for tiling can be explained by additional compilations of functions only needed for tiling as a first hypothesis. An additional look into the data shows further that simulations without tiling max out their bond dimension and therefore encounter only a limited number of combinations.

These results concerning the precision are not *per se* a statement against TPUs as the scaling of the computation with the bond dimension χ is promising. Further optimization steps remain unexplored. For example, removing trivial dimensions before jit-compiling functions, enabling jited-functions in our library instead of completely relying on the JAX-backend. The smallest size of the TPU used here also allows one to further scale it up as successfully shown for linear algebra in Ref. (Lewis et al., 2022). A comparison with newer hardware is another future step; TPU v4-8 has been released in 2021.

3.4 Block-sparse tensors for conserved symmetries

As the last part of the benchmark, we demonstrate that the abstract tensor class extends into block-sparse tensors. These block-sparse tensors enable us to handle quantum systems with conserved quantities. The Hamiltonian in Eq. (1) has a $\mathbb{Z}_2$ Abelian symmetry. The block-sparse tensors rely on the abstract tensor in two ways. First, block-sparse tensors have to comply with the abstract tensor class so that the TTN algorithms can employ them as tensors for a TN. Second, the block-sparse tensors have to contain a tensor for each block; these are dense tensors based on NumPy/CuPy, PyTorch, JAX, or TensorFlow.

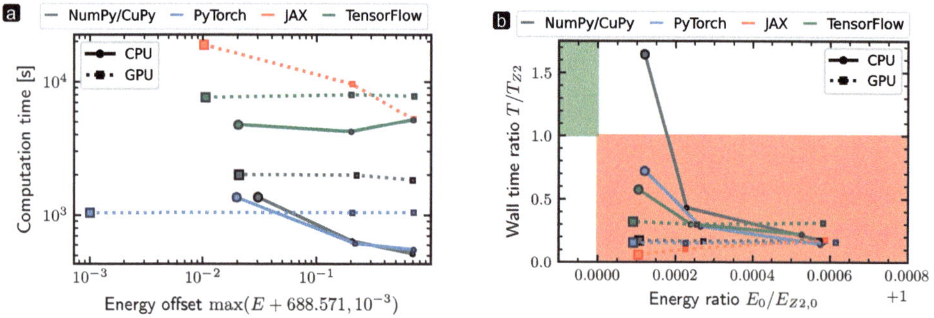

Figure 6: *Block-sparse tensor benchmark for conserved symmetries.* a We analyze the TTN with a conserved $\mathbb{Z}_2$ symmetry and its energies and runtimes for both CPU and GPU. As linear algebra operations are on smaller problems, GPUs do not yet show a speedup for $\chi \leq 64$. b We compare the data with and without symmetries via the ratios of the energy and wall time. Ratios in the red (green) rectangle are a decline (improvement) with respect to both energy and wall time. CPUs profit with respect to the wall time.

In Figure 6a), we show the computation time over the energy of the ground state with symmetry for different bond dimensions $\chi \in \{16, 32, 64\}$. In Figure 6b) we compare to the same simulation without the $\mathbb{Z}_2$ symmetry. By taking the ratio of energies and wall times, we see whether both aspects improved (see green rectangle) or whether both aspects deteriorate (red rectangle). For $\chi = 64$, we find a speedup in computation time for CPUs with NumPy when using block-sparse tensors, although convergence is still slightly worse. The expected speedup of block-sparse tensors depends on the exploited symmetry. Our Hamiltonian only splits into two blocks and the upper bound for a speedup is 4. Because the matrix dimension for linear algebra operations is effectively smaller when using symmetric tensors, the GPU has less impact in comparison with the CPU for the bond dimensions $\chi \leq 64$ shown here. To summarize, the concept of abstract classes extends to symmetric tensors, however, parallel loops of decompositions are not exploited yet and have the potential for an additional speedup in the future.

4 Conclusions

We have demonstrated a benchmark for tensor network algorithms used to simulate many-body quantum systems. Due to the uprise of quantum-inspired methods, this class of algorithms has raised interest beyond quantum systems, e.g., for optimization or machine learning problems. We identify seven aspects that have the potential to reduce computation time spanning different hardware, i.e., CPUs, GPUs, and TPUs, backend libraries, and precision of the underlying arithmetic.

When using CPUs, we find that the most important aspect is the choice of the linear algebra library. Additionally, using lower precision for initial iterations also provides a sizeable speedup. Combined with the other approaches like parallelization, this strategy leads to a speedup factor of 34 compared to the initial baseline.

For GPUs, we demonstrate an additional speedup of 2.76 for the PyTorch-backend over the best CPU implementation (4 threads, SSSSDD sweep pattern, skip ERGT). The overall speedup from the initial starting point to the optimal GPU implementation is 94.

We see further potential in matching the strengths of the linear algebra libraries with the type of hardware. An example is the TPU architecture, where we achieve a working example, but no significant speedup at sufficient precision yet. Extracting the best computational performance requires in the future considering just-in-time compilation and rewriting functions with this aspect in mind. This approach then benefits both TPUs and GPUs.

Corresponding Author

Daniel Jaschke: daniel-1.jaschke@uni-ulm.de
Institute for Complex Quantum Systems, Ulm University, Germany

ORCID

Daniel Jaschke https://orcid.org/0000-0001-7658-3546
Marco Ballarin https://orcid.org/0000-0002-3215-3453
Nora Reinić https://orcid.org/0000-0002-9490-2536
Luka Pavešić, https://orcid.org/0000-0002-9800-9200
Simone Montangero https://orcid.org/0000-0002-8882-2169

Data availability

The scripts and source code are available via References (Bacilieri et al., 2024) and (Ballarin et al., 2024). We provide the datasets and figures via Reference (Jaschke et al., 2024).

Acknowledgements

We thank Alessandro Lonardo, Francesco Simula, Ilaria Siloi, and Pietro Silvi for discussions and feedback. We acknowledge financial support from the Italian Ministry of University and Research (MUR) via PRIN2022 project TANQU, and the Departments of Excellence grant 2023-2027 Quantum Frontiers; from the European Union via H2020 projects EuRyQa and textarossa, the QuantERA projects QuantHEP and T-NISQ, and the Quantum Flagship project Pasquans2, from the German Federal Ministry of Education and Research (BMBF) via the funding program quantum technologies – from basic research to market – project QRydDemo, and from the World Class Research Infrastructure – Quantum Computing and Simulation Center (QCSC) of Padova University. N. R. received support from the European Union via the UNIPhD programme (Horizon 2020 under Marie Skłodowska-Curie grant agreement No. 101034319 and NextGenerationEU). We also acknowledge computation time supported support by the state of Baden-Württemberg through bwHPC and the German Research Foundation (DFG) through grant no INST 40/575-1 FUGG (JUSTUS 2 cluster), on Cineca's *leonardo* machine, the dibona cluster via the project textarossa, and via Google's TPU Research Cloud program.

References

Abadi, M. et al. (2015). *TensorFlow: Large-Scale Machine Learning on Heterogeneous Systems.* Software available from tensorflow.org. URL: https://www.tensorflow.org/.

Ansel, J. et al. (2024). »PyTorch 2: Faster Machine Learning Through Dynamic Python Bytecode Transformation and Graph Compilation«. In: *29th ACM International Conference on Architectural Support for Programming Languages and Operating Systems, Volume 2 (ASPLOS '24).* ACM. DOI: 10.1145/3620665.3640366.

Bacilieri, D. et al. (2024). *Quantum TEA: qtealeaves.* Version 1.2.30. DOI: 10.5281/zenodo.13383350.

Ballarin, M., D. Jaschke, S. Montangero, L. Pavešić and N. Reinić (2024). *Quantum TEA: qredtea.* Version 0.0.15. DOI: 10.5281/zenodo.13385250.

Bañuls, M. C. (2023). »Tensor Network Algorithms: A Route Map«. In: *Annual Review of Condensed Matter Physics* 14.1, pp. 173–191. DOI: 10.1146/annurev-conmatphys-040721-022705.

Bradbury, J. et al. (2018). *JAX: composable transformations of Python+NumPy programs.* Version 0.3.13. URL: http://github.com/google/jax.

Gourianov, N. et al. (2022). »A quantum-inspired approach to exploit turbulence structures«. In: *Nature Computational Science* 2.1, pp. 30–37. ISSN: 2662-8457. DOI: 10.1038/s43588-021-00181-1.

Harris, C. R. et al. (2020). »Array programming with NumPy«. In: *Nature* 585.7825, pp. 357–362. DOI: 10.1038/s41586-020-2649-2.

Jaschke, D., M. Ballarin, N. Reinić, L. Pavešić and S. Montangero (2024). *Simulation data and figures for "Benchmarking Quantum Red TEA on CPUs, GPUs, and TPUs".* Version v0.0.15. DOI: 10.5281/zenodo.13386420.

Lewis, A. G. M. et al. (2022). »Large-scale distributed linear algebra with tensor processing units«. In: *Proceedings of the National Academy of Sciences* 119.33, e2122762119. DOI: 10.1073/pnas.2122762119.

Lucas, A. (2014). »Ising formulations of many NP problems«. In: *Frontiers in Physics.* ISSN: 2296-424X. DOI: 10.3389/fphy.2014.00005.

Montangero, S. (2018). *Introduction to Tensor Network Methods.* Cham, CH: Springer Nature Switzerland AG. DOI: 10.1007/978-3-030-01409-4.

NVIDIAUsersGuide (2023). *User's Guide | NVIDIA Docs: Matrix Multiplication Background*. URL: https://docs.nvidia.com/deeplearning/performance/pdf/Matrix-Multiplication-Background-User-Guide.pdf.

Okuta, R., Y. Unno, D. Nishino, S. Hido and C. Loomis (2017). »CuPy: A NumPy-Compatible Library for NVIDIA GPU Calculations«. In: *Proceedings of Workshop on Machine Learning Systems (LearningSys) in The Thirty-first Annual Conference on Neural Information Processing Systems (NIPS)*. URL: http://learningsys.org/nips17/assets/papers/paper_16.pdf.

Orús, R. (2014). »A practical introduction to tensor networks: Matrix product states and projected entangled pair states«. In: *Annals of Physics* 349, pp. 117–158. ISSN: 0003-4916. DOI: 10.1016/j.aop.2014.06.013.

Sachdev, S. (2011). *Quantum Phase Transitions*. 2nd. Cambridge, United Kingdom: Cambridge University Press. DOI: 10.1017/CBO9780511973765.

Schollwöck, U. (2011). »The density-matrix renormalization group in the age of matrix product states«. In: *Annals of Physics* 326.1. January 2011 Special Issue, pp. 96–192. ISSN: 0003-4916. DOI: 10.1016/j.aop.2010.09.012.

Silvi, P. et al. (2019). »The Tensor Networks Anthology: Simulation techniques for many-body quantum lattice systems«. In: *SciPost Phys. Lect. Notes*, p. 8. DOI: 10 . 21468 / SciPostPhysLectNotes.8.

Stoudenmire, E. M. (2018). »Learning relevant features of data with multi-scale tensor networks«. In: *Quantum Science and Technology* 3.3, p. 034003. DOI: 10.1088/2058-9565/aaba1a.

KI-Morph – User-friendly large-scale image analysis & AI on bwHPC systems

Alexander Zeilmann, Vincent Heuveline

Engineering Mathematics and Computing Lab (EMCL), Heidelberg University, and
Data Mining and Uncertainty Quantification Group (DMQ), Heidelberg Institute for Theoretical Studies (HITS) gGmbH, Heidelberg, Germany

Abstract

Artificial Intelligence (AI) has become indispensable for analyzing large-scale datasets, particularly in the realm of 3D image volumes. However, effectively harnessing AI for such tasks often requires advanced algorithms and high-performance computing (HPC) resources, presenting significant challenges for non-technical users. To overcome these barriers, we present KI-Morph, a novel software platform tailored for large-scale image analysis on the bwHPC infrastructure. Our goal is to help researchers analyze 3D image data as efficiently as possible. To this end, KI-Morph offers a user-friendly interface that seamlessly integrates with HPC resources, enabling sophisticated AI-driven analysis without requiring deep technical expertise in either AI or HPC. The platform prioritizes data privacy and sovereignty, ensuring that users retain full control over their data. Additionally, the components developed for KI-Morph support researchers not only with advanced data analysis but also with science outreach and communication by enabling the creation of interactive online visualizations, for example, using the 2D, 3D, and augmented reality viewers.

1 Introduction

The integration of artificial intelligence (AI) into scientific research is poised to revolutionize the analysis and interpretation of complex, large-scale datasets, especially in the realm of volumetric imaging. The enormous size of these datasets – where a single volume of a biological specimen can easily reach several hundred gigabytes – presents significant challenges in data processing and analysis. High-performance computing (HPC) systems provide the computational power needed to manage such vast amounts of data. However, effectively leveraging AI within these HPC environments remains a considerable hurdle, particularly for users who lack expertise in both technologies.

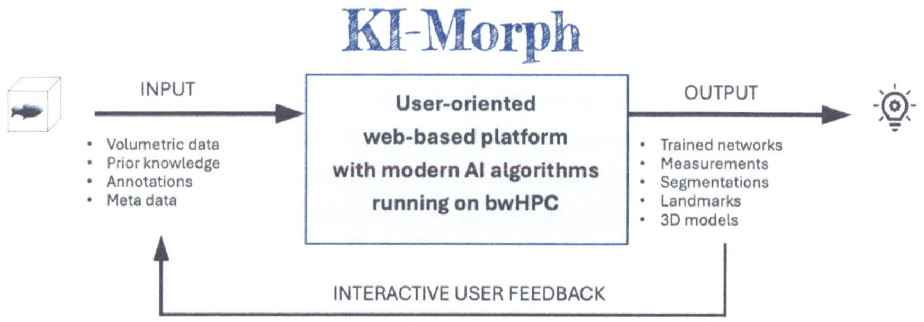

Figure 1: Graphical Abstract: KI-Morph supports researchers to produce insights from volumetric image data. Often researchers have large amounts of volumetric image data, possible with a few annotations or other meta data, that is too time intensive to analyze by hand. Using KI-Morph they can generate a variety of results using an user oriented web-based platform with modern AI algorithms running on bwHPC systems.

Despite advancements by our group and collaborators in developing sophisticated pipelines for data acquisition (Vogelgesang et al., 2016) and tomographic reconstruction (Faragó et al., 2022), which have dramatically reduced initial processing times to mere minutes, the subsequent analysis remains predominantly manual. This manual effort often extends over several days to weeks for a single volume (Weinhardt et al., 2018). To address this, our research group has developed Biomedisa (Lösel et al., 2020), an application designed to accelerate this process. However, as data sizes have increased exponentially, there is a growing need for more efficient utilization of HPC resources and the incorporation of modern AI algorithms, such as active and interactive learning.

In response to these challenges, various solutions – both commercial and open-source – have emerged, aiming to streamline the integration of AI into HPC environments for volumetric imaging.

1.1 Commercial AI platforms and their challenges

There are several commercial AI solutions available, including WEBKNOSSOS, Dragonfly, CVAT, and Labelbox[1]. While these platforms typically offer robust, out-of-the-box tools for a range of applications, they can fall short for scientific research due to several key limitations:

Limited suitability for scientific data Many commercial AI platforms are optimized for processing natural images and consumer-oriented data, making them less effective for handling the complex and specialized datasets typical of scientific research. Specifically, 3D data such as volumetric imaging from MRI scans or 3D microscopy is a niche application supported by only a few commercial platforms.

Lack of adaptability Most commercial AI platforms lack extensibility and allow users only to run those algorithms on the data that are implemented by the platform. This limitation means that researchers may be constrained to outdated algorithms and unable to use state-of-the-art approaches in the rapidly evolving field of AI.

High costs The financial burden of commercial AI platforms can be substantial, with high licensing fees and ongoing subscription costs that may be prohibitive for academic and research institutions. These costs are frequently calculated based on the required computational power and storage capacity, which can create limitations. As a result, researchers may be driven to rely more on manual processing rather than automated algorithms, as well as potentially impeding effective data management by restricting the volume of data that can be stored.

Data privacy concerns Commercial platforms may utilize user data to train their own AI systems, raising significant concerns about data privacy, especially when dealing with sensitive or proprietary research data.

Data sovereignty and vendor lock-in The challenge of extracting data from commercial platforms can lead to vendor lock-in, where researchers are compelled to continue using the platform to retain access to their results, limiting their control over data management.

Some commercial solutions offer hybrid models, in the sense that some of the code is open source, which can be used like the open source AI solutions we will discuss next.

[1] webknossos.org, dragonfly.comet.tech, www.cvat.ai, labelbox.com

1.2 Open source AI solutions and their challenges

Similar to the commercial solutions, there are many open source AI solutions[2] available ranging from general machine learning frameworks like PyTorch and TensorFlow to image analysis libraries and applications like Fiji, ITK, OpenCV, 3D Slicer and Project MONAI and in particular MONAI Label (Diaz-Pinto et al., 2024). While these approaches often provide a viable alternative to commercial solutions, offering flexibility and cost-effectiveness, most open source AI solutions are provided as libraries (focus on one particular technical problem) or frameworks (focus on few related technical problems) but not platforms (solving an application problem completely). Accordingly, the setup and maintenance present challenges, particularly for non-experts:

Hardware configuration and integration with HPC systems This setup requires specialized knowledge to properly set up and optimize hardware components to work seamlessly with high-performance computing environments. This involves configuring networking, storage, and processing units to ensure efficient data handling and computational performance.

Software installation and dependency management Software installation can often be complicated due to the need for precise configuration and dependency management. Installing software on HPC systems typically involves navigating intricate setup procedures, including the installation and maintenance of necessary libraries, modules, and system dependencies.

Lack of unified workflow and user interface Open source platforms often consist of a variety of plugins and extensions that may not be fully compatible with each other. This lack of an overarching architecture can result in compatibility issues and make it difficult to create a cohesive workflow.

Documentation and support Some open source platforms lack comprehensive documentation and user support, making it challenging for researchers to troubleshoot issues and optimize their workflows.

[2] pytorch.org, www.tensorflow.org, fiji.sc, itk.org, opencv.org, www.slicer.org, monai.io

Legacy code base The development of some open source libraries started many years, with a focus on classical image analysis techniques (i.e., image analysis without AI) and single images instead of entire datasets. Restructuring the architecture to integrate the latest AI advancements and dataset handling is often not possible without significant effort and refactoring large parts of the code base.

1.3 Introducing the KI-Morph platform

To address the limitations inherent in both commercial and open-source AI approaches, we introduce the KI-Morph platform, which is a user-centric solution tailored for handling image analysis on extensive 3D image volumes. We specifically designed KI-Morph to overcome the aforementioned challenges by offering KI-Morph as a cost-effective and managed platform taking care of both hardware and software management. This allows users to leverage sophisticated AI capabilities without needing in-depth technical expertise in AI development or HPC management. Every aspect of the workflow – from data input and processing to analysis and visualization – is directly supported within the KI-Morph platform. Additionally, all data processed through KI-Morph is hosted securely in Heidelberg, Germany, in the user's Scientific Data Storage (SDS@hd) project, ensuring complete data privacy and sovereignty.

In the following, we describe the technical infrastructure in Section 2 and the design decisions in Section 3. In Section 4 we explain the rough workflow in KI-Morph before concluding in Section 5.

2 Technical infrastructure of KI-Morph and bwHPC

To develop KI-Morph, we leverage the robust HPC infrastructure available in Heidelberg, Germany, and adapt it to better support interactive GUI applications and AI use cases. In particular, we are focusing on the computations with the bwForCluster Helix, remote visualizations using bwVisu, and data storage on SDS@hd.

2.1 bwForCluster Helix — high performance computing

The bwForCluster Helix[3] is a high-performance computing (HPC) resource located at Heidelberg University, available to all members of universities in Baden-Württemberg. It is designed to facilitate a wide range of scientific research, providing flexible and powerful hardware nodes capable of supporting diverse computational tasks. By integrating this cluster into KI-Morph, we ensure that users have access to the computational power necessary for processing large-scale image datasets and running sophisticated AI algorithms.

2.2 bwVisu — remote visualization

The bwForCluster Helix is optimized for running non-interactive scripts that are scheduled by the Slurm workload manager. However, interactive applications, which require rapid initiation and responsiveness, necessitate a different approach. To accommodate these needs, the Heidelberg Computing Center offers bwVisu (Schnetter et al., 2023), a remote visualization service that enables the execution of native GUI applications directly on the HPC infrastructure. bwVisu also supports the deployment of web applications, which is the foundation for delivering the KI-Morph platform (see Subsection 3.4). Thus, this service ensures that users can interact with high-performance resources in real time while having a familiar graphical user interface.

2.3 SDS@hd — scientific data storage

SDS@hd (Scientific Data Storage at Heidelberg) (Richling et al., 2022) is a specialized data storage service provided by the Computing Center at Heidelberg University, designed to meet the rigorous demands of scientific research. As an integral part of the bwHPC infrastructure, SDS@hd offers secure, privacy-preserving, high-capacity storage solutions that are well integrated with both the bwForCluster Helix and bwVisu. Researchers across all universities in Baden-Württemberg can create projects called *Speichervorhaben* on SDS@hd, and users from many more institutions can join existing ones.

[3] https://www.urz.uni-heidelberg.de/de/service-katalog/hochleistungsrechnen/bwforcluster-helix

3 Technical design decisions for KI-Morph

In this section, we outline the key technical design decisions that shaped the development of KI-Morph. These decisions were guided by the overarching goal of **making advanced AI-driven image analysis accessible to a broad range of users, while also enhancing the platform's capabilities for science outreach and communication.**

3.1 Managed platform: simplifying user experience

KI-Morph is designed as a fully managed platform, not merely a framework or library. This approach ensures that the platform is accessible to non-technical users with minimal setup requirements. By managing the entire hardware and software stack, we eliminate the need for users to purchase or maintain hardware or install software. This design choice simplifies the user experience, allowing researchers to focus on their work without the overhead of technical configuration.

3.2 Multi-purpose data storage: full data sovereignty & privacy

To ensure full data sovereignty, users have access to their input and output data at any time by accessing the corresponding SDS@hd project. Although the data storage in KI-Morph is tightly integrated into the platform, the storage system functions independently, enabling its use across a wide range of applications, whether running locally or on the HELIX cluster. Complete data privacy is maintained, as we have no access to user settings or research data unless the corresponding SDS@hd project is explicitly shared with the KI-Morph maintainers.

3.3 Client-server architecture: balancing performance and usability

In contrast to approaches that run completely on either HPC infrastructure or the user hardware, KI-Morph utilizes a client-server architecture (see Figure 2) to balance computational efficiency with good user interaction. The server component, running on the Helix cluster via bwVisu, handles computationally intensive tasks such as data preprocessing, neural network training and inference. On the other hand, the client part manages the user interface, performing tasks such as annotation and visualization on hardware that is close to the user ensuring a responsive user experience.

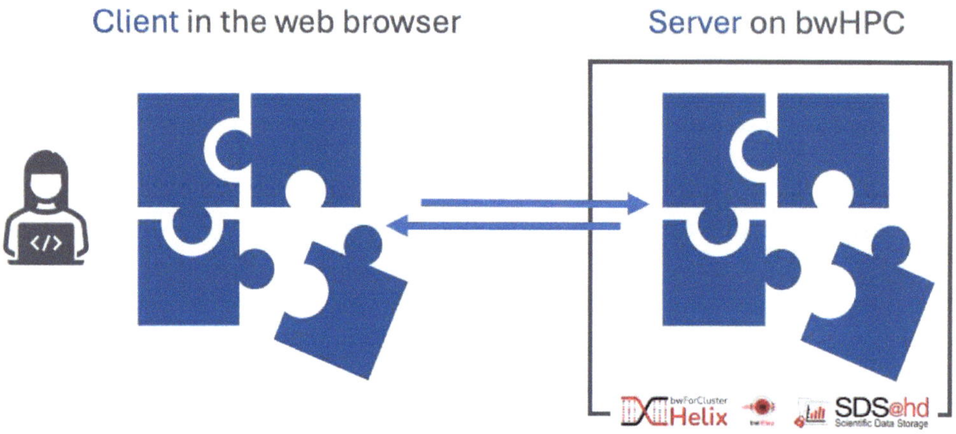

Figure 2: Componentized client-server architecture. KI-Morph uses a client-server architecture. All code related to user interaction is running directly in the web browser of the user, whereas computationally expensive code is running on the Helix cluster via bwVisu. The code is strongly componentized, ensuring the reusability of different parts of the platform.

3.4 Web application: cross-platform and simplified maintenance

Rather than deploying as a native application, KI-Morph is implemented as a web application. Native apps, which require separate distributions and updates for each operating system and hardware configuration, can significantly increase development complexity. In contrast, web applications offer a more streamlined approach, running on any device with a web browser and enabling seamless updates with each page load. The web platform also provides robust tools for building user interfaces, leveraging web technologies, which are specifically designed for UI development. Additionally, the web ecosystem offers the largest collection of component frameworks and programming libraries, enhancing the flexibility and scalability of the platform. This trend towards web-based solutions is evident in other AI platforms as well, with newer tools like OHIF and Labelbox favoring web apps over traditional native applications. KI-Morph follows this modern approach, utilizing a state-of-the-art web technology stack.[4]

[4] typescriptlang.org, react.dev, nextjs.org, primereact.org, tailwindcss.com, threejs.org, r3f.docs.pmnd.rs

3.5 Componentization: modular flexibility and reusability

KI-Morph is built with a strong emphasis on componentization, both in its technical structure and user workflows. Instead of relying on a single, monolithic workflow, KI-Morph offers a suite of modular tasks that can be customized and combined according to the specific needs of the user, the input data, and the desired outcomes. The user interface is similarly modular. For example, the viewer component used for data annotation can also be employed for visualization and data preprocessing, showcasing the flexibility and reusability of the platform's interface elements. Using this componentization, we ensure the platform's adaptability towards the rapidly changing AI landscape.

4 Using the KI-Morph platform

This section provides a high-level overview of the typical workflows involved in using KI-Morph, from initial registration and login to advanced data management, collaborative project handling, annotation processes, and visualization. Rather than serving as detailed documentation or a step-by-step tutorial, we intend to give users a broad understanding of how to interact with the platform and effectively utilize its features.

4.1 Registration, login and launch

To access KI-Morph through bwVisu, users must first register for the SDS@hd data storage service and set up the required credentials as outlined in the bwHPC Wiki[5]. Additionally, users intending to perform computationally intensive tasks on the Helix cluster must complete a separate registration process therefore. Subsequently, users can log in via the bwVisu website[6] and launch the KI-Morph application. The platform is then accessible through a personalized URL in the web browser.

[5] https://wiki.bwhpc.de/
[6] https://bwvisu-web.urz.uni-heidelberg.de/

4.2 Data management and sharing

All research data and user settings are stored on SDS@hd, which users can add, remove, or download at any time, ensuring they retain full data sovereignty, i.e., control over their data. After initializing a new project in KI-Morph, the user copies the research data to the newly created project folder on SDS@hd. A typical step in a KI-Morph workflow then involves loading the corresponding data from this project folder, running algorithms on the data, and then writing the results, such as segmentations, trained models, or measurements, back to SDS@hd.

Although KI-Morph is launched for each user as a separate Singularity container, collaborative work between several users is possible if two users share the same SDS folder. In this case, all KI-Morph projects in this folder are shared and the corresponding data, trained models, segmentations, and measurements are accessible to all users with access to this SDS.

	Volume ⇅	Accuracy ⇅	Precision (macro avg) ⇅	Precision (weighted avg) ⇅	Recall (macro avg) ⇅	Recall (weighted avg) ⇅	F1-Score (macro avg) ⇅	F1-Score (weighted avg) ⇅
>	672.tif	0.9962	0.2397	0.9962	0.2397	0.9962	0.2397	0.9962
˅	673.tif	0.9969	0.2395	0.9969	0.2395	0.9969	0.2395	0.9969

Metrics by label for volume 673.tif

Label	Precision ⇅	Recall ⇅	F1-Score ⇅	Support ⇅
Background	0.9986	0.9986	0.9986	8,944,441
Optic nerves	0.0177	0.0177	0.0177	1,016
Optical Tectum	0.1113	0.1113	0.1113	4,446
Forebrain	0.3503	0.3503	0.3503	3,980
Midbrain	0.4003	0.4003	0.4003	5,528

Figure 3: User interface for the depiction of different metrics (state September 2024). All metrics are computed for all volumes and all labels as well as averages over all them. The users can sort the tables by the metrics and pick the volumes or labels that should be considered next for additional annotations.

4.3 Efficient annotation process through dedicated tools

AI-driven workflows often require extensive data annotation, a task that is both time-consuming and labor-intensive. However, recent advancements like active and interactive learning have reduced the necessity for exhaustive annotation. To optimize this process, KI-Morph includes various tools like the automatic computing of different metrics (see Figure 3) that guide users in prioritizing which volumes and labels should be annotated next. The platform's viewer also highlights specific areas within images that warrant further attention, enabling users to focus their efforts where it is most needed, thereby streamlining the annotation workflow.

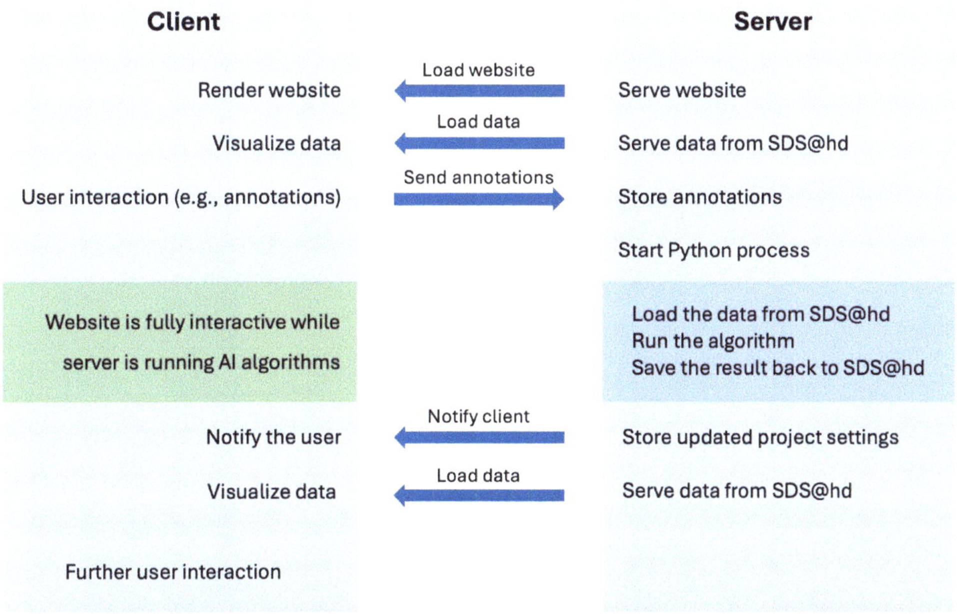

Figure 4: Client-server communication. When a user accesses the KI-Morph platform, the server transmits the website and associated data to the client, where they are rendered. User actions, such as annotations, are then sent back to the server and stored within the project settings. If computational processing is required, the server initiates a Python process that retrieves the necessary data from SDS@hd, executes the algorithm, and writes the results back to SDS@hd. Throughout the algorithm's execution, the platform remains fully interactive and navigable. Once processing is complete, the user is notified, and the results are displayed.

4.4 Advanced visualization capabilities

KI-Morph provides a robust suite of tools for visualizing volumetric images, featuring an advanced 3D viewer with a customizable interface (see Figure 5). We support the volumetric rendering of the input data and segmentation masks as well as the surface rendering of the generated 3D models and the marking of annotations and landmarks.

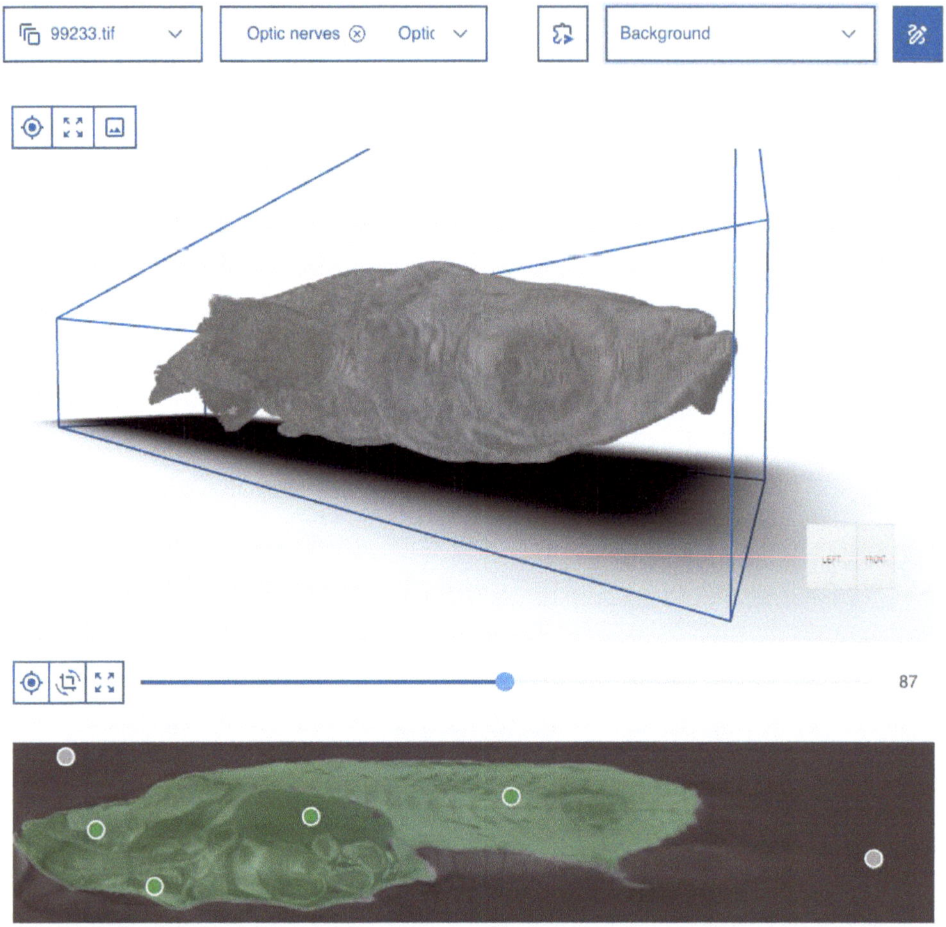

Figure 5: User interface for the visualization and annotation of the volumetric images (state September 2024). We currently support a 3D view with an augmented reality mode as well as displaying 2D slices along the axis directions. Annotations can be made directly in these viewers without the need for any external applications. The annotations (in this example green and gray circles, green for label Medaka and gray for background) are then sent to the back end where the segmentation (green highlighted area) is computed. If the segmentation does not meet the user's expectations, the existing annotations can be modified or new ones added until the resulting segmentation is satisfactory.
The Medaka fish volume in the figure was originally published in (Weinhardt et al., 2018).

The 3D viewer includes an augmented reality (AR) mode on supported devices with which the users can view the 3D rendering directly in front of them. The 2D viewer provides the ability to explore 2D slices along the principal axes. This viewer also supports the display of segmentations, landmarks, and other computed image properties, enabling a streamlined annotation process and facilitating comprehensive analysis.

4.5 Interactive annotation of volumes

In the 2D viewer, users can not only visualize but also add and edit sparse pointwise annotations. Usually, for most (not too complicated) segments, a few point annotations suffice to produce a meaningful segmentation. The user can then send the annotations to the server where a segmentation is generated, returned to the front end and visualized. In the case of faulty segmentations, the user can add more annotations and continuously refine the result.

4.6 Training neural networks

While KI-Morph operates on the Helix cluster via bwVisu, it is allocated a limited portion of the cluster's resources, which is sufficient for the segmentation of a few small volumes. However, when more computationally intensive operations, such as training or fine-tuning of complex neural networks, are required, users can seamlessly transition these computations to the main portion of the Helix cluster, where additional computational power is available. KI-Morph facilitates this transition by automatically generating the necessary Slurm scripts and commands, thus streamlining the submission and execution of these demanding tasks on the broader cluster infrastructure.

5 Conclusion

In this paper, we introduced KI-Morph, a robust platform specifically designed for large-scale image analysis and artificial intelligence applications on the bwHPC infrastructure. KI-Morph distinguishes itself as a managed platform, thus remaining accessible even to researchers with little to no prior knowledge in AI or HPC. It not only facilitates advanced data analysis but also supports subsequent visualizations, making it a valuable tool for both research and science outreach.

KI-Morph leverages a modern, established web technology stack combined with a carefully thought-out design. Its client-server architecture optimizes hardware utilization, adapting to the specific demands of tasks ranging from computationally intensive processes like neural network training to real-time interactive visualizations. The platform's high degree of componentization ensures that it remains adaptable and future-proof, capable of evolving alongside advances in image analysis and AI.

Looking ahead, KI-Morph will continue to be developed, not only with volumetric image analysis in mind, but also with the goal of serving as a prototype for similar platforms and research projects within the bwHPC infrastructure. Its success could inspire future innovations, demonstrating how complex computational tools can be made more accessible to a broader range of researchers by using platforms with graphical user interface on HPC systems.

Corresponding Author

Alexander Zeilmann: alexander.zeilmann@iwr.uni-heidelberg.de
Engineering Mathematics and Computing Lab (EMCL), Heidelberg University, and
Data Mining and Uncertainty Quantification Group (DMQ), Heidelberg Institute for Theoretical Studies (HITS) gGmbH, Heidelberg, Germany

ORCID

Alexander Zeilmann https://orcid.org/0000-0002-8119-0349
Vincent Heuveline https://orcid.org/0000-0002-2217-7558

Acknowledgements

The authors gratefully acknowledge funding by the Federal Ministry of Education and Research (BMBF) under the Project KI-Morph (05D2022). Furthermore, the authors acknowledge support by the state of Baden-Württemberg through bwVisu and bw-HPC as well as the bwForCluster Helix and the storage service SDS@hd supported by the Ministry of Science, Research and Arts Baden-Württemberg (MWK) and the German Research Foundation (DFG) through grants and INST 35/1503-1 FUGG and INST 35/1597-1 FUGG.

References

Diaz-Pinto, A. et al. (2024). »MONAI Label: A framework for AI-assisted interactive labeling of 3D medical images«. In: *Medical Image Analysis* 95, p. 103207. DOI: 10.1016/j.media.2024.103207.

Faragó, T. et al. (2022). »Tofu: a fast, versatile and user-friendly image processing toolkit for computed tomography«. In: *Journal of Synchrotron Radiation* 29.3, pp. 916–927. DOI: 10.1107/s160057752200282x.

Lösel, P. D. et al. (2020). »Introducing Biomedisa as an open-source online platform for biomedical image segmentation«. In: *Nature Communications* 11.1. DOI: 10.1038/s41467-020-19303-w.

Richling, S., S. Siebler, A. Balz, R. Kühl and M. Baumann (2022). *Managing large research data with SDS@hd*. de. DOI: 10.11588/HEIBOOKS.979.C13759.

Schnetter, E. et al. (2023). »bwVisu: A Scalable Remote Service for Interactive Data Processing and Training for Scientists«. In: *E-Science-Tage 2023*. Ed. by V. Heuveline, N. Bisheh and P. Kling. heiBOOKS, pp. 161–173. DOI: 10.11588/heibooks.1288.c18073.

Vogelgesang, M. et al. (2016). »Real-time image-content-based beamline control for smart 4D X-ray imaging«. In: *Journal of Synchrotron Radiation* 23.5. DOI: 10.1107/s1600577516010195.

Weinhardt, V. et al. (2018). »Quantitative morphometric analysis of adult teleost fish by X-ray computed tomography«. In: *Scientific Reports* 8.1. DOI: 10.1038/s41598-018-34848-z.

II HPC Operations and Resource Management

The operating models of the High Energy Physics groups at the University of Freiburg

For the utilisation of NEMO and NEMO2

Michael Boehler, Anton J. Gamel, Markus Schumacher

Physikalisches Institut, Albert-Ludwigs-Universität, Freiburg, Deutschland

Abstract

After 8 successful years of operation and use of the High-Performance Compute (HPC) Cluster NEMO, NEMO2 is scheduled to go into operation in autumn 2024. Since 2005, we have been operating the ATLAS-BFG High-Throughput Computing (HTC) cluster for the ATLAS collaboration as part of the Worldwide LHC Computing Grid. Synergies, such as a shared parallel storage system or the centralised provisioning of worker node images, were identified and used efficiently, particularly in the area of locally used resources of the HTC cluster and HPC cluster.

In this article, we summarise how the resources provided by NEMO to the ATLAS groups at the University of Freiburg were used. In addition, the operating model of this utilisation and the intended operating model for the follow-up project NEMO2 will be explained in detail. To this end, historical data will be analysed and conclusions drawn to discuss the strengths and weaknesses of the High Energy Physics (HEP) operating model at NEMO.

1 Introduction

Before the research cluster for Neuroscience, Elementary Particle Physics, Microsystems Engineering and Materials Science (NEMO) (Janczyk et al., 2019) was inaugurated at the computer centre in Freiburg on 1st August 2016, the Black Forest Grid (BFG) has been successfully operated for more than a decade. The BFG was launched in 2005 at the University of Freiburg to meet the growing demand for computing resources for scientific computing from various areas of the university and its environment. From around 2010, the local ATLAS group provided around 80% of these resources. Other shareholders from various specialist disciplines were able to co-finance the cluster. Within the distributed computing system of the Worldwide LHC Computing Grid (WLCG) (Bos et al., 2005), a further distinction is made between so-called Tier-2 (T2) resources, which are resources pledged to the global collaboration for computing, and the so-called Tier-3 (T3) resources, which are dedicated to the local ATLAS working groups. At that time the ATLAS-BFG storage and compute was a combination of ATLAS-T2, ATLAS-T3 and other local working groups. Since especially the ATLAS experiment is collecting continuously data at the Large Hadron Collider at CERN in Geneva, both the disk storage as well as the compute capacity has to grow accordingly. Figure 1 shows the increase of the pledged storage and compute capacity over the last 15 years.

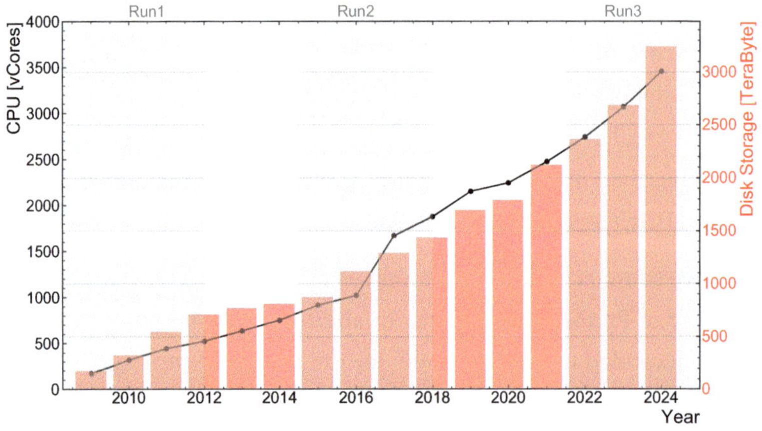

Figure 1: Pledged storage and compute capacity of the ATLAS-BFG over the last 15 years. For comparison, the NEMO cluster had 900 nodes with 20 physical cores, which makes 18000 cores in the operated setup and a parallel storage that has 768 TB of usable capacity.

With the start of NEMO, the ATLAS-BFG became an almost pure ATLAS-T2 computing cluster. The computing capacity for the local ATLAS users was realised in the form of computing projects on the NEMO cluster. In order to facilitate a typical ATLAS user analysis, a dedicated software stack has to be installed on a compute cluster. This installation was circumvented by starting pre-installed virtual machines (Bührer et al., 2019), hereinafter referred to as virtual research environments (VRE), on the NEMO cluster orchestrated by the OpenStack Cloud computing Infrastructure[1].

Provisioning and decommissioning of the VRE dynamically according to demand was managed by the meta-schedulers ROCED[2], later upgraded to CobalD/TARDIS (Fischer et al., 2023; Giffels et al., 2024).

With NEMO2, the current operation model will be completely revised. Since NEMO2 will be equipped with the Slurm (Yoo et al., 2003) scheduling system and the CERN Virtual Machine File System (CVMFS)(Buncic et al., 2010) provided by CERN, ATLAS users will in future be able to work directly on NEMO2 and the additional virtualisation layer using VREs will no longer be necessary.

In this paper we will first describe the operating model of the ATLAS groups on NEMO, and then present the new operating model on NEMO2 and the main changes, before giving a short summary.

2 Operating model of the Freiburg ATLAS groups for utilising NEMO

To make the access for ATLAS users to NEMO as easy as possible, the user administration, the users' home directories, the connection to the ATLAS storage file system (dCache) (Fuhrmann et al., 2006) and the Slurm batch scheduler were retained from the ATLAS BFG cluster. To enable this, the local ATLAS administrators ensured that the familiar working environment was made available and kept up to date in the form of VREs, which were automatically started as virtual machines (VMs) on NEMO.

[1] OpenStack: https://www.openstack.org/
[2] ROCED: https://github.com/roced-scheduler/ROCED, visited on 03.08.2024

In particular, this meant that users could continue to use the user interfaces as login nodes and their existing user homes without having to move their analysis code. New VMs were started on NEMO via service accounts of the individual ATLAS groups to ensure that the resources are properly accounted for the authorised groups. When the utilization of the NEMO resources fell under a defined threshold , the VMs were automatically shut down (see Figure 2).

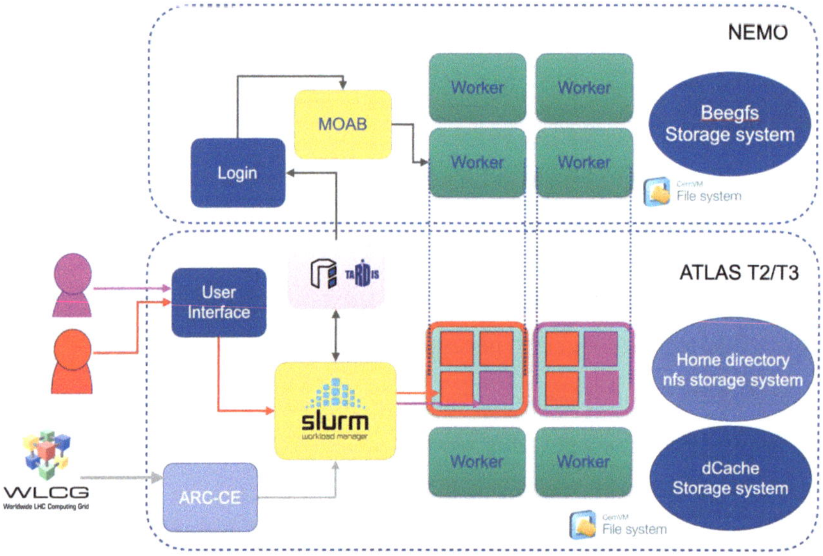

Figure 2: The upper box shows a simplified representation of the NEMO cluster. The main components are the login nodes (blue rectangle), the batch system scheduler MOAB (yellow rectangle), the worker nodes (green rectangles) and the parallel storage system BeeGFS[3] (blue ellipse), which is mounted under /work on the NEMO login nodes, the NEMO worker nodes, ATLAS-BFG login nodes, the worker nodes, and the VMs. The ATLAS-BFG is shown in the lower box. Local ATLAS users and their work flows are shown in red and magenta. VMs that are started on NEMO with VREs connect to the ATLAS-BFG scheduler Slurm and provide their compute resources. These resources are shared by the local ATLAS groups indicated with the red and magenta squares. Jobs that are sent by the WLCG to the ATLAS-T2 are accepted by the ARC-CE servers and submitted exclusively to the worker nodes in the ATLAS-BFG. The ATLAS file system dCache is accessible both from the VMs and from the ATLAS-BFG worker nodes.

A usual policy on HPC clusters, also on NEMO, is the so-called single-user policy. I. e. as long as a user's job runs on a compute node, this node is reserved for the very same user and his other potential jobs no matter how few resources are actually used by the first

[3] BeeGFS: https://www.beegfs.io, visited on 03.08.2024

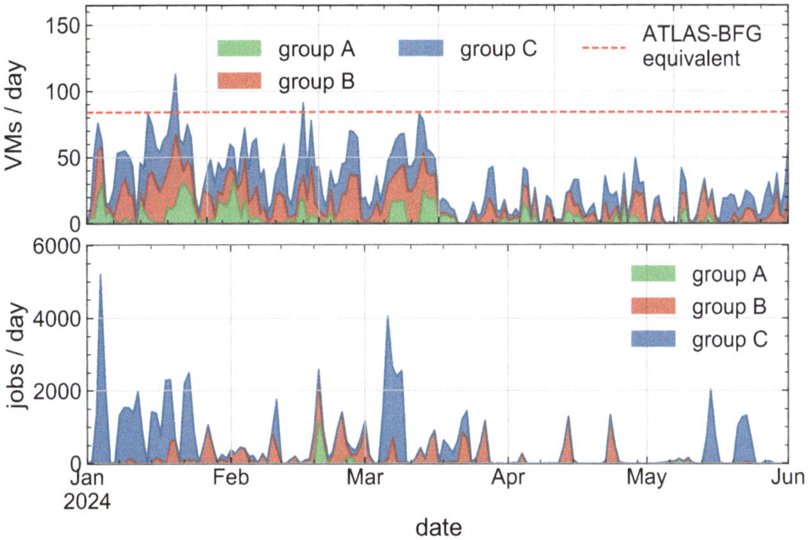

Figure 3: The upper distribution shows the number of VMs started on the NEMO cluster per day in 2024. The lower plot shows the number of ATLAS analysis jobs executed on these VMs in the same period.

job. As the workflows of local ATLAS analyses often do not utilise an entire worker node, the resources of the VMs were shared within the local ATLAS groups in order utilise the resources as efficiently as possible. Figure 3 shows the number of jobs that started VMs on the NEMO cluster in the upper plot. The lower figure shows the number of ATLAS jobs that ran on these VMs within the same day.

Since users of the local ATLAS groups could use resources both via the ATLAS-BFG and directly on NEMO, the group priority of the shared ATLAS resources in the ATLAS-BFG was regulated by the priority plugin (Boehler et al., 2024a) of the accounting ecosystem AUDITOR (Boehler et al., 2024b). New priority was adjusted based on the amount of resources provided on NEMO by the respective group. Figure 4 shows the provided vCore hours and the adjusted group priorities from January to August 2024. The »provided vCore hours« take into account the total number of vCore hours provided in the previous 14 days. Based on this number, the new group priorities are calculated for each of the three ATLAS groups A,...,C and adjusted in Slurm.

To minimise the administration effort, the ATLAS-BFG login node (also referred to as user interface) and the ATLAS-T2 worker nodes were provisioned via a so-called Preboot eXecution Environment (PXE) (Henry et al., 1999), which allows to boot the oper-

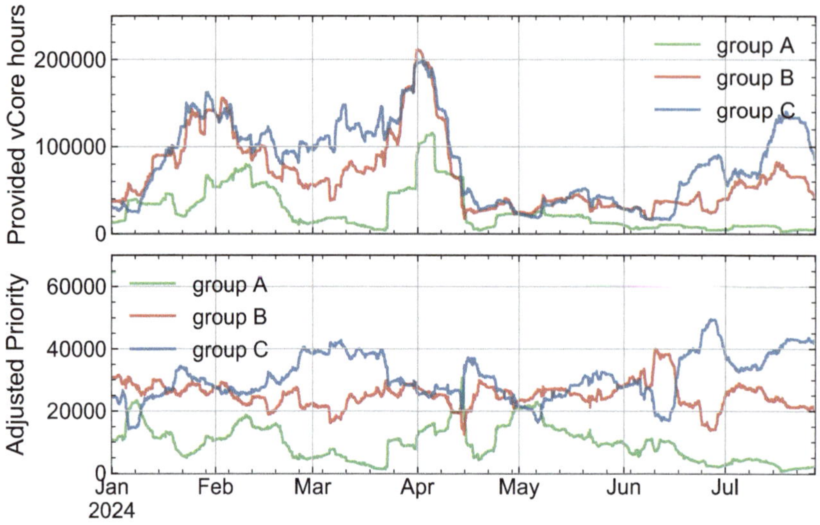

Figure 4: The top plot shows the integral over the CPU core hours of the last 14 days per group. The bottom plot shows the computed priority per group using the `ScaledBySum` mode of the AUDITOR Priority Plugin.

ating system from images via network without installation on disk. These images where provided by the packer-software[4] and automatically configured via a central instance of the configuration management tool Puppet[5]. The VMs that were started on NEMO as pre-installed images managed by the same Puppet instance. To ensure that security updates can be rolled out in situ at runtime, both the VMs and the other compute nodes are connected to the same Puppet instance (Sammel et al., 2023).

3 Planned operating model of the Freiburg ATLAS groups for utilising NEMO2

Since NEMO2 is provided with the batch system scheduler Slurm, which is well known in the particle physics community, as well as with the software stack required by ATLAS users, there is no need anymore to provide the ATLAS specific environment using VREs. Therefore, the ATLAS-BFG will completely discontinue local user support and all the

[4] Packer: https://www.packer.io, visited on 03.08.2024
[5] Puppet: https://www.puppet.com, visited on 03.08.2024

local users of the ATLAS community with an University of Freiburg computing account will register as regular users of NEMO2. This not only simplifies the operation of the ATLAS-BFG, but infrastructures in NEMO2 can also be dismantled. For example, the operation of an OpenStack instance was necessary in order to be able to start VMs on NEMO. Access to the ATLAS-specific storage system dCache will be included.

The ATLAS-BFG will not have to operate a local user administration, the servers that hosted the user home directories and ATLAS-BFG login nodes will be switched off when NEMO2 goes live. After the support of local users is terminated, the batch scheduler system will be switched from Slurm to HTCondor[6]. HTCondor is a scheduler that has been specially optimised for HTC workflows and has the great advantage that resources are not only accepted as compute nodes or VMs, but that individual containers can also serve as compute resources. This makes it much easier to integrate resources from HPC clusters, as no cloud infrastructure such as OpenStack is required.

As described in Section 2, three flavours of installations had to be maintained: the image of the operating system for the ATLAS-BFG worker nodes, the login nodes and the VMs deployed on NEMO. The new model only requires one flavour for ATLAS-BFG worker nodes. As the latest hardware generation has many more compute cores per node, the previous 84 worker nodes could be replaced by 12 powerful new machines. Therefore, PXE provisioning via the network is also replaced by a local installation, which can still be continuously updated with Puppet.

As part of the reassessment of the provision of university computing resources within the KET (Committee for Elementary Particle Physics) computing strategy (Elementarteilchenphysik, 2022), computing resources will no longer be installed at the university computing centres in future, but will be acquired by means of applications for computing time at the national High-Performance computing centres NHR. The associated operating model is shown in the bottom box in Figure 5. Similar to the NEMO operating model, containers are started on the NHR computing resources, which report their resources to the new HTCondor batch scheduler and are then filled with jobs from the WLCG.

[6] HTCondor: https://htcondor.org, visited on 03.08.2024

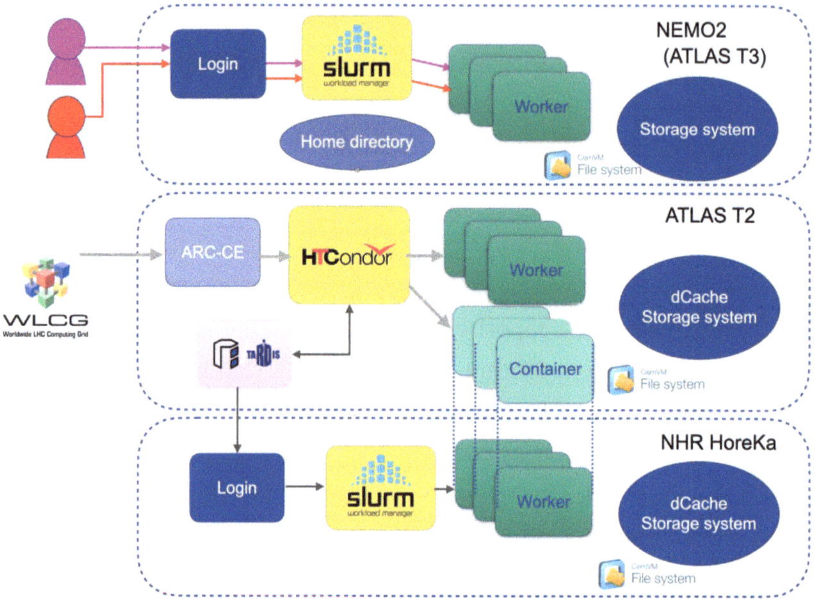

Figure 5: The ATLAS operating model for the use of Nemo 2 envisages that the local ATLAS users will now switch completely to NEMO2 and that the ATLAS-BFG will discontinue user support. Users can only log in directly to the Nemo login node and submit their analysis jobs there. Jobs from the WLCG will continue to be accepted by the ARC-CEs and sent to the cluster via the new scheduler HTCondor. No new hardware will be purchased for the ATLAS-BFG, but resources from computing projects at the NHR cluster HoreKa will be dynamically integrated via COBalD/TARDIS into the ATLAS-BFG.

4 Conclusion

The operation of NEMO in symbiosis with the ATLAS-BFG was extremely successful. In order to run local ATLAS jobs on a cluster with a single-user policy as efficiently as possible, it was necessary to share the resources of the ATLAS groups with each other. This policy is no longer implemented in NEMO2, especially as compute nodes with more and more cores no longer allow this policy to be applied. The use of NEMO resources in the form of VMs was the most user-friendly operating model at the time of NEMO, whereby the introduction of Slurm and the provision of the ATLAS software via CVMFS minimised the changeover hurdle for ATLAS users. Thanks to the experience the ATLAS admins have gained with the provision of NEMO resources via VMs, we are also well equipped for the changeover of the operating model according to the plans of the KET community. We are looking forward to the launch of NEMO2 with great anticipation.

Acknowledgements

This work was supported by the Federal Ministry of Education and Research (BMBF) within the project 05H21VFRC2 »Entwicklung, Integration und Optimierung von digitalen Infrastrukturen für ErUM« in the context of the collaborative research centre »Föderierte Digitale Infrastrukturen für die Erforschung von Universum und Materie (FIDIUM)«.

The HPC-cluster NEMO in Freiburg is supported by the Ministry of Science, Research and Arts Baden-Württemberg through the bwHPC grant and by the German Research Foundation (DFG) through grant no INST 39/963-1 FUGG.

Corresponding Author

Michael Boehler: michael.boehler@physik.uni-freiburg.de
Physikalisches Institut, Albert-Ludwigs-Universität Freiburg,
Hermann-Herder-Str. 3, 79104 Freiburg, Deutschland

ORCID

Michael Boehler https://orcid.org/0000-0001-9734-574X
Anton J. Gamel https://orcid.org/0000-0002-7044-8324
Markus Schumacher https://orcid.org/0000-0002-1733-8388

References

Boehler, M. et al. (2024a). »AUDITOR: Accounting for opportunistic resources«. In: *EPJ Web of Conferences* 295. Ed. by R. De Vita, X. Espinal, P. Laycock and O. Shadura, p. 04008. ISSN: 2100-014X. DOI: 10.1051/epjconf/202429504008.

Boehler, M. et al. (2024b). *The accounting ecosystem AUDITOR*. en. DOI: 10.5281/ZENODO.12653483.

Bos, K., N. Brook, D. Duellmann and et al (2005). *LHC computing Grid: Technical Design Report. Version 1.06 (20 Jun 2005)*. Geneva. URL: http://cds.cern.ch/record/840543.

Bührer, F. et al. (2019). »Dynamic Virtualized Deployment of Particle Physics Environments on a High Performance Computing Cluster«. In: *Computing and Software for Big Science* 3.1. ISSN: 2510-2044. DOI: 10.1007/s41781-019-0024-5.

Buncic, P. et al. (2010). »CernVM – a virtual software appliance for LHC applications«. In: *Journal of Physics: Conference Series* 219.4, p. 042003. ISSN: 1742-6596. DOI: 10.1088/1742-6596/219/4/042003.

Elementarteilchenphysik, K. für (2022). *Bereitstellung der Computing-Ressourcen in Deutschland für Speicherung und Auswertung der Daten des Large Hadron Colliders*. URL: https://www.ketweb.de/sites/site_ketweb/content/e199639/e312771/KET-Computing-Strategie-HL-LHC-final.pdf.

Fischer, M. et al. (2023). *MatterMiners/cobald: v0.14.0*. DOI: 10.5281/ZENODO.1887872. URL: https://zenodo.org/record/1887872.

Fuhrmann, P. and V. Gülzow (2006). »dCache, Storage System for the Future«. In: *Lecture Notes in Computer Science*. Springer Berlin Heidelberg, pp. 1106–1113. ISBN: 9783540377849. DOI: 10.1007/11823285_116.

Giffels, M. et al. (2024). *MatterMiners/tardis: 0.8.2*. DOI: 10.5281/ZENODO.2240605.

Henry, M., E. Dittert, D. Koeppen and V. Viswanathan (1999). *Intel Preboot Execution Environment*. Hillsboro, OR 97124. URL: https://datatracker.ietf.org/doc/id/draft-henry-remote-boot-protocol-00.txt.

Janczyk, M., D. von Suchodoletz and B. Wiebelt (2019). »bwForCluster NEMO. Forschungscluster für die Wissenschaft«. In: *Proceedings of the 5th bwHPC Symposium. HPC Activities in Baden-Württemberg*. Freiburg, September 2018. 5th bwHPC Symposium. Ed. by M. Janczyk, D. von Suchodoletz and B. Wiebelt. TLP, Tübingen, pp. 29–50. DOI: 10.15496/publikation-29041.

Sammel, D., M. Boehler, A. J. Gamel and M. Schumacher (2023). »Lightweight Integration of a Data Cache for Opportunistic Usage of HPC Resources in HEP Workflows«. In: *Computing and Software for Big Science* 7.1. ISSN: 2510-2044. DOI: 10.1007/s41781-023-00100-1.

Yoo, A. B., M. A. Jette and M. Grondona (2003). »SLURM: Simple Linux Utility for Resource Management«. In: *Lecture Notes in Computer Science*. Springer Berlin Heidelberg, pp. 44–60. ISBN: 9783540397274. DOI: 10.1007/10968987_3.

AUDITOR: Accounting for opportunistic resources

Performance Optimisation

Raghuvar Vijayakumar, Michael Boehler, Dirk Sammel, Markus Schumacher

Physikalisches Institut, Albert-Ludwigs-Universität, Freiburg, Deutschland

Abstract

In response to the increasing demand for computing resources in High Energy Physics, we have integrated under-utilized computing resources opportunistically using COBalD/TARDIS. However, resource sharing requires robust accounting. We present AUDITOR (AccoUnting DatahandlIng Toolbox for Opportunistic Resources), a flexible and extensible accounting ecosystem tailored to address a broad range of use cases and infrastructures.

AUDITOR employs specialised collectors that monitor, capture and record accounting data, subsequently stored in a database. The recorded data are then made accessible to plugins, which analyse the accounting information to perform specific tasks, such as setting the priorities for user groups and forwarding the accounting data to other accounting systems.

In this article, we highlight how we improved AUDITOR's architecture, particularly in retrieving of accounting data. These performance improvements position AUDITOR to scale effectively, accommodating the demands of larger computing sites with increased data loads.

1 Introduction

The growing computational needs in High Energy Physics (HEP) and other research areas, alongside increasing concerns about energy efficiency, are driving efforts to enhance resource utilization. COBalD/TARDIS (Fischer et al., 2023) (Giffels et al., 2024) facilitates dynamic, opportunistic sharing of resources across HPC-HTC clusters, and cloud providers, integrating resources only when needed. To manage accounting in such dynamic environments, AUDITOR (Boehler et al., 2024) has been developed as an open-source tool. It collects and processes accounting data via collectors and plugins, enabling flexible tracking and management of resource usage. AUDITOR's extensible design supports diverse use cases and integrates with existing systems through a REST interface.

In order to measure the performance of AUDITOR, its data retrieval capabilities are benchmarked. The results of the benchmark showed that the query time was getting slower as the scale of the database increased. Therefore, the database schema was changed to improve the performance of the data query. Through this article, we discuss the implications of changing the schema and the tangible performance improvements which resulted from these changes.

2 AUDITOR

AUDITOR is centered around a database that stores records containing accounting information collected from sources like schedulers. Plugins then request a subset of records from AUDITOR to perform specific tasks. These components interact with AUDITOR via a REST interface, and client libraries are provided for Rust (Developers, 2024) and Python (Van Rossum et al., 1995) to simplify development.

A record in AUDITOR represents a single piece of accountable information. It can be created and submitted to AUDITOR through a direct REST API call or via client tools and is then stored in a database with a unique record ID. The record's fields are provided through a meta field, a hashmap that maps string keys to arrays of string values. Components within a record specify the types and amounts of resources (e.g., CPU cores, RAM, disk space, GPUs) being accounted for. Components can also have scores attached, such as HEPScore23 (Giordano et al., 2024), to measure the normalized CPU performance. Each score has a name and value. The start and stop times define when the resources were available, and AUDITOR calculates the runtime, the difference between start time and stop time in seconds. Below is a summary of the fields (Boehler et al., 2024):

- `record_id` (String, unique)
- `[meta]` (HashMap[String → [String]])
- `[components]` (Array)
  - `name` (String)
  - `amount` (Integer)
  - `[scores]` (Array)
    - `name` (String)
    - `value` (Float)
- `start_time` (Datetime, UTC)
- `stop_time` (Datetime, UTC)
- `runtime` (Integer,seconds, output-only)

3 Schema Change

Until AUDITOR v0.5.0, the database schema is designed with the database normalisation concept. As seen in the Figure 1, meta and component record fields are put in a separate table with one-to-many and many-to-many relations. Though this structure follows the guidelines for normalising the data into different tables, it did not help AUDITOR's use case. The crux of AUDITOR's database is to save and retrieve the record in the same structure and there is no partial retrieval of data from a record. Therefore, having three joins in a query to retrieve the record data using filters would result in longer query time and unnecessary operations as the database grows.

The new schema, as shown in Figure 2, consists of meta and component information in JSONb column type in a single table. This eliminates the complex join operations of different tables and data while querying the record. Moreover, it improves the query string readability and reduces the complexity for the user.

The AUDITOR-client provides a REST interface to retrieve records using advanced query techniques. The individual fields of the records mentioned in the previous section can be

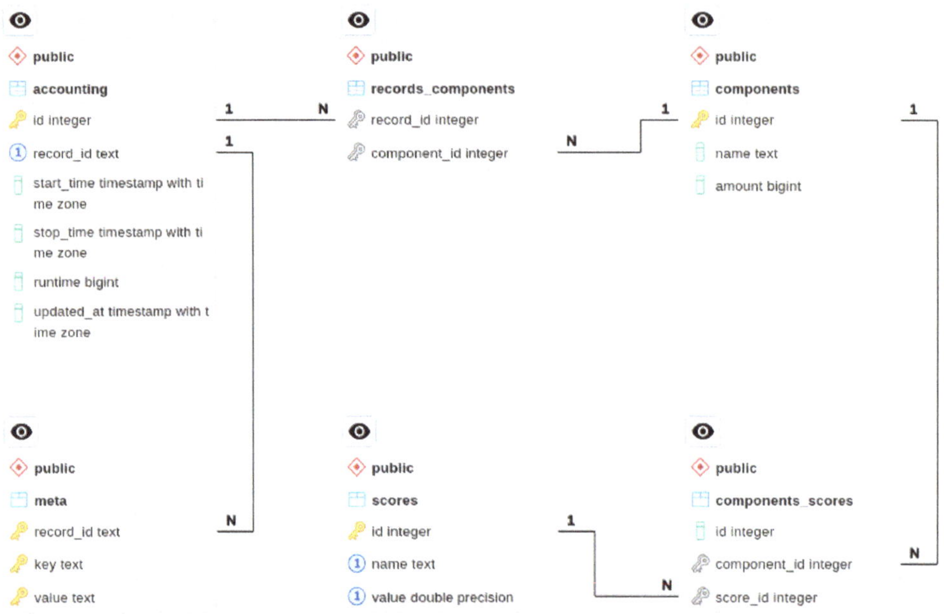

Figure 1: The database schema of AUDITOR v0.5.0 was designed with the database normalisation concept.

queried with any combinations from the database. This is helpful for faster and precise retrieval of records. Therefore, the following sets of queries are chosen for testing the performance improvements for the schema change by measuring the time taken for the query to execute and also to reflect the real case query scenario.

The real case scenario is simulated by filling the database with records resembling the actual records. The actual use case requires the retrieval of accounting data for a whole month or up to 2 months. In addition, the data records are also sorted according to different locations or HEP collaborations.

- **all** – Get all the records from the database
- **time range** – Filter records within a start time within a select time range of 120 days
- **time range and site id** – Filter the time range and a specific site id
- **component** – Filter component such as CPU with its score
- **time range + meta + comp** -Filter records with a time range, a meta field like site id and a component
- **time range + 2 meta + comp** – Filter with time range, a meta field like site id and two components

Figure 2: The new database schema, available from AUDITOR v0.6.2, consists of meta and component information in JSONb column type in a single table. It improves the query string readability and reduces the complexity for the user.

4 Benchmarks

The time taken to retrieve records from AUDITOR is a crucial aspect of the functioning of various plugins. Therefore, bench-marking the query time and the execution of queries from the AUDITOR-client is a necessity. The benchmarks are used to measure the performance of the AUDITOR database and the client response to the query.

4.1 Setup and Specifications

The benchmark is setup and run on a VM instance with the specifications as summarised in the Table 1.

In Figure 3, the AUDITOR server is launched and establishes a connection to the PostgreSQL database. The benchmark script is run using the command cargo bench (Developers, 2024). This command executes the AUDITOR benchmarking client. Criterion is a rust package which is a statistics driven benchmarking tool (Brookman, 2024). This library is used to analyze the query time to fetch records from AUDITOR database us-

Table 1: Technical Specifications

Component	Configuration
Processor	Intel(R) Xeon(R) CPU E5-2630 v4 @ 2.20GHz
Memory	4 GB
Storage	40 GB
vCPU	2

ing the AUDITOR benchmarking client. The results from the benchmarks are stored in JSON (Pezoa et al., 2016) files for each of the benchmark groups.

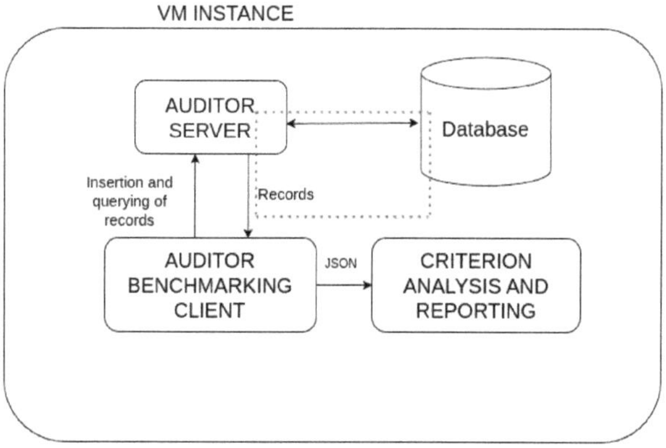

Figure 3: Benchmark setup

4.2 Benchmark comparison

To compare the performance improvement from v0.5.0 to v0.6.2, different queries with varying amounts of data in the database are executed and the query time is measured. However, running the benchmarking script using the criterion package will benchmark the time taken to get the query to the client endpoint. Though these measurements reflect the real case scenario of how a client would interact with AUDITOR, the time measured in this case would include the HTTP response time along with the database query time. Therefore, the query time is also directly measured from the PostgreSQL database. The improvement in the schema changes are measured by comparing the v0.5.0 with v0.6.2 version of AUDTIOR.

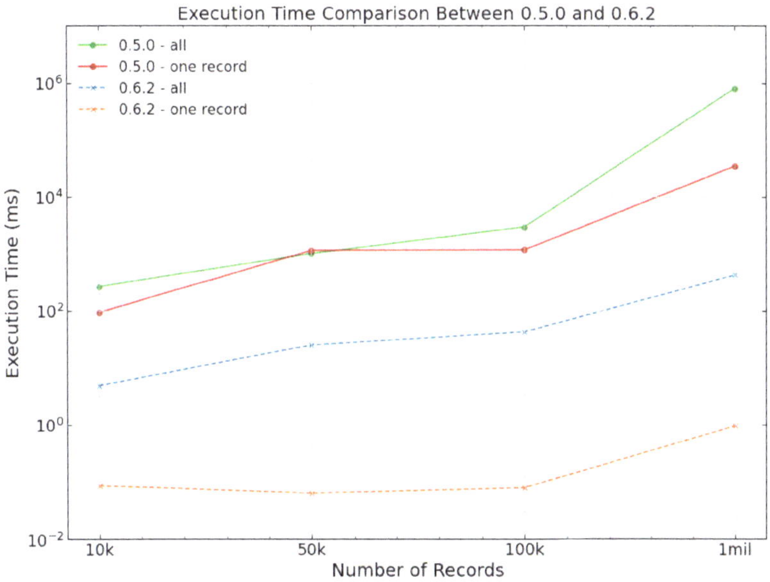

Figure 4: Comparison of query performance. The x-axis describes the number of records in the database against the y-axis that depicts the time for execution of the query. The query time for retrieving all records is reduced by a factor of more than 20.

The graph in Figure 4 shows the comparison of the old schema and the new schema. AUDITOR v0.5.0 is compared against v0.6.2. The x-axis describes the number of records in the database against the y-axis that depicts the time for execution of the query. The query time for retrieving all records is reduced by a factor of more than 20.

Table 2 shows the measurements of query time measured directly from the database.

Table 2: Comparison of database query time of AUDITOR v0.5.0 and v0.6.2 (All measurements are in milli seconds)

	10k		50k		100k		1 mil	
	0.5.0	0.6.2	0.5.0	0.6.2	0.5.0	0.6.2	0.5.0	0.6.2
all records	267.7	4.8	1007.3	25.0	2929.9	42.2	791457.6	421.1
time range	100.5	0.6	686.6	2.5	1814.3	24.4	41948.1	188.7
time range and meta	88.8	1.0	814.6	4.1	2500.0	25.2	76142.9	232.6
component	99.7	7.8	564.5	42.6	2366.5	31.1	41905.9	1648.8
time range + meta + comp	77.0	0.5	499.6	3.2	1159.0	25.0	29114.5	496.0
time range + 2 meta + comp	80.5	0.6	567.6	2.5	2285.6	25.7	23803.7	187.3
one record	92.3	0.1	1136.4	0.1	1164.6	0.1	34045.7	1.0

Table 3 shows the measurement from the benchmark results which is measured with the criterion package. These query results are the output which the user gets from the

Table 3: Comparison of response time for different queries from AUDITOR benchmarking client (All measurements are in milli seconds)

	10k		50k		100k	
	0.5.0	0.6.2	0.5.0	0.6.2	0.5.0	0.6.2
all records	313.2	220.9	1540.8	1083.5	4113.8	2368.9
time range	41.8	4.7	1011.7	8.5	3037.4	32.5
time range and meta	42.0	3.4	391.1	4.7	1982.9	40.0
component	38.0	5.9	209.4	24.1	1428.9	49.1
time range + meta + comp	29.5	6.5	194.4	6.3	1265.6	39.8
time range + 2 meta + comp	28.9	7.9	194.9	4.7	1255.5	47.0

AUDITOR client. Since there are overheads due to HTTP method handling, we can see a difference in performance measurements between Tables 2 and 3. However, v0.6.2 has performed better and we were able to achieve significant improvements in record retrieval time.

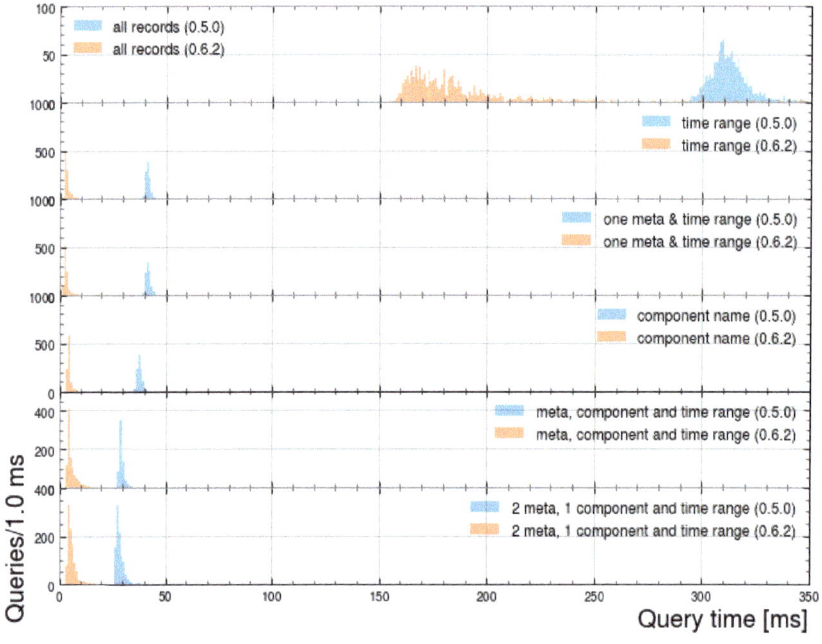

Figure 5: Comparison of distribution data of query times of 10k records. The x-axis shows number of queries while the y-axis shows the query execution time (ms). Notably, query time for retrieving all records is reduced by a factor of 1.42 and higher for all queries

Figures 5 and 6 show the distribution of benchmark results for the versions v0.5.0 and v0.6.2 of AUDITOR, based on tests with 10k and 100k records, respectively. Each figure illustrates the distribution for each query mentioned in Table 3, with 1,000 benchmark iterations per query. The distributions for AUDITOR v0.6.2 are generally less dispersed than those for v0.5.0, except for the »all records« query, which exhibits more consistent record retrieval times. The wider distribution observed for the »all records« query in both v0.5.0 and v0.6.2 can be attributed to several factors. The benchmark process was conducted on a minimal hardware setup with 4 GB of RAM, which introduces significant overhead. Additionally, the Criterion library, used for benchmarking, concurrently executes multiple requests to sample query times. The large query data size increases the overhead due to the need for serializing the data into structs before sending the HTTP response to the client.

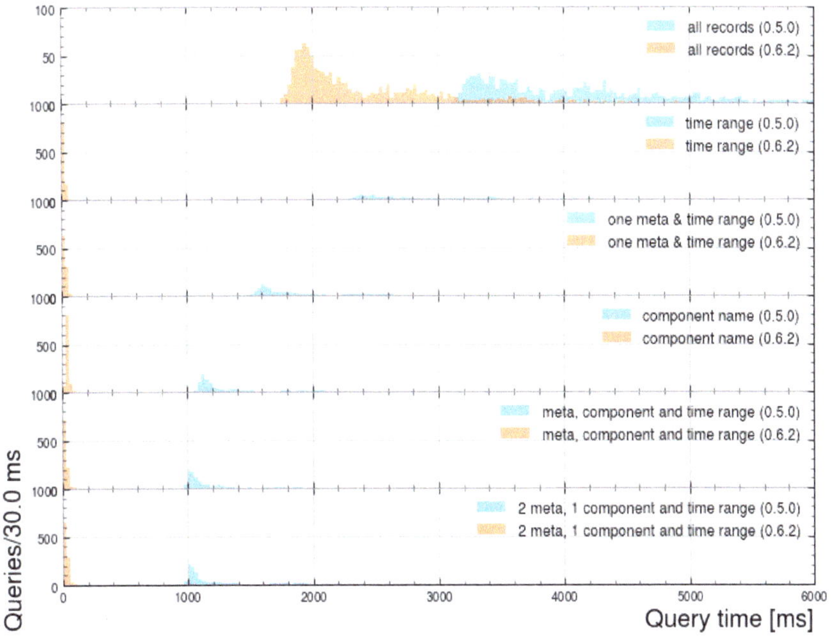

Figure 6: Comparison of distribution data of query times of 100k records. The x-axis shows number of queries while the y-axis shows the query execution time (ms). Notably, query time for retrieving all records is reduced by a factor of 1.74 and higher for all queries

5 Conclusion and Outlook

In this article, we evaluated AUDITOR, an accounting system designed for managing opportunistic resources in HEP environments. Our work focused on improving the performance of AUDITOR by optimizing its database schema and benchmarking the improvements.

The transition from the normalized schema in AUDITOR v0.5.0 to the more efficient schema in v0.6.2 has led to significant improvements in query performance. The benchmarking results demonstrate a reduction in query execution time by a factor of 12.78 to 923 in certain cases. This enhancement not only improves the retrieval of accounting records but also enables the system to scale effectively as the volume of data grows.

Additionally, exploring the implementation of more advanced data retrieval techniques such as db indexing and indexing methods could yield further performance gains.

Acknowledgements

This work was supported by the Federal Ministry of Education and Research (BMBF) within the project 05H21VFRC2 »Entwicklung, Integration und Optimierung von digitalen Infrastrukturen für ErUM« in the context of the collaborative research centre »Föderierte Digitale Infrastrukturen für die Erforschung von Universum und Materie (FIDIUM)«.

Corresponding Author

Raghuvar Vijayakumar: raghuvar.vijayakumar@physik.uni-freiburg.de
Experimentelle Teilchenphysik – Abteilung Prof. Schumacher,
Albert-Ludwigs-Universität Freiburg, Deutschland

ORCID

Raghuvar Vijayakumar https://orcid.org/0009-0000-0103-8105
Michael Boehler https://orcid.org/0000-0001-9734-574X
Dirk Sammel https://orcid.org/0000-0003-4484-1410
Markus Schumacher https://orcid.org/0000-0002-1733-8388

References

Boehler, M. et al. (2024). *The accounting ecosystem AUDITOR*. en. DOI: 10.5281/ZENODO.12653484.

Brookman, B. (2024). *Criterion: Statistics-driven micro-benchmarking library for Rust*. https://crates.io/crates/criterion. Version 0.4.0.

Developers, T. R. P. (2024). *The Rust Programming Language*. https://www.rust-lang.org/.

Fischer, M. et al. (2023). *MatterMiners/cobald: v0.14.0*. DOI: 10.5281/ZENODO.1887872. URL: https://zenodo.org/record/1887872.

Giffels, M. et al. (2024). *MatterMiners/tardis: 0.8.2*. DOI: 10.5281/ZENODO.2240605.

Giordano, D., J.-M. Barbet, T. Boccali and et al (2024). *HEPScore: A new CPU benchmark for the WLCG*. Ed. by R. De Vita, X. Espinal, P. Laycock and O. Shadura. DOI: 10.1051/epjconf/202429507024.

Pezoa, F., J. L. Reutter, F. Suarez, M. Ugarte and D. Vrgoč (2016). »Foundations of JSON schema«. In: *Proceedings of the 25th International Conference on World Wide Web*. International World Wide Web Conferences Steering Committee, pp. 263–273.

Van Rossum, G. and F. L. Drake Jr (1995). *Python reference manual*. Centrum voor Wiskunde en Informatica Amsterdam.

A Resource-aware Scheduling Concept for an OpenStack-based VDI

Manuel Bentele[*], Manuel Messner[*], Dirk von Suchodoletz[*],
Radosław Piliszek[†]

[*]University of Freiburg, Germany
[†]7bulls.com, Warsaw, Poland

Abstract

Using Virtual Machines (VMs) with dedicated rendering and remote access capabilities, virtual workplaces can be created, and can then be accessed from anywhere at any time. If this is to happen on a large scale in the cloud, so-called Virtual Desktop Infrastructures (VDIs) for the dynamic provisioning of virtual desktops play an increasingly important role. A sustainable VDI should be freely available to everyone for modification and redistribution at no cost, be scalable, and should support various desktop use cases with different resource requirements. Some use cases involve hundreds of similar VMs running in parallel, which requires proper resource planning ahead. A timed long-term resource scheduling of VM placements on compute nodes on an OpenStack cloud represents a major development challenge. Further requirements arise from long-term reservations, capabilities of the available compute nodes, conditions imposed by the guest OS, and remote access. Summarizing the state-of-the-art placement and outlining the use cases for a VDI on OpenStack, this paper discusses the necessary considerations and steps to extend existing OpenStack services and develop scheduling components for a timed operation to operate a fully Open Source VDI (OSVDI) for various use cases in the academic field. The suggested approach works towards separated building blocks to allow re-use in similar scenarios.

1 Introduction

Virtual Desktop Infrastructures (VDIs) are an attractive solution to streamline large-scale machine operation, the centralization of resources, and the flexible responding to various user demands. Additionally, VDIs help to bring interaction nearer to (large-scale) data sets, provides controlled environments and thus fosters to improve system security. For example, a VDI can significantly enhance teaching in academia by automatically providing virtual desktop workplaces for exercises and exams. Additionally, researchers can utilize a VDI to access custom desktop workplaces tailored to their specific research needs, with necessary applications and tools pre-installed. Here, a VDI provides researchers with the necessary resources for customized desktop environments and effortless remote access from any location, relieving researchers from the burden of adjusting hardware configurations for specialized applications and tools.

As many VDI use cases require temporary resources, cloud operation is a resource-efficient means. As of today, many cloud platforms focus on the consolidation of traditional server tasks and temporary resources for testing and development. Thus, the scheduling of resources in platforms like OpenStack concentrates on the on-demand placement of VMs in a setup mostly without GUI components. VDI is a sought after candidate to better utilize existing cloud infrastructure in academia: it allows courses to take place during the semester at specific times or a workshop scheduled for a couple of days well ahead to be run on existing infrastructural resources.

Adding VDI capabilities to OpenStack is not a novel idea (J.-Y. Li et al., 2017; Redondo Gil et al., 2014; Rot et al., 2018), but the efforts so far did not achieve wide take-up for a series of shortcomings (Shukur et al., 2020). In this paper, we will dig deeper into one of the central aspects of an OSVDI outlined in our previous overview (Bentele et al., 2022) and focus primarily on timed resource scheduling and related aspects. It will demonstrate that existing scheduling mechanisms and some OpenStack modules need to be modified or extended and new components to be developed. After presenting our use cases and a state-of-the-art analysis, initial concepts and ideas for medium- to long-term resource planning will be discussed. The discussion outlines the necessary changes and additions that will modify and extend the basic OpenStack infrastructure, including the implementation of additional components. With the contribution of this paper, an OpenStack infrastructure can be upgraded to a fully functional OSVDI for academia.

2 VDI use cases

To motivate suitable solutions, various VDI use cases are taken into account. This further includes the consideration of numerous inputs on resource scheduling required by factors like hardware and remote access protocol capabilities, expectations of the guest OS, and the provided host systems. From these concepts, a long-term, time-based resource scheduling is derived and evaluated for implementation. We identified three distinct VDI use cases with individual characteristics to consider for our proposed scheduling concept. For the three use cases, we take up some findings from our lecture room PC orchestration service bwLehrpool (Bauer et al., 2019; Suchodoletz et al., 2021; Trahasch et al., 2015) with its remote access functionality.

2.1 Traditional desktop workplaces for single-user access

The traditional VDI example is an end-user PC replacement in the form of a virtual desktop. The virtual desktop is implemented as a stateful VM which is assigned to an individual user. For a university, this could be a student or a researcher working on a time-limited project. It would allow individual configuration of the various VM parameters, like the amount of CPU cores or memory and disk space, to match the actual user's requirements. Such a configured VM is typically persistent over a certain period of time and is not discarded after a single session. Often, the VM would be linked directly to an OpenStack user or project, manageable via OpenStack's default dashboard. Such a setup is described in more detail by earlier approaches to VDI.[1] A simplified dashboard composed of icons would also be conceivable, which allows a user to control an assigned VM with some basic operations, e.g., starting, pausing, stopping, and restarting the VM.

2.2 Discardable desktop workplaces for temporary sessions

Further significant use cases evolve around discardable virtual desktops where a configured resource (in the form of a VM) is not assigned to a dedicated user or project in a 1:1 relationship. In such setups, users change frequently like for training, temporary sessions (e.g., e-assessments), or resources, to access remote compute resources with a

[1] See OpenStack Summit – Boston, MA (2017): https://www.openstack.org/videos/summits/boston-2017/virtual-desktop-infrastructure-vdi-with-openstack (visited on 19.07.2025)

graphical user interface. In the context of the cross-university e-learning project PePP,[2] a general training desktop environment is to be provided or students should be able to take an e-assessment in a full curated and controlled desktop environment from home or some generic computer in a PC lab. In such a use case, a student (or a larger group of them participating a certain course) is scheduled to take an e-assessment at a specific point in time. An event like this usually happens at the end of the semester (in the official examination period), or some courses might schedule self-assessments using the course software environment in a controlled manner.

Resources for e-assessments should be made available ad-hoc in the sense that they are not linked to the user but are provided via a link to a special access gateway. Access to such environments is not directly granted by OpenStack itself but could be handled through an access gateway dealing with user authentication through an external Authentication and Authorization Infrastructure (AAI) linked to it. After successful user authentication, the access gateway should redirect the user to web-based desktop access of an assigned VM.

For training and e-assessments, the (formal) scheduling is usually done ahead of time by the organizer or lecturer who reserves a matching number of VMs for a given time slot. Such reservations could be initiated and managed via third-party systems, e.g., through a Campus Management System (CMS) or Learning Management System (LMS). These systems could handle the automatic management of resources for training and e-assessments. The participants need to be informed about ways to access the resource to a given point in time by a link (e.g., a one-time URL which is just valid once for the specific time slot of an e-assessment). Optimally, the link points directly to an already provisioned VM and does not require any VM or session selection.[3]

Similarly, a growing number of research projects require standardized training environments of identical setups for courses meant to be held in typical desktop environments. For example, this is the case for the National Research Data Infrastructure (NFDI) consortia of *DataPLANT* and *NFDI4BIOIMAGE* in their training and educational subprojects.[4] This use case extends upon the PC lab operation model (Bentele et al., 2022) in which a lecturer curates a course requiring specially configured VMs. The configura-

[2] Partnership for innovative E-Assessments – Joint Project of the Baden-Württemberg Universities, see https://www.hnd-bw.de/projekte/pepp (visited on 17.07.2025)

[3] As the session chooser, called VMchooser, in the bwLehrpool project (Bentele et al., 2022).

[4] See https://nfdi4plants.org (visited on 17.07.2025) and https://nfdi4bioimage.de (visited on 17.07.2025)

tion for course-related resources can be specified by a lecturer in an individual environment template. These specified resources need to be available at a certain predefined point in time. All use cases for temporary sessions are typically characterized by their discardable nature to fully clean up the allocated resources after a session is completed.

2.3 Powerful desktop workplaces for graphic visualizations

Researchers as well as students often deal with graphic-intensive applications or large-scale data sets where dedicated compute or rendering capabilities are required. This kind of task can be characterized by an interactive processing and visualization of data. In this use case, virtual desktops based on powerful VMs with dedicated resource capabilities replace the need for locally available high-performance workstations with often limited resource capabilities. Especially (large-scale) data sets can be accessed and visualized near their cloud data store more easily because the data sets are either huge and cannot be transferred fast enough to a remote workstation, or the data sets are sensitive and should not leave a secured cloud environment at all. In the case of sensitive data sets, remote access to dedicated virtual desktops where data processing takes place can be secured through a safe access gateway. Trustworthy users are able to access such data sets in dedicated virtual desktops whereas a transfer of sensitive data for guests can be denied based on a fine-grained data access policy.

3 Related Work

Most work related to scheduling of resources for cloud infrastructures address the traditional cloud computing model rather than a VDI centered setup. In the cloud computing model, resources can be requested to execute compute-only tasks on one or several compute nodes. Support for dedicated rendering capabilities and virtual displays for virtual desktops are not considered in this case but might be partly available, e.g., for accelerated computing based on Graphics Processing Units (GPUs).

3.1 VDI solutions

Ready-to-use VDI solutions as outlined in Table 1 – commercial as well as (partly) open-source – often introduce the notion of desktop pools, which allocate scheduled resources for virtual desktops over a specified period. The partly open-source solution *flexVDI*,[5] as well as commercial VDI solutions offered by VMware or Citrix, focus mainly on the single user VDI use case where virtual desktops are provisioned on-demand for personal workplaces.

Table 1: Overview of VDI solutions and their capabilities and licensing.

Solution	Features and Limitations	Licensing
Commercial (VMware, Citrix)	✓ Single-user VDI for on-demand personal desktops. ✗ Lacks resource scheduling for timed VDI use cases. ✓ Provides vGPU support for dedicated rendering.	Proprietary
flexVDI[5]	✓ Single-user VDI for on-demand personal desktops. ✗ Lacks resource scheduling for timed VDI use cases. ✗ Misses vGPU support for dedicated rendering.	Partly open-source (GPL 2.0 / 3.0)
Bumblebee[6] (separate VDI service for OpenStack)	✓ Provides on-demand virtual desktops. ✗ Lacks resource scheduling for timed VDI use cases. ✗ Misses vGPU support for dedicated rendering. ✗ No storage management for discardable desktops.	Open-source (Apache 2.0)
OpenStack plugins[1] (broker services for external remote desktop gateways)	✓ Provide on-demand virtual desktops. ✓ Can deploy pre-provisioned VMs from a pool. ✗ Lack resource scheduling for timed VDI use cases. ✗ Miss vGPU support for dedicated rendering.	Partly open-source (Apache 2.0)

Also, the open-source project *Bumblebee*[6] can provision virtual desktops on-demand and is the backbone VDI for the ARDC Nectar Research Cloud.[7] Resource scheduling in all those solutions lacks appropriate support for our temporary and timed VDI use cases. Currently, flexVDI, as well as Bumblebee, do not provide any support for dedicated rendering capabilities, such as vGPU support for graphic-intensive virtual desktops, nor an appropriate storage implementation for discardable (temporary) virtual desktops. However, Bumblebee is closely related to this work since it is a separate VDI service for an OpenStack-based cloud infrastructure. This work is closely related to existing

[5] See https://flexvdi.com (visited on 18.07.2025)
[6] See https://github.com/NeCTAR-RC/bumblebee (visited on 18.07.2025)
[7] See https://ardc.edu.au/services/nectar-research-cloud (visited on 18.07.2025)

efforts that develop *plugins*[1] to integrate external remote desktop gateways – such as Citrix XenDesktop, Microsoft RDS, and Apache Guacamole[8] – with OpenStack. The plugins act as brokers that interface with an OpenStack infrastructure to facilitate the on-demand provisioning of VMs for virtual desktop workplaces. However, these plugins do not provide a resource scheduling for our temporary and timed VDI use cases, lack support for dedicated rendering capabilities, and primarily serve as interfaces to incorporate existing remote desktop solutions rather than delivering a fully integrated or native VDI solution within OpenStack.

3.2 Scheduling strategies

One central aspect in cloud platforms like OpenStack is the scheduling of dynamically allocated resources. Resource scheduling in terms of a cloud infrastructure determines where and when to place and provision dynamically requested resources for computations on available compute nodes. Machines are often provided in the form of VMs with further allocated resources, such as hardware accelerators like GPUs, disk storage, and dedicated network capabilities. Most work related to resource scheduling follows a certain objective.

A major part of related work addresses **resource scheduling for workflow tasks**. Tasks from workflows are interconnected together through compute or data dependencies. A resource scheduling for those tasks has to map each task to a set of provisioned resources (mostly VMs) so that all dependencies of all tasks are satisfied. Various scheduling optimizations have been proposed to achieve energy-efficient (Kaur et al., 2016; H. Li et al., 2016; Yuan et al., 2021) or cost-aware (Cai et al., 2019; Calheiros et al., 2014; Haidri et al., 2020; Z. Li et al., 2018; Ma et al., 2019; Wu et al., 2017) workflow schedules, as well as considering time-sensitive constraints such as soft (Calheiros et al., 2014) or hard deadlines (Hu et al., 2018; Rodriguez et al., 2014; Wu et al., 2017) for workflow tasks. Other scheduling objectives, especially for offloading compute-intensive tasks of mobile applications to cloud resources, are presented in a wide literature review by Ramanathan et al., 2020. Scheduling of workflow tasks is not directly related to VDI resource scheduling but solves the same scheduling problems at a higher level of abstraction. Instead of mapping tasks to compute resources (mostly VMs), VDI resource

[8] See OpenStack VDI Broker https://github.com/cloudbase/vdi-broker (visited on 18.07.2025)

scheduling attempts to place VM resources to compute nodes. It is worth mentioning here that the startup-time-aware resource provisioning (Zhu et al., 2016) is closely related to this paper, since its algorithm is beneficial for this work to overcome the challenge of timely and efficient provision of resources in long-term schedules.

Other work refers to **resource scheduling for cloud computing** platforms like OpenStack. Various resource scheduling strategies address different objectives to optimize resource allocation and VM placements on cloud computing nodes for optimal networking (Lucrezia et al., 2015; Scharf et al., 2015; Stein et al., 2017), high availability (Moghaddam et al., 2016), increased performance (Sahasrabudhe et al., 2015), balanced compute node workload (Gohil et al., 2021; Xu et al., 2016; Zhai et al., 2021), consideration of service requirements (Parakh et al., 2018; Xu et al., 2016), and a trustworthy and secure operation (Abbadi et al., 2013; Jilhawar et al., 2015) as well as robustness (Zhai et al., 2021). A further approach by Kim et al., 2020, uses live migration of VMs to gain good performance if an unbalanced resource placement w.r.t. performance occurs during operation. All of those scheduling strategies are well suited to implement an efficient and safe cloud infrastructure for further VDI use cases but they do not address any VDI-related improvements. However, Hwang et al., 2012, present an optimized VM scheduling on the level of a hypervisor to improve performance for VDI setups, but their work does not contribute any research regarding VDI resource scheduling on the level of VMs and compute nodes.

So far, all strategies for cloud computing purposes follow the approach of an on-demand request of resources. This approach allocates and provisions resources immediately after a request was triggered. Thereby, a timed long-term resource scheduling for our temporary and timed VDI use cases cannot be established.

3.3 OpenStack platform

OpenStack is an open-source platform for large-scale cloud infrastructure.[9] The platform is composed of many services, each handling a specific use case in the field of Infrastructure-as-a-Service (IaaS) setups: from identity management, VM scheduling, image services, over Software Defined Networking (SDN), to more abstract modules, implementing orchestration methods and workflow management. The main resource

[9] See https://www.openstack.org (visited on 19.07.2025)

scheduling components of OpenStack, namely the *Placement*[10] and the *Nova*[11] service, are briefly introduced for the purpose of this paper. The OpenStack services are listed in Table 2 with a description of their provided functionality. In addition, we also present the services *Watcher*[12], *Blazar*[13], and *Cyborg*[14], which are integral to the overall resource management within OpenStack. Effective resource management will be particularly important w.r.t. the presented VDI use cases.

Table 2: Overview of related OpenStack services and their functionalities.

Service	Functionality
Placement[10]	Accounting service that tracks installed resources and their usage across compute nodes and storage pools. The service manages resource classes (like CPU, memory, and disk) and traits (describing qualitative aspects of resources).
Nova[11]	Compute service that manages VMs and containers. The service is responsible for the VM's and container's life cycle.
Watcher[12]	Optimization service to improve the performance of an OpenStack infrastructure via retroactive resource placement and intelligent VM migration.
Blazar[13]	Reservation service to provide resource reservations for various resource types including VMs, storage volumes, and physical hosts. The service allows to reserve, schedule, and manage resources within an OpenStack infrastructure.
Cyborg[14]	Management service for accelerator resources that provisions specialized hardware devices like GPUs on compute nodes. The service allows to efficiently allocate and utilize these resources for high-performance workloads.

The *Placement* service **tracks installed resources and their current usage or availability**, categorized into resource classes and traits. Resource classes represent countable resources, e.g., the hypervisor's installed disk space and memory, as well as their current usage, whereas traits are boolean properties. Traits represent specific (non-countable) features of a hypervisor, e.g., the support of special CPU extensions. Resource classes and traits are used among other things as a baseline for the scheduling process.

[10] See https://docs.openstack.org/placement/yoga (visited on 19.07.2025)
[11] See https://docs.openstack.org/nova/yoga (visited on 19.07.2025)
[12] See https://docs.openstack.org/watcher/yoga (visited on 19.07.2025)
[13] See https://docs.openstack.org/blazar/yoga (visited on 19.07.2025)
[14] See https://docs.openstack.org/cyborg/yoga (visited on 19.07.2025)

The *Nova* service is the service that is **responsible for the VM's life cycle**. It provides all functionality around running VMs, connecting it with artifacts from other services, such as networks or storage, and especially important for this paper, it provides OpenStack with a VM scheduler.

Before the OpenStack Wallaby release, a generic scheduler interface enabled the implementation of custom schedulers. With Wallaby, this API has been removed and the only allowed scheduler remaining is Nova's built-in scheduler known as *nova-scheduler*, which follows a bin packing strategy (Janagoudar et al., 2020). The **default scheduling procedure of the nova-scheduler** is implemented using a filter chain approach visualized in Figure 1.

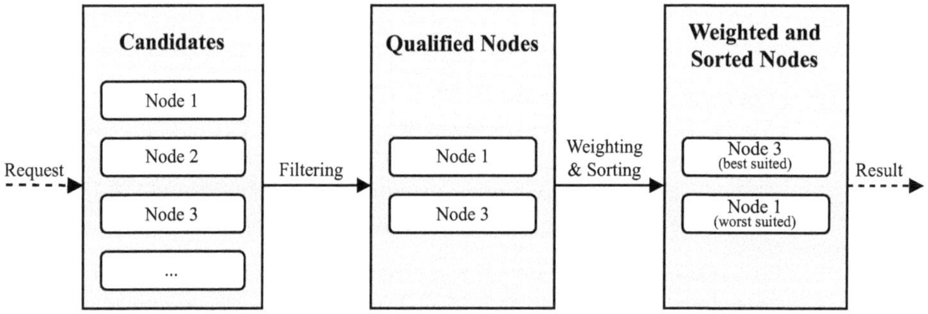

Figure 1: Default scheduling procedure of the OpenStack nova-scheduler.

When receiving a scheduling request, the nova-scheduler fetches all available compute node candidates from the Placement service. This node list is then reduced by various installed and enabled filters to a list of qualified nodes. Then, the list is weighted and sorted by available metadata to find the best-suited nodes out of all qualified ones. As of OpenStack Yoga, there are many available filters. The ones enabled by default are depicted (in order from top to bottom) in Table 3.

The weighting of compute nodes follows a worst fit strategy, i.e., the nova-scheduler always prefers the nodes with the most resources available (Janagoudar et al., 2020). In most cases, this strategy is sufficient enough and strongly recommended. This scheduling might produce an unbalanced resource distribution. There is an OpenStack service, called *Watcher*,[12] which tries to optimize the placement of resources retroactively, by migrating these resources to potentially better suited compute nodes later on.

For a **timed resource allocation and provisioning**, OpenStack provides the *Blazar* service.[13] This service reserves requested resources (VMs, physical compute nodes, and

Table 3: Resource scheduling filters enabled by default in OpenStack.

Filter	Functionality
AvailabilityZoneFilter	Selects compute nodes of the requested availability zone.
ComputeFilter	Selects compute nodes that are enabled and available.
ComputeCapabilitiesFilter	Selects compute nodes with matching node capabilities.
ImagePropertiesFilter	Selects compute nodes matching the VM's image properties including architecture, hypervisor type, or VM mode.
ServerGroupAntiAffinityFilter	Selects compute nodes that are not hosting VMs belonging to the same affinity group as the VM to be started.
ServerGroupAffinityFilter	Selects compute nodes which are in a configured group.

floating IP addresses) for a specific duration determined by a start and end time. Reservations are based on time leases that can be created for each of those resource types. In the case of time leases for VMs, a specific flavor with a resource reference to the reservation is created automatically if a lease is added. Such a flavor can then be used to create a VM instance only during the specified time lease.

Compute nodes in heterogeneous infrastructures are often equipped with various hardware-based **accelerator resources**. These resources can be exposed as dedicated compute resources to speed up specific computations like graphics rendering or AI-based computations. OpenStack provides the additional *Cyborg* service which is intended to discover and manage specific accelerator devices on all compute nodes.[14] This information is used to help the OpenStack Placement service to receive more precise allocation candidates (suitable compute nodes) for OpenStack's scheduler, e.g., a vGPU instance can be only acquired on a compute node with available vGPU capabilities. Accelerator resources are fully managed by OpenStack with extensive resource accounting.

In addition to managing dedicated accelerator resources for graphic rendering, OpenStack also supports emulated or para-virtualized graphic adapters provided by the underlying hypervisor. Such lower-performance GPUs are more flexible since no dedicated hardware capabilities are involved. They fit perfectly for normal office-like VDI use cases without any graphic-intensive rendering requirements. Graphic adapters are currently managed differently than accelerator resources by OpenStack, which leads to a more complicated resource accounting. A resource accounting for graphic adapters was already implemented once but was removed in the past.[15] The additional memory consumption of an emulated or para-virtualized graphic adapter is currently not included in the total memory consumption of a VM. This can lead to serious scheduling errors, especially if the requested graphic memory for a VM exceeds the available amount of memory. In this case, the cloud administrator has to manually take care of memory over-provisioning, which is a major drawback for various VDI use cases.

In conjunction with the open-source hypervisor QEMU,[16] OpenStack has additional functionalities to control and configure GPU accelerator resources in the form of a direct GPU passthrough for VMs and a simple management for vGPUs where a physical GPU can be partitioned into several vGPUs of the same vGPU type. Currently, the implemented GPU partitioning support in OpenStack lacks support for dedicated capabilities of physical GPUs providing advanced partitioning technologies in a more fine-grained manner, e.g., different vGPU partition types per physical GPU. The current implementation also lacks dynamic resource scheduling with attached vGPU memory demands, which limits flexibility and efficient GPU resource usage required for VDI use cases.

GPU partitioning is currently a significant topic for cloud infrastructures and is becoming increasingly prominent. Some manufacturers, such as Nvidia, already offer GPU products that support partitioning for VDI use cases. However, Nvidia's products are subject to a complex and unfavorable licensing model for the cost-effective operation of VDI cloud environments.[17] Fortunately, upcoming alternatives from other vendors like Intel and AMD have been announced, introducing new approaches to GPU partitioning. For example, Intel's GVT-g technology (Tian et al., 2014; Xue et al., 2016) enables dynamic partitioning of GPUs into several vGPUs of distinct vGPU types based on resource demand, making these solutions particularly attractive for various VDIs use cases.

[15] See https://review.opendev.org/c/openstack/nova/+/483133 (visited on 19.07.2025)
[16] See https://www.qemu.org (visited on 19.07.2025)
[17] See https://docs.nvidia.com/vgpu/16.0/grid-licensing-user-guide/index.html (visited on 19.07.2025)

4 VDI resource scheduling and placement

For the implementation of a resource scheduling and VM placement for an OpenStack-based VDI, we propose a new OpenStack service with an architecture similar to the TIMER-Cloud framework (Begam et al., 2020) and the Aardvark tool (Moreira et al., 2019). Implementing resource scheduling as a separate service allows code encapsulation and leaves the base functionality of OpenStack unchanged. This preserves the traditional cloud computing infrastructure model provided by a fresh deployment of the OpenStack platform. Any VDI resource scheduling support can then be retrofitted.

4.1 Service architecture

A VDI resource scheduling service should implement an orchestrator composed of three components: a *VM dispatcher*, a *resource scheduler*, and a *resource monitor* (as depicted in Figure 2).

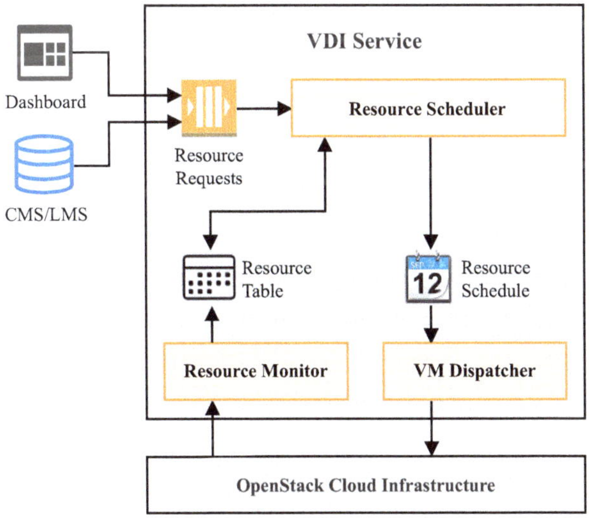

Figure 2: The general VDI service architecture considered for implementation.

The VM dispatcher communicates with a deployed OpenStack cloud through appropriate APIs, e.g., OpenStack's provided public RESTful APIs, and dispatches VM and resource requests scheduled by a resource scheduler component. The scheduler component should implement various resource scheduling algorithms to meet the requirements of our different VDI use cases. Here, an automatic selection dependent on the desired use case should be considered to obtain a good allocation of resources when needed. For optimized planning, the scheduler should receive feedback from the cloud infrastructure via a resource monitor. The resource monitor should keep track of the current resource allocation and placement of the cloud infrastructure by receiving feedback through appropriate APIs. Its main task is to provide the following mandatory input information for various VDI resource scheduling strategies.

4.2 Scheduling inputs

Input and feedback information for VDI resource scheduling strategies can be derived from our VDI use cases where the following inputs are mandatory.

The **type of the preferred use case** plays an important role in the resource scheduling strategy. This information as input determines the selection of a preconfigured resource template. Such a resource template can reuse OpenStack's underlying concept of flavors and properties to allocate, configure, and provision resources accordingly. In addition, this input informs the VDI resource scheduler and the VM dispatcher to choose an optimized resource scheduling strategy and to configure suitable remote access to a user's virtual desktop. The remote access can be provided either through a dedicated dashboard or direct access to a remote access gateway allowed via a link (e.g., an URL) to support the access from native (non web browser based) remote desktop clients.

For temporary and timed VDI sessions like courses and e-assessments, a **timed long-term resource scheduling** is necessary. This scheduling strategy requires as input a (long-term) time schedule that contains all planned time slots and the number of participants for each time slot. Reserved time slots of such events could be described by a start time and a certain duration where the event itself requests specified resources for its time slots. Such information can be automatically obtained from an external CMS or LMS which is managed by an organizer or directly by a lecturer (see Figure 3).

In a heterogeneous cloud infrastructure, there are various hardware resources on compute nodes available which provide numerous **compute node capabilities**. E.g. some compute nodes could be equipped with specific hardware accelerators, such as dedicated GPUs, for specific computations and VDI rendering purposes. This information can be obtained from already implemented OpenStack services, namely the *Placement* and the *Cyborg* service. Both services provide a full inventory list which also shows the granularity of virtualizable resources, e.g., vGPU partition types and number of vGPUs.

Further specific compute node capabilities include video encoding resources to speed up and optimize remote video transport for graphic-intensive virtual desktop sessions. All information should be exposed by the resource monitor so that the scheduling component is aware of all available resources from an OpenStack cloud infrastructure. This knowledge could be used by the resource scheduler to avoid unfulfillable resource allocations as well as over-provisioning.

Further mandatory information for VDI resource scheduling are the **requirements of the guest OS** in conjunction with the selected use case. Depending on the selected VDI use case, various additional resources could be exposed to a VM so that the guest OS is able to access them. Here, proper access to additional resources is only possible if the guest OS in a VM image is correctly prepared meaning that necessary drivers for the exposed resources are installed. In addition to that, a guest OS often requires hardware-related properties which must be met for proper operation, e.g., the virtualized or emulated hardware architecture must match the hardware architecture supported by the guest OS. Such crucial information should be included in the VDI resource scheduling as well to prevent most common guest OS startup failures and pitfalls in a production-ready OpenStack cloud infrastructure.

Remote access to provisioned virtual desktops can be implemented using different technologies and thus optimized for certain VDI use cases. Most of the remote access requirements can be derived from a preferred VDI use case. Additional resources in the cloud environment might be allocated to implement the selected remote access technology, e.g., an optimized remote transport of graphic-intensive desktop content requires efficient video encoding. Such an additional allocation demand of video encoding resources should be considered by the resource scheduler as well but should not be made publicly available to any users of virtual desktops. Further interaction-specific features like shared clipboard support or USB redirection might be required to obtain a good user experience while working with remote virtual desktops. Here, it could be desirable that features like shared clipboard support must be limited in specific VDI use cases to guarantee security in general or to avoid cheating during e-assessments.

4.3 Scheduling strategies

Derived from our VDI use cases, we propose two major resource scheduling strategies. Both strategies differ in their aspect of when resources should be made available in a temporal manner.

For the VDI use case addressing single-user access to virtual desktops, we propose as a resource scheduling strategy an **on-demand allocation and dispatching** of VMs. In this case, there is no special resource scheduling algorithm needed since the on-demand resource provisioning can be passed to OpenStack's on-demand resource scheduling and placement (cf. Figure 3). Using OpenStack's resource scheduling and placement has the benefit that cloud operators can configure the scheduling and placement in more detail to optimize the default resource provisioning for the underlying cloud infrastructure. Such a scheduling strategy is useful if a researcher requires a stateful and persistent on-demand virtual desktop, e.g., for remote visualization or image analysis.

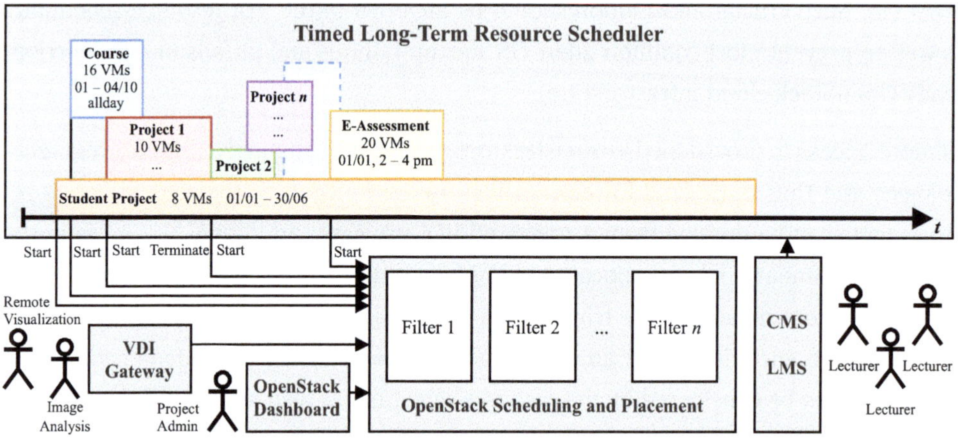

Figure 3: On-demand (short-term) resource scheduling using the filtering procedure in OpenStack vs. timed long-term resource scheduling considerations.

To handle the more specific VDI use cases, a **timed long-term resource scheduling** is to be developed as it is not yet implemented in the standard OpenStack (cf. Figure 3).

As one option, VM resources can be allocated and provisioned for predefined time slots just before an event takes place. To achieve the expected outcome, the timed long-term resource scheduling should guarantee a startup-time-aware resource scheduling and VM provisioning within a certain time before a specified startup-time deadline will be hit. In our VDI use cases, the startup-time deadline is set to the start time of a time slot from a course or e-assessment. More formally, a proper operation of requested resources for a specified time slot is guaranteed, if the startup-time deadline for the time slot is met and all requested resources are fully provisioned and operational. This guarantee is a strong requirement for VDI use cases like e-assessments since all resources must be allocated and provisioned shortly before an e-assessment takes place, so that the e-assessment can start on time. If a provisioning attempt exceeds the startup-time deadline (e.g., through a failure), there is no guarantee given and the provisioning success rate gets worse. Various optimizations could be used to keep the provisioning success rate up, such as resource replications or parallel VM placements. The approach of resource replication is similar to task replication (Calheiros et al., 2014) and suggests to allocate and provision more resources than needed for safety reasons, whereas parallel VM placements can reduce the resource provisioning duration (Cohen et al., 2020).

As another option, VM resources could be automatically reserved for predefined time slots. The difference from the first option lies in the timing of the resource creation. Each requested VM resource for a specific time slot would be created immediately and not before a time slot's start time. After a VM resource is created, the resource would be advertised to OpenStack but not accessible otherwise. This approach would significantly increase the provisioning success rate since such resources are already created, making a timely reactivation of those resources faster than a full allocation and provisioning from scratch.

Both scheduling strategies should not only plan resource allocations and provisioning for resource requests but should also consider cleanup strategies to free unused or unusable resources (e.g., from failed provisioning or hanging VMs). Further steps could include resource usage optimization and migration of VMs while preserving placement constraints (Kim et al., 2020) to achieve more optimal placements for a specific VDI use case (e.g., a scheduled large-scale course or e-assessment). If resources are running low, other VMs marked with a lower priority or labeled as opportunistic could be shelved temporarily to be reactivated later or powered off immediately.

4.4 Multi-cloud and further infrastructure orchestration

The prototype we started to develop and test could be extended in further steps to allow orchestration of our VDI use cases across multiple OpenStack infrastructures, similar to the MELODIC platform (Horn et al., 2018). This might require further inputs like the desired geolocation of a certain resource and the available communication resources between geolocations. In further steps, the module could get extended to be able to handle other cloud infrastructures besides OpenStack, as well as backends to use Linux/KVM hypervisors directly or the bwLehrpool infrastructure (Bauer et al., 2019; Bentele et al., 2022).

4.5 OpenStack modifications

The proposed VDI resource scheduling concept can be implemented as a standalone VDI service within the OpenStack ecosystem. For the technical foundation, inspiration can be drawn from existing services such as Bumblebee[6] or the OpenStack VDI Broker[8]. However, implementing this service requires some modifications to OpenStack's code base to orchestrate virtual desktops within a traditional cloud computing infrastructure.

A mandatory modification involves implementing resource accounting for emulated or para-virtualized graphic adapters. These adapters are preferred for office-like VDI use cases where lightweight rendering capabilities are sufficient. Adding this feature allows the resource monitor to accurately track emulated graphic resources, such as GPU memory of emulated graphics adapters. Without the feature, the resource monitor would be unable to accurately track these resources, which might lead to serious resource scheduling issues such as fatal overprovisioning where the total memory of a compute node is exceeded. The resource accounting for graphic adapters has been successfully implemented in previous OpenStack versions and can serve as a reference for integrating it into the current OpenStack code base.[15]

Another important modification involves enhancing the management of GPUs with more fine-grained partitioning support, enabling flexible utilization of virtualizable GPU resources for various VDI use cases. Implementing this could extend the management of existing GPU virtualization technologies such as Intel's GVT-g (Tian et al., 2014; Xue et al., 2016) to support dynamic GPU partitioning at a fine-grained level. This may require hypervisor enhancements for live re-partitioning or hot-plugging, as well as updates to resource management services like Cyborg to accurately track and handle these partitions. Such features would also benefit traditional cloud computing environments, providing more flexible and efficient resource allocation and utilization. Inspiration can be drawn from high-performance computing, where technologies like Nvidia's Multi-Instance GPU (MIG) and AMD's Multi-User GPU (MxGPU) provide hardware support for resource slicing. Their management software can dynamically adjust resource allocations, which helps maximize hardware utilization across different workloads.

Further modifications include collaboration with the OpenStack Blazar service to expand its resource reservation capabilities beyond VMs to include accelerator resources like vGPUs. Since reserving these accelerator resources is essential for enabling a timed long-term scheduling of VDI workloads with specific GPU demands, this extension is crucial for our proposed VDI service. To implement this enhancement, Blazar must be extended to handle GPU partitioning in order to support the reservation of vGPUs from partitioned GPUs. The existing implementation for VM resource reservations may serve as a useful guide to integrate reservation support for allocator resources like vGPUs.

An extension of OpenStack's live migration support is a desirable feature, as current capabilities are limited to VM resources. When accelerator resources such as vGPUs are assigned to a VM, a migration of these resources to another compute node is not yet supported. Enabling migration of accelerator resources requires comprehensive support across multiple layers. OpenStack must be extended so that the Cyborg service can maintain accurate resource accounting when moving resources between compute nodes. Additionally, the Nova service must be extended to properly control the underlying hypervisor. Support is also needed at the level of the hypervisor implementation and in the hardware of the accelerator device. Intermediate states across all layers must be accurately tracked and saved before resource migration can take place. The saved state must then be restored on the target compute node to continue resource operations seamlessly. Challenges include minimizing downtime and latency during migration, especially to avoid noticeable disruptions during active virtual desktop sessions. Technologies in the QEMU hypervisor and in GPU products from Nvidia are expected to provide prototype support for vGPU live migrations in upcoming versions. Proper integration of vGPU migration into OpenStack is planned for a future version.[18] The announced prototyping work helps to keep the modification effort required for the vGPU migration support manageable, making its incorporation into the proposed VDI service feasible.

[18] See https://blueprints.launchpad.net/nova/+spec/libvirt-mdev-live-migrate (visited on 20.07.2025)

5 Outlook

The adaptation of existing components and the implementation of the additional OpenStack service will be tackled on different strands with the objective to advance individual aspects independently and improve the current status of the development. To allow rapid testing we embed these activities into our revised bwCloud-OS[19] operation model consisting of a completely separated production and prototyping installation. These installations will be swapped for updates between each other. This setup allows for a near-production environment for development and testing with experienced adventurous early adopters invited to try out new features. A first demonstrator for the e-assessment use case of the PePP project is being developed focusing on the various scheduling challenges and necessary modules. It follows the minimum viable product approach and is planned just as a software-backed graphical rendering and stream encoding, and to be available by the end of 2024. Additionally, it provides an evaluation playground for more fine-grained requirements engineering.

Further development cycles beyond the scheduling focus on developing remote access and client side implementations both as stand-alone and web applications. One objective is to improve bwLehrpool Remote by adding channels for audio and improve rendering and streaming performance, as well as extending the operation to be cloud-native. Using the insights on hardware partitioning of the latest Intel GPU line, we exploit the features of the ATS-M GPU to implement both accelerated rendering within the VM as well as hardware assisted video stream encoding (Scherle et al., 2026). These activities are orchestrated in the context of the NFDI4BIOIMAGE consortium started in 2023 and the bwCloud 3 project started in 2023. Furthermore we hope to combine the various project efforts for programming of well-defined software modules with future extensions to the timed long-term resource scheduling service. The extensions should include interfaces (e.g., RESTful APIs) for various resource management systems.

Acknowledgments

Part of the activities and insights presented in this paper were made possible through the collaboration in the PePP project (FBM2020-VA77-8-01241) funded by the German

[19] See https://bwcloud-os.de/ (visited on 20.07.2025)

foundation »Stiftung Innovation in der Hochschullehre« and work in the bwCloud 3 project supported by the Baden-Württemberg Ministry of Science, Research, and Arts, and the support of DataPLANT (NFDI 7/1 – 442077441) and NFDI4BIOIMAGE (NFDI 46/1 – 501864659) as part of the German National Research Data Infrastructure.

Corresponding Author

Dirk von Suchodoletz: dirk.von.suchodoletz@rz.uni-freiburg.de
University of Freiburg, Germany

ORCID

Manuel Bentele https://orcid.org/0009-0003-4794-958X
Manuel Messner https://orcid.org/0009-0009-0138-066X
Dirk von Suchodoletz https://orcid.org/0000-0002-4382-5104
Radosław Piliszek https://orcid.org/0000-0003-0729-9167

References

Abbadi, I. M. and A. Ruan (2013). »Towards Trustworthy Resource Scheduling in Clouds«. In: *Transactions on Information Forensics and Security* 8.6, pp. 973–984. DOI: 10.1109/TIFS.2013.2248726.

Bauer, J. et al. (2019). »bwLehrpool -- A Jointly Managed and Financed Inter-University It Project«. In: *EDULEARN19 Proceedings*. EDULEARN. IATED, pp. 5548–5555. DOI: 10.21125/edulearn.2019.1360.

Begam, R. et al. (2020). »TIMER-Cloud: Time-Sensitive VM Provisioning in Resource-Constrained Clouds«. In: *Transactions on Cloud Computing* 8.1, pp. 297–311. DOI: 10.1109/TCC.2017.2777992.

Bentele, M. et al. (2022). »Towards a GPU-Accelerated Open Source VDI for OpenStack«. In: *Cloud Computing*. Ed. by M. R. Khosravi, Q. He and H. Dai. Springer, pp. 149–164. DOI: 10.1007/978-3-030-99191-3_12.

Cai, Z. et al. (2019). »Resource Provisioning for Task-Batch Based Workflows with Deadlines in Public Clouds«. In: *Transactions on Cloud Computing* 7.3, pp. 814–826. DOI: 10.1109/TCC.2017.2663426.

Calheiros, R. N. and R. Buyya (2014). »Meeting Deadlines of Scientific Workflows in Public Clouds with Tasks Replication«. In: *Transactions on Parallel and Distributed Systems* 25.7, pp. 1787–1796. DOI: 10.1109/TPDS.2013.238.

Cohen, I. et al. (2020). »Poster Abstract: Parallel VM Placement with Provable Guarantees«. In: *Conference on Computer Communications Workshops*. INFOCOM WKSHPS. IEEE, pp. 1298–1299. DOI: 10.1109/INFOCOMWKSHPS50562.2020.9162912.

Gohil, B. N. et al. (2021). »Fair Fit – A Load Balance Aware VM Placement Algorithm in Cloud Data Centers«. In: *Advances in Communication and Computational Technology*. Ed. by G. S. Hura, A. K. Singh and L. Siong Hoe. ICACCT. Springer, pp. 437–451. DOI: 10.1007/978-981-15-5341-7_35.

Haidri, R. A. et al. (2020). »Cost effective deadline aware scheduling strategy for workflow applications on virtual machines in cloud computing«. In: *Journal of King Saud University - Computer and Information Sciences* 32.6, pp. 666–683. DOI: 10.1016/j.jksuci.2017.10.009.

Horn, G. and P. Skrzypek (2018). »MELODIC: Utility Based Cross Cloud Deployment Optimisation«. In: *International Conference on Advanced Information Networking and Applications Workshops*. WAINA. IEEE, pp. 360–367. DOI: 10.1109/WAINA.2018.00112.

Hu, Z. et al. (2018). »FlowTime: Dynamic Scheduling of Deadline-Aware Workflows and Ad-Hoc Jobs«. In: *International Conference on Distributed Computing Systems*. ICDCS. IEEE, pp. 929–938. DOI: 10.1109/ICDCS.2018.00094.

Hwang, J. and T. Wood (2012). »Adaptive dynamic priority scheduling for virtual desktop infrastructures«. In: *International Workshop on Quality of Service*. IWQoS. IEEE, pp. 1–9. DOI: 10.1109/IWQoS.2012.6245988.

Janagoudar, N. V. et al. (2020). »Multi-Objective Scheduling using Logistic Regression for OpenStack-based Cloud«. In: *Procedia Computer Science* 171, pp. 1429–1438. DOI: 10.1016/j.procs.2020.04.153.

Jilhawar, Y. V. and M. Emmanuel (2015). »Trustworthy Resource Scheduling using Openstack in Cloud«. In: *Spvryan's International Journal of Engineering Sciences & Technology* Special Issue.104. URL: http://spvryan.org/splissue/ipgcon/104.pdf (visited on 22. 07. 2025).

Kaur, T. and I. Chana (2016). »Energy aware scheduling of deadline-constrained tasks in cloud computing«. In: *Cluster Computing* 19.2, pp. 679–698. DOI: 10.1007/s10586-016-0566-9.

Kim, S. and Y.-r. Choi (2020). »Constraint-aware VM placement in heterogeneous computing clusters«. In: *Cluster Computing* 23.1, pp. 71–85. DOI: 10.1007/s10586-019-02966-6.

Li, H. et al. (2016). »Energy-Aware Scheduling of Workflow in Cloud Center with Deadline Constraint«. In: *International Conference on Computational Intelligence and Security*. CIS. IEEE, pp. 415–418. DOI: 10.1109/CIS.2016.0101.

Li, J.-Y. et al. (2017). »The Implementation of a GPU-Accelerated Virtual Desktop Infrastructure Platform«. In: *International Conference on Green Informatics*. ICGI. IEEE, pp. 85–92. DOI: 10.1109/ICGI.2017.42.

Li, Z. et al. (2018). »Cost and Energy Aware Scheduling Algorithm for Scientific Workflows with Deadline Constraint in Clouds«. In: *Transactions on Services Computing* 11.4, pp. 713–726. DOI: 10.1109/TSC.2015.2466545.

Lucrezia, F., G. Marchetto, F. Risso and V. Vercellone (2015). »Introducing network-aware scheduling capabilities in OpenStack«. In: *Proceedings of the Conference on Network Softwarization*. NetSoft. IEEE, pp. 1–5. DOI: 10.1109/NETSOFT.2015.7116155.

Ma, X., H. Gao, H. Xu and M. Bian (2019). »An IoT-based task scheduling optimization scheme considering the deadline and cost-aware scientific workflow for cloud computing«. In: *Journal on Wireless Communications and Networking* 2019.249, pp. 1–19. DOI: 10.1186/s13638-019-1557-3.

Moghaddam, F. F., A. Gherbi and Y. Lemieux (2016). »Self-Healing Redundancy for OpenStack Applications through Fault-Tolerant Multi-Agent Task Scheduling«. In: *International Conference on Cloud Computing Technology and Science*. CloudCom. IEEE, pp. 572–577. DOI: 10.1109/CloudCom.2016.0099.

Moreira, B., S. Trigazis and T. Tsioutsias (2019). »Optimizing OpenStack Nova for Scientific Workloads«. In: *EPJ Web of Conferences* 214, p. 07031. DOI: 10.1051/epjconf/201921407031.

Parakh, P., D. G. Narayan, M. M. Mulla and V. P. Baligar (2018). »SLA-aware Virtual Machine Scheduling in OpenStack-based Private Cloud«. In: *International Conference on Computational Systems and Information Technology for Sustainable Solutions*. CSITSS. IEEE, pp. 259–264. DOI: 10.1109/CSITSS.2018.8768760.

Ramanathan, S. et al. (2020). »A survey on time-sensitive resource allocation in the cloud continuum«. In: *it - Information Technology* 62.5-6, pp. 241–255. DOI: 10.1515/itit-2020-0013.

Redondo Gil, C., P. Vega Prieto, M. Silva and A. M. Teixeira (2014). »Virtual Desktop Infrastructure (VDI) Technology: FI4VDI Project«. In: *New Perspectives in Information Systems and Technologies, Volume 2*. Ed. by Á. Rocha, A. M. Correia, F. B. Tan and K. A. Stroetmann. WorldCIST. Springer, pp. 35–42. DOI: 10.1007/978-3-319-05948-8_4.

Rodriguez, M. A. and R. Buyya (2014). »Deadline Based Resource Provisioning and Scheduling Algorithm for Scientific Workflows on Clouds«. In: *Transactions on Cloud Computing* 2.2, pp. 222–235. DOI: 10.1109/TCC.2014.2314655.

Rot, A. and P. Chrobak (2018). »Benefits, Limitations and Costs of IT Infrastructure Virtualization in the Academic Environment. Case Study using VDI Technology«. In: *Proceedings of the International Conference on Software Technologies*. ICSOFT. INSTICC. SciTePress, pp. 704–711. DOI: 10.5220/0006934707380745.

Sahasrabudhe, S. and S. S. Sonawani (2015). »Improved filter-weight algorithm for utilization-aware resource scheduling in OpenStack«. In: *International Conference on Information Processing*. ICIP. IEEE, pp. 43–47. DOI: 10.1109/INFOP.2015.7489348.

Scharf, M., M. Stein, T. Voith and V. Hilt (2015). »Network-Aware Instance Scheduling in OpenStack«. In: *International Conference on Computer Communication and Networks*. ICCCN. IEEE, pp. 1–6. DOI: 10.1109/ICCCN.2015.7288436.

Scherle, M., A. Saur, V. Kasireddy, R. Gieschke and D. von Suchodoletz (2026). »SPICE for hardware accelerated remote desktop access. Central building Block of an open source VDI«. In: *Proceedings of the 10th bwHPC Symposium. HPC Activities in Baden-Württemberg*. Freiburg, September 2024. 10th bwHPC Symposium. Ed. by M. Janczyk, D. von Suchodoletz, B. Wiebelt and M. Frank. KIT Scientific Publishing, Karlsruhe, pp. 127–141. DOI: 10.58895/ksp/1000169488-9.

Shukur, H. et al. (2020). »Cloud Computing Virtualization of Resources Allocation for Distributed Systems«. In: *Journal of Applied Science and Technology Trends* 1.3, pp. 98–105. DOI: 10.38094/jastt1331.

Stein, M., M. Scharf and V. Hilt (2017). »SDN policy-driven service chain placement in OpenStack«. In: *Symposium on Integrated Network and Service Management*. IM. IEEE, pp. 760–765. DOI: 10.23919/INM.2017.7987374.

Suchodoletz, D. von, J. Leendertse, B. Wiebelt, M. J. Messner and M. Janczyk (2021). »Stateless System Remote-Boot als Business-Continuity-Konzept«. German. In: *Sicherheit in Vernetzten Systemen: 28. DFN-Konferenz*. Ed. by A. Ude. Hamburg: Books on Demand, F1–F21. DOI: 10.6094/UNIFR/218386.

Tian, K., Y. Dong and D. Cowperthwaite (2014). »A Full GPU Virtualization Solution with Mediated Pass-Through«. In: *Proceedings of the Conference on USENIX Annual Technical Conference*. USENIX ATC. USENIX Association, pp. 121–132. URL: https://www.usenix.org/conference/atc14/technical-sessions/presentation/tian.

Trahasch, S., D. von Suchodoletz, J. Münchenberg, S. Rettberg and C. Rößler (2015). »bwLehrpool: Plattform für die effiziente Bereitstellung von Lehr- und Klausurumgebungen«. German. In: *Die 13. E-Learning Fachtagung Informatik*. Ed. by H. Pongratz and R. Keil. DeLFI. Gesellschaft für Informatik e.V., pp. 291–297. URL: https://dl.gi.de/handle/20.500.12116/2060 (visited on 22. 07. 2025).

Wu, Q., F. Ishikawa, Q. Zhu, Y. Xia and J. Wen (2017). »Deadline-Constrained Cost Optimization Approaches for Workflow Scheduling in Clouds«. In: *Transactions on Parallel and Distributed Systems* 28.12, pp. 3401–3412. DOI: 10.1109/TPDS.2017.2735400.

Xu, Z. et al. (2016). »An VM Scheduling Strategy Based on Hierarchy and Load for OpenStack«. In: *International Conference on Cloud Computing and Big Data*. CCBD. IEEE, pp. 58–63. DOI: 10.1109/CCBD.2016.022.

Xue, M. et al. (2016). »gScale: Scaling up GPU Virtualization with Dynamic Sharing of Graphics Memory Space«. In: *Proceedings of the Conference on Usenix Annual Technical Conference*. USENIX ATC. USENIX Association, pp. 579–590. URL: https://www.usenix.org/conference/atc16/technical-sessions/presentation/xue.

Yuan, H., H. Liu, J. Bi and M. Zhou (2021). »Revenue and Energy Cost-Optimized Biobjective Task Scheduling for Green Cloud Data Centers«. In: *Transactions on Automation Science and Engineering* 18.2, pp. 817–830. DOI: 10.1109/TASE.2020.2971512.

Zhai, Y. et al. (2021). »Towards Robust Multi-Tenant Clouds Through Multi-Constrained VM Placement«. In: *International Symposium on Quality of Service*. IWQoS. IEEE, pp. 1–6. DOI: 10.1109/IWQOS52092.2021.9521344.

Zhu, X., H. Chen, G. Liu and L. Liu (2016). »STARS: Startup-Time-Aware Resource Provisioning and Real-Time Task Scheduling in Clouds«. In: *International Conference on High Performance Computing and Communications*. HPCC. IEEE, pp. 309–316. DOI: 10.1109/HPCC-SmartCity-DSS.2016.0052.

SPICE for hardware accelerated remote desktop access

Central building block of an open source VDI

Michael Scherle*, Armin Saur*, Vivek Kasireddy†, Rafael Gieschke*,
Dirk von Suchodoletz*

*eScience, University of Freiburg, Freiburg, Germany
†Intel Corporation, United States

Abstract

This paper presents an accelerated remote desktop and visualization solution using SPICE, leveraging hardware acceleration for both encoding/decoding and content rendering within the guest operating system. A virtual GPU is passed to the virtual machine through VFIO or PCI passthrough, enabling direct access to the framebuffer. The remote transport is further optimized by utilizing modern GPU architectures for frame rendering and video encoding. This enhanced SPICE architecture overcomes the limitations of traditional open-source remote GUI protocols such as VNC, X11, and Xpra, offering a more efficient solution for HPC remote visualization and imaging applications that require high-performance transport and interaction.

We explore the state-of-the-art in remote access technologies, discuss the rationale behind the chosen solution, and describe the implementation strategies with a focus on Intel hardware. Key challenges, including framebuffer capture and low-latency encoding, are addressed. The proposed system is designed for modern environments, supporting multiple instances of visualization with robust user isolation. The server-side implementation is built on Linux QEMU/KVM and compatible hardware. To achieve the desired performance and functionality, several components and modules within SPICE need to be enhanced or developed.

1 Introduction

Remote access to machine screens, including both console output and graphical desktops, has been ubiquitous for more than three decades. While X11/Xorg[1] primarily serves Unix-like architectures, Citrix Independent Computing Architecture (ICA)[2] as well as Microsoft Remote Desktop Protocol (RDP)[3] addresses similar needs in the Windows ecosystem. Virtual Network Computing (VNC) and derivates like X Persistent Remote Applications (Xpra)/VirGL offer broad remote access approaches across a wide range of Operating system (OS), with clients available for many platforms.[4]

For many years, the Free and open source (FOSS) community has sought a high-performance, efficient RAPs. A Remote access protocol (RAP) is responsible for transmitting graphical content, audio, and input signals between (usually) a Virtual Machine (VM) and an end-user device. Simple Protocol for Independent Computing Environments (SPICE) is presented here as a *type I* RAP in Figure 1, running in Quick Emulator (QEMU). Within this work, the authors present a light Virtual Desktop Infrastructure (VDI), serving VMs able to grab their desktops directly from the GPU. Each VM has access to a passed through GPU partition. This approach enables GPU hardware-accelerated frame rendering and stream encoding, resulting in enhanced efficiency and performance. The design presented in this work addresses the quality and hardware acceleration limitations of traditional RAP.

After deriving the requirements for modern remote access by considering the expectations of the intended user base, this paper provides an overview of the current state-of-the-art. We then justify the use of SPICE as the next-generation solution for remote visualization on virtual machines running in QEMU (Figure 1). Section four describes a new Open Source VDI (OSVDI) architecture with an optimized RAP, incorporating

[1] See https://x.org/wiki/, visited on 19.09.2024
[2] See https://www.citrix.com/, visited on 19.09.2024
[3] See https://learn.microsoft.com/en-us/troubleshoot/windows-server/remote/understanding-remote-desktop-protocol, visited on 19.09.2024
[4] See SPICE project page, https://www.spice-space.org/download.html, visited on 19.09.2024

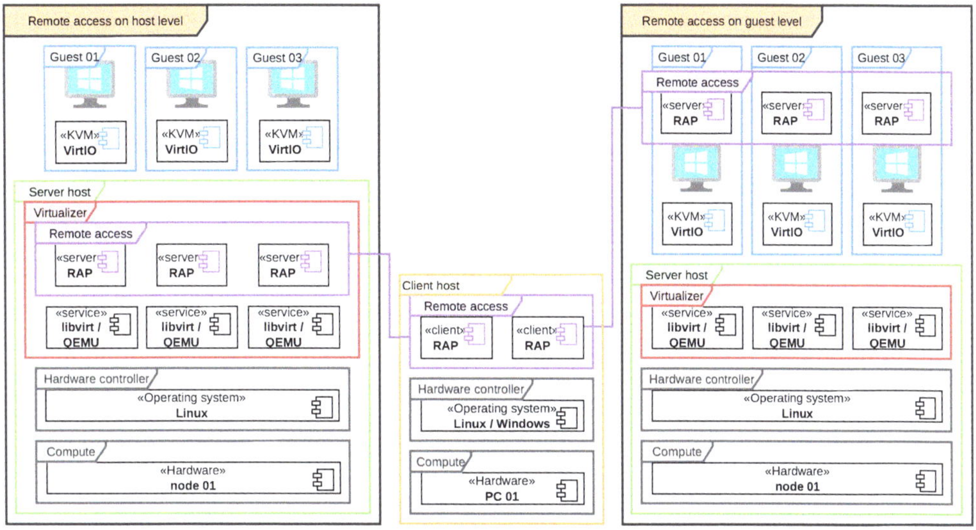

Figure 1: Two different concepts for a VDI. While in *type I* the RAP-Server is engaged with the host virtualizer QEMU, is it in *type II* running within the VM. A RAP-Client connects to the RAP-Server with respect to the RAP.

framebuffer capture, GPU passthrough, hardware partitioning and stream encoding. Finally, we conclude with a discussion of preliminary quality and evaluation findings.

2 Problem statement

Every operation in the RAP pipeline, from grabbing the framebuffer, encoding, transmitting over the network, decoding and rendering it on the client side, must be optimized for efficiency and performance. Implementing versatile and robust access to remote graphical user environments requires careful consideration of multiple aspects, from efficiently capturing and transmitting GPU-accelerated screen content over diverse network conditions to ensuring compatibility across a wide range of end-user devices. Key considerations for modern use cases include:

A reliable remote access is resilient and can adapt to different environments. It ensures the transmission of critical processes, such as system boot sequences, and is designed to prevent inadvertently disruption of the stream.

Comprehensive channel management for modern remote interactions is required to manage various aspects of the user interface: Generally an (automatic or user controlled) negotiation of parameters between the client and VM is desirable.

Video streaming has emerged as the most efficient method for transporting fast-changing complex graphical content, like live 3D editing or high-resolution image processing. Unlike traditional 2D graphic primitives (e.g., elements like lines and texts), modern applications (e.g., Imaris[5]) expect different approaches. However, the video streaming system must be fast in the sense of minimal delay.

Efficient resource allocation and scalability is essential to optimize resource utilization to be both cost-efficient and environmentally friendly. This involves making the most of available resources while ensuring the system remains flexible enough to adapt to changing demands.

Cloud or VM deployability addresses the shift towards mobile devices and centralized cloud infrastructures, not only arising from the need to manage and store increasing volumes of data efficiently. Large datasets cannot easily be transferred or synced across long distances, necessitating processing close to the data's storage location.

High GPU performance for cloud and virtualized environments for complex software stacks often necessitates GPU passthrough. Applications like CAD, AI, simulations, and large-scale data visualization require substantial GPU computational power and the complete feature set of modern GPUs. In these scenarios, GPU emulation or paravirtualization falls short, making direct GPU passthrough essential for performance and functionality.

To achieve this, we must address the lack of free and FOSS RAP that can meet the minimal latency requirements. Screen Resolution and Video RAM (VRAM) management must be handled carefully, as virtual machines do not have direct access to the client-side physical screen. In environments like OpenStack,VRAM and framebuffer requirements are often inadequately addressed; these resources are typically grouped with general RAM scheduling. This oversight can lead to suboptimal scheduling decisions and potential performance bottlenecks, especially in scenarios that demand high-resolution graphics beyond basic VGA standards. The authors of this paper propose that a high-quality RAP should have an interaction latency of less than 80 ms, a minimum resolution

[5] Special purpose visualization software, see: https://imaris.oxinst.com/, visited on 29.09.2024

of 1080p, and image quality that closely mirrors the source. Additionally, for efficiency, it should utilize the minimal possible bandwidth (Casas et al., 2013; Magaña et al., 2019).

3 State of the art in open source remote access

A RAP defines the client-side application for remote desktop rendering, the server-side infrastructure, and the transport protocol that enables communication between a remote (virtual) machine and the end user's interface. These protocols establish a bidirectional communication channel. In the simplest implementations, one direction is used to transfer graphical output from an application or a desktop session on a remote (virtual) machine to a renderer for display purposes. The opposite direction transmits user inputs (e.g., keyboard, pointer, and gesture events) from the user's device to the remote (virtual) machine. (F. Li et al., 2023; Magaña et al., 2019) Transport protocols like VNC (Richardson et al., 1998), which implement the Remote Framebuffer Protocol (RFB) protocol (Richardson et al., 2011), can be characterized by the range of graphics primitives they support for rendering on the remote machine.

A similar protocol to VNC is the Thin-Client Internet Computing (THINC) protocol, which implements more low-level graphic primitives, improving RFB and resulting in better video performance (Baratto et al., 2005). ICA and RDP are proprietary remote desktop transport protocols developed by Citrix and Microsoft, respectively. They support a wide range of high-level graphic primitives, including optimizations such as caching previously transferred primitives and support for glyphs. The X Window System (X11, later Xorg), developed at MIT in 1984, became the standard cross-platform display server for Unix-based systems (Scheifler, 2004). Xorg abstracts hardware specifics, enabling applications to render graphics, manage GUI elements, and process input via the X protocol, which defines communication between the X server and client applications. While Xorg became the default display server primarily on Linux, it lacks full GPU hardware acceleration, has limited support for modern technologies like OpenGL 3+ and Vulkan, and is not widely available on platforms such as Windows and mobile devices. X11 is gradually being superseded by Wayland,[6] which follows a modular approach and focuses solely on low-level display and input processing.

[6] See https://wayland.freedesktop.org/, visited on 29.09.2024

Xpra[7] is an Open Source remote access application to execute X11 programs (or a complete desktop) on a remote host and direct the output to the own machine. A running accelerated Xorg server is required, which will render the Xpra sessions using VirtualGL. The Xpra server application integrates a built-in HTML5 client, hardware acceleration, multi-user support, graphical tools and various configuration options. Xpra offers a proxy which can act as a front end for multiple server sessions or relay. There are disadvantages of the VirtualGL transport as it is designed to be used with remote Xorg servers, thus it relies on the chatty remote X11 protocol to send the 2D graphic primitives of the application's renderer. As a result, the VirtualGL transport is not recommended for use on high-latency or low-bandwidth networks. The client is not stateless. As with any remote X11 application, if the connection drops, then the application will be exited as well.

The SPICE[8] is an open-source alternative to the proprietary ICA and RDP. Similarly, SPICE supports high-level graphic primitives and is intended and optimized for remote access to a VM. Other optimizations include an additional display mode to improve Quality of Experience (QoE) (Liu et al., 2018) and further interaction features like full duplex audio support, folder sharing, USB redirection, and reduced response time (W. Li et al., 2016). It provides comprehensive support for various input devices such as mouse, keyboard, USB, and smartcard passthrough. In terms of security, SPICE incorporates robust measures including Transport Layer Security (TLS) for encrypted communication and Simple Authentication and Security Layer (SASL) for secure authentication processes.

Guacamole, an open-source project,[9] bridges both VNC and RDP to enable browser-based access. In its deployment for bwLehrpool, additional functionalities for authentication and session brokerage were integrated, enhancing security and tailoring it for institutional use (Bentele et al., 2022). Open-source VNC clients, and to a lesser degree RDP clients, are widely available across all major end-user devices. Most of these implementations are open-source, offering high flexibility and accessibility. However, protocols like RDP and SPICE have more limited availability on certain platforms, which can restrict their use cases. Xpra stands out by offering both cross-platform support and

[7] See xpra.org, maintained at https://github.com/Xpra-org, visited on 29.09.2024
[8] Simple Protocol for Independent Computing Environment, see https://www.spice-space.org, originally developed by RedHat; visited on 29.09.2024; (F. Li et al., 2023)
[9] See https://guacamole.apache.org/, visited on 18.09.2024

a browser-based HTML5 streaming option. It provides native clients for Linux, macOS, and Windows, ensuring seamless integration across these operating systems. One of Xpra's unique features is its ability to allow users to disconnect from X11 programs and reconnect from the same or another device without losing the application's state.

4 Concept

We evaluate and implement GPU deployment for assisted rendering and stream encoding to enhance performance and user experience, relying on efficient access to the (virtual) machine's framebuffer using SPICE as an open-source RAP. For virtualization, we make use of QEMU, a powerful and versatile open-source Hypervisor with Kernel-based Virtual Machine (KVM) and built-in SPICE support. QEMU can take advantage of hardware acceleration, significantly boosting performance and enabling near-native execution speed. It has an active and large development community, ensuring regular updates, security patches, and new features.

4.1 GPU passthrough and hardware partitioning

To achieve high GPU performance and full feature support, the most effective approach is PCI passthrough, which passes GPUs directly to the VM. To improve resource allocation and scalability, we partition the physical GPU into smaller virtual GPUs, tailored to the specific needs of each application. The core technologies required for GPU passthrough and partitioning in virtualized environments are DMA,(Harvey et al., 1991) IOMMU[10] for translating virtual device addresses to physical ones, VFIO[11] for allowing user-space processes like QEMU to securely access devices, and SR-IOV (Intel LAN Access Division, 2011) for presenting a single physical PCI device as multiple virtual devices. All three major data center GPU manufacturers – AMD, Nvidia, and Intel – support GPU partitioning, but their implementations differ. AMD's support is limited to a few models with minimal public documentation. Nvidia offers extensive support across many models but requires additional licensing fees for each virtual GPU, on top of the initial GPU cost.

[10] On IOMMU in Linux Kernel: https://lenovopress.lenovo.com/lp1467.pdf, visited on 29.09.2024
[11] VFIO, »Virtual Function I/O«, https://docs.kernel.org/driver-api/vfio.html, visited on 29.09.2024

Our initial implementation focuses on Intel data center GPUs. Key parameters for creating Intel virtual GPUs include the amount of reserved VRAM for each virtual GPU, ensuring some VRAM remains for the physical GPU. Another critical parameter is the execution time allocated to each virtual GPU, which can be adjusted individually. Additionally, the GPU scheduler can be set to either fixed or dynamic, allowing the GPU to quickly move to the next virtual GPU when the current one finishes its tasks. These parameters provide flexibility in optimizing performance and resource allocation for varying workloads.

4.2 Framebuffer grabbing

To achieve our goal of robustness, relying solely on a service for screen capturing within the VM would be insufficient. For consistent and resilient video transmission at all times, including during booting and other critical stages, it is crucial to capture the framebuffer from outside the VM like implemented for SPICE in QEMU. The current method relies on a graphics device that implements the Virtual Device (VD) Interface, with the QXL device being the most commonly used. QXL is a paravirtual graphics driver supporting 2D graphics. When an application issues a draw request (e.g., X or GDI), the request is passed to the QXL driver (see Figure 2). The driver translates the request into QXL-specific commands and sends them to the Commands Ring of the QXL device. The SPICE server retrieves these commands from the Command Ring, adds them to the Display Tree (which holds commands for display content), and converts them into SPICE protocol messages sent to the client. The server optimizes performance by culling unnecessary commands, such as those related to hidden content. The client then executes the commands to generate the image. Once no longer needed, commands are pushed to the Release Ring, allowing the QXL driver to reclaim the associated resources.

Modern applications often use 3D GPU functions to render GUIs, even for simple 2D interfaces. In these cases, SPICE cannot send draw commands directly to the client as it would for 2D rendering. Instead, the framebuffer changes from these applications appear to SPICE as frequent bit block transfers (bit blits). As a result, SPICE updates the image using bitmaps, which is less efficient than sending draw commands, leading to higher bandwidth usage and reduced performance. Additionally, the VD Interface implementation does not support capturing the framebuffer from a passed-through virtual GPU.

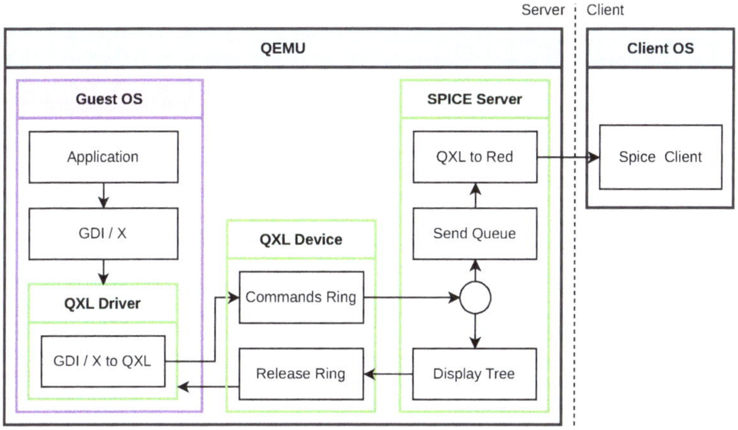

Figure 2: SPICE QXL architecture in QEMU, adapted from https://www.spice-space.org/spice-for-newbies.html.

Intel engineers have proposed two designs for zero-copy access to a VM's framebuffer on the host. The first design[12] enhances Mesa's KMSRO, originally developed for handling split GPU SoCs, where Display and Render/Media blocks come from different vendors. KMSRO ensures that the scanout buffer (framebuffer) is allocated by the Display driver but imported by the 3D DRI driver for rendering. The goal of the first design is to use KMSRO to ensure the Virtio-GPU driver allocates the scanout buffer, which is then imported by the Iris DRI driver for rendering. Since the Virtio-GPU driver allocates the scanout buffer in system RAM, it can share the Direct Memory Access (DMA) addresses and lengths with QEMU's Virtio-GPU backend, which translates them into file offsets associated with the VM's memory file. These offsets are given to the user space mappable DMA buffer (udmabuf) driver on the host, which pins the pages and creates a Direct Memory Access buffer file descriptor (DMA-BUF fd) for sharing across modules.

Due to QEMU's modular design, the DMA-BUF fd for the VM's scanout buffer is eventually shared with the UI module, either SPICE for remote display or GTK UI for local display. The main advantage of this design is that it only requires changes to KMSRO, without modifying any Guest Compositors (e.g., Xorg or Wayland). However, a significant drawback is that since the Virtio-GPU driver can only allocate scanout buffers

[12] See https://gitlab.freedesktop.org/mesa/mesa/-/merge_requests/9592#note_851314, visited on 19.12.2025

in system RAM, it works well for integrated GPUs (iGPUs) but leads to performance degradation for discrete GPUs (dGPUs).

Discrete GPUs prefer to store all buffers in VRAM for optimal performance, as accessing buffers in System RAM via the PCI bus incurs overhead. To achieve the best performance with dGPUs, it is ideal for the VM's scanout buffer to be created directly in VRAM, avoiding the need for migration to System RAM. This requires the Virtual GPU driver to allocate the scanout buffer. To meet this goal, a platform-agnostic design is needed that pins the scanout buffer in the Virtual GPU's preferred memory region, working seamlessly with both iGPUs and dGPUs. The second proposed design[13] achieves this by enhancing the Virtio-GPU driver to import scanout buffers from other GPU drivers, leveraging the behavior of modern Wayland compositors when multiple GPUs are present. For example, when Mutter (the default GNOME compositor) detects multiple GPUs, it designates one as primary and others as secondary. The primary GPU is responsible for allocating and rendering the framebuffers for all outputs, including those associated with secondary GPUs, which then import their respective framebuffers. By making the Virtual GPU the primary and enabling the Virtio-GPU driver to import its framebuffer, we can access the DMA addresses backing the buffer.

When the Virtio-GPU backend in QEMU receives these DMA addresses, it determines whether they belong to System RAM or VRAM. If the former, it uses the udmabuf driver to create a DMA-BUF fd. If the latter, it translates the VM's DMA addresses into PCI memory region offsets, which are shared with the VFIO PCI driver. This driver converts the offsets into PCI Bus addresses, maps them to Host-compatible DMA addresses, and returns a DMA-BUF fd. A patch that adds the VFIO_DEVICE_FEATURE_DMA_BUF feature to the VFIO PCI driver is under review.

For dGPUs, when the Host GPU accesses the VM's framebuffer provided by SPICE via GStreamer for encoding, it is considered P2P DMA, as one GPU accesses another's VRAM. This is valid since both devices belong to the same physical GPU and are compatible. This design also works with Windows guests when Virtio-based Display Virtualization drivers are included. The main drawback is that it doesn't work with legacy Xorg-based VM compositors that don't support primary/secondary GPU designations.

[13] See https://lore.kernel.org/dri-devel/20241126031643.3490496-1-vivek.kasireddy@intel.com, https://lists.nongnu.org/archive/html/qemu-devel/2025-11/msg03611.html, https://lore.kernel.org/dri-devel/20251120-dmabuf-vfio-v9-0-d7f71607f371@nvidia.com, and https://lore.kernel.org/dri-devel/20250915072428.1712837-1-vivek.kasireddy@intel.com, visited on 19.12.2025

However, this design works well with major Linux distributions (e.g., Ubuntu, RedHat), where Wayland-based GNOME compositors are the default, with no changes needed to userspace components.

4.3 Frame decoding/encoding

SPICE obtains a DMA-BUF fd pointing to the scanout buffer from the Virtio-GPU backend for video encoding (see Figure 3). The GStreamer media framework handles video encoding, directly importing DMA-BUF fds and encoding them into a video stream. These encoded frames are then transmitted via SPICE to the client, where they are decoded and displayed. Both software and hardware encoding are supported in SPICE through GStreamer.

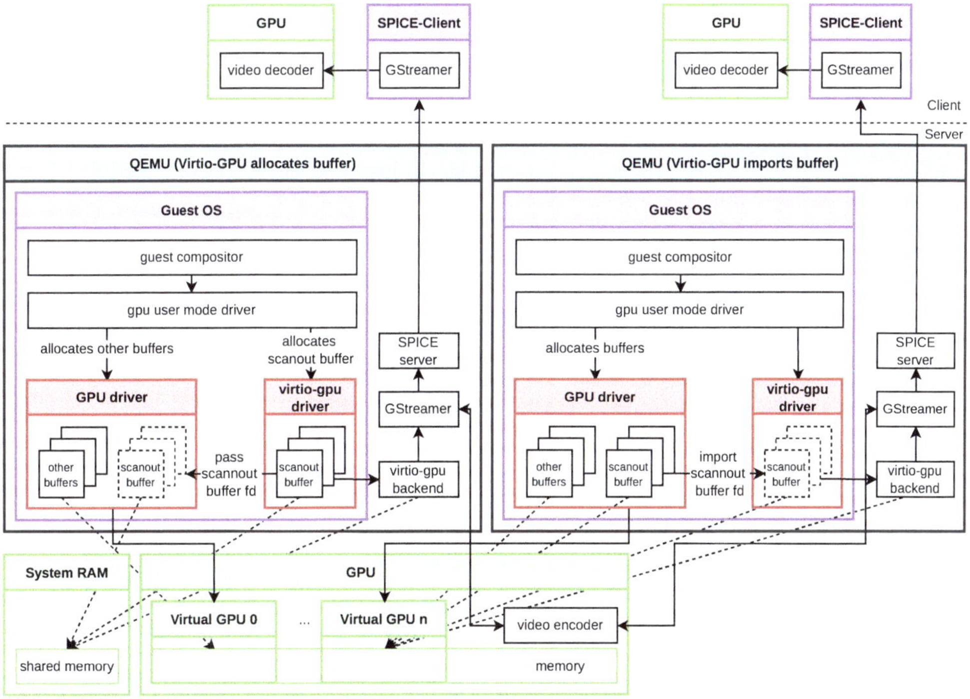

Figure 3: Framebuffer grabbing and transmission architecture.

Hardware encoding/decoding is preferred due to its lower latency, higher efficiency, and reduced CPU usage. For newer codecs like H265 or AV1, real-time decoding is essential. For hardware encoding, SPICE supports Intel Media SDK (MSDK) and Video

Acceleration API (VA-API), with VA-API drivers available for Intel, AMD, and Nvidia GPUs. Thanks to GStreamer's flexible pipeline architecture, adding new encoders or codecs is straightforward. The SPICE protocol is also flexible enough to support new codecs.

4.4 Remote desktop client and general platform

A software framework (Figure 4) is required to realize OSVDI remote access for the use cases outlined (Bentele et al., 2022). In general it might be favorable to start with a browser session as it allows simple interfaces for authentication, session selection and session routing before firing up the client application for interaction (e.g. see bwLehrpool Guacamole example).

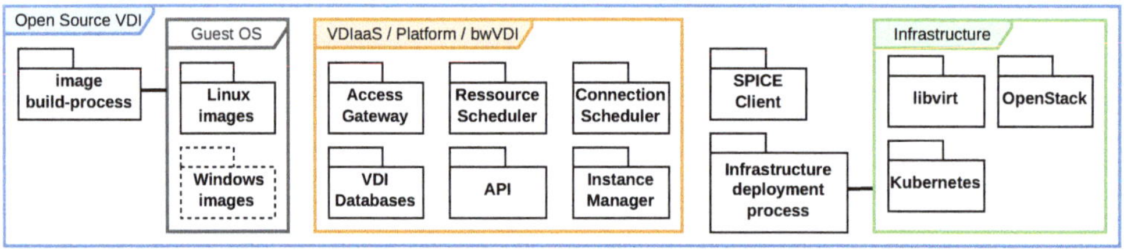

Figure 4: The OSVDI components designed to use different infrastructural backends.

Several remote desktop clients are available for SPICE, including spice-gtk, an open-source GTK client library that supports all SPICE features, including video stream decoding, when compiled with GStreamer. Spice-gtk is integrated into several SPICE-capable desktop clients, such as Remmina and Virt-Viewer. For mobile devices, the aSPICE client is available for both Android and iOS, supporting video streaming to a certain degree. Although there are web-based clients for SPICE, their feature sets are currently limited and will need further development to meet the requirements of our project.

5 Discussion and Outlook

During initial testing with Intel GPUs – chosen for their strong open-source driver support – we observed a display delay exceeding 400 ms. To measure this delay more accurately, we developed a custom tool. Further analysis revealed a substantial hardcoded delay, intended for buffering and synchronizing audio and video. After discussing this with the SPICE developers, the delay was removed, reducing the latency to approximately 100 ms at 1080p resolution (with a 1 ms network delay). Additional optimizations reduced decoding time by two frames, or about 32 ms for 60 fps content.

Looking ahead, we plan to implement an overlay for debug statistics. As expected, GPU performance was excellent, significantly outpacing software rendering, even with multiple virtual GPUs. The current method for negotiating bandwidth and codec selection still needs refinement. Overall image quality remained high, even with rapidly changing content, though further improvements are possible with newer codecs and optimized settings.

A specific issue we observed with image quality was that the hardware encoder/decoder implementation defaults to chroma subsampling (4:2:0), resulting in noticeable artifacts, especially with colored fonts (see Figure 5).[14] To address this, we developed a prototype allowing users to select their preferred codec and chroma sampling directly from the RAP client. For older hardware that supports only chroma subsampling decoding, we implemented an upsampling method that improves image quality to near 4:4:4 (no subsampling). However, this approach increases bandwidth usage and computational requirements due to the larger image data.

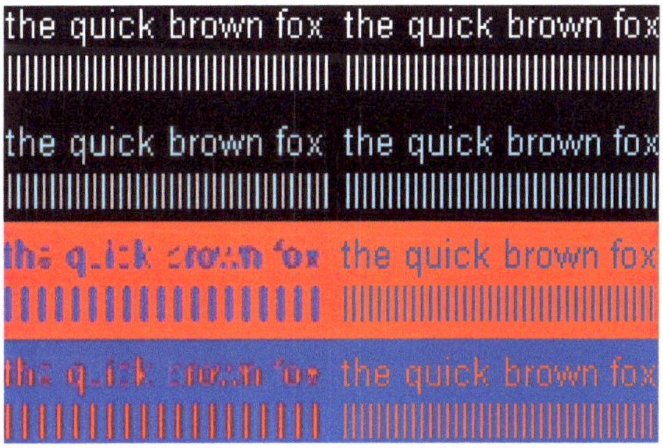

Figure 5: Chroma subsampling issues, left side 4:2:0 and right side 4:4:4.

The project involves multiple components, each essential for its functionality. On the compute side, in addition to specialized versions of QEMU and SPICE, we require customized GPU drivers, media drivers, and a tailored version of Mesa. Given the complex-

[14] Test graphic from https://www.rtings.com/tv/learn/chroma-subsampling

ity and need for specialized components, we are developing a build pipeline to automate the creation of these images.

While our current implementation is somewhat dependent on Intel hardware, particularly for framebuffer-grabbing, GPUs from Nvidia and AMD do not yet meet our requirements due to limitations and quality in open source driver support as well as constricting licensing. We selected Intel for its advantages mentioned earlier, but this hardware dependency is limited mainly to the framebuffer-grabbing aspect of the project.

Acknowledgment

Part of the activities and insights presented in this paper were made possible through the collaboration in the PePP project (FBM2020-VA77-8-01241) funded by the *Foundation for Innovation in Higher Education*, the contributions provided by the projects bwLehrpool, bwCloud 3 and bwHPC-S5 that are supported by the Ministry of Science, Research and Arts Baden-Württemberg and the funds provided through NFDI 46/1 – 501864659 (NFDI4BIOIMAGE), and NFDI 7/1 – 442077441 (DataPLANT) as part of the German National Research Data Infrastructure.

Corresponding Author

Michael Scherle: michael.scherle@rz.uni-freiburg.de
eScience Abteilung, Rechenzentrum Albert-Ludwigs-Universität Freiburg,
Hermann-Herder-Str. 10, 79104 Freiburg, Deutschland

ORCID

Armin Saur https://orcid.org/0009-0003-8037-7288
Michael Scherle https://orcid.org/0009-0008-6652-0697
Vivek Kasireddy https://orcid.org/0009-0004-3754-7066
Rafael Gieschke https://orcid.org/0000-0002-2778-4218
Dirk von Suchodoletz https://orcid.org/0000-0002-4382-5104

References

Baratto, R. A., L. N. Kim and J. Nieh (2005). »THINC: A Virtual Display Architecture for Thin-Client Computing«. In: *Proceedings of the Twentieth ACM Symposium on Operating Systems Principles*. SOSP '05. New York, NY, USA: Association for Computing Machinery, pp. 277–290. ISBN: 1595930795. DOI: 10.1145/1095810.1095837.

Bentele, M., D. von Suchodoletz, M. Messner and S. Rettberg (2022). »Towards a GPU-Accelerated Open Source VDI for OpenStack«. In: *Cloud Computing*. Ed. by M. R. Khosravi, Q. He and H. Dai. Cham: Springer International Publishing, pp. 149–164. ISBN: 978-3-030-99191-3. DOI: 10.1007/978-3-030-99191-3_12.

Casas, P., M. Seufert, S. Egger and R. Schatz (2013). »Quality of experience in remote virtual desktop services«. In: *2013 IFIP/IEEE International Symposium on Integrated Network Management (IM 2013)*. IEEE, pp. 1352–1357. ISBN: 978-3-901882-50-0. URL: https://ieeexplore.ieee.org/abstract/document/6573191.

Harvey, A. F. and Data Acquisition Division Staff (1991). *DMA Fundamentals on Various PC Platforms*. Tech. rep. National Instruments. URL: https://cires1.colorado.edu/jimenez-group//QAMSResources/Docs/DMAFundamentals.pdf.

Intel LAN Access Division (2011). *PCI-SIG SR-IOV Primer*. Tech. rep. Intel. URL: https://cdrdv2-public.intel.com/321211/pci-sig-sr-iov-primer-sr-iov-technology-paper.pdf.

Li, F. et al. (2023). »Transportation of Service Enhancement Based on Virtualization Cloud Desktop«. In: *Electronics* 12.7. ISSN: 2079-9292. DOI: 10.3390/electronics12071572. URL: https://www.mdpi.com/2079-9292/12/7/1572.

Li, W. et al. (2016). »The optimization of Transparent-Desktop service mechanism based on SPICE«. In: *Concurrency and Computation: Practice and Experience* 28.18, pp. 4543–4556. DOI: 10.1002/cpe.3858.

Liu, X., M. Zhu, L. Xiao and Y. Jiang (2018). »A VM-shared desktop virtualization system based on OpenStack«. In: *AIP Conference Proceedings* 1955.1, p. 040137. DOI: 10.1063/1.5033801.

Magaña, E., I. Sesma, D. Morató and M. Izal (2019). »Remote access protocols for Desktop-as-a-Service solutions«. In: *PLOS ONE* 14.1, pp. 1–28. DOI: 10.1371/journal.pone.0207512. URL: https://doi.org/10.1371/journal.pone.0207512.

Richardson, T. and J. Levine (2011). *The Remote Framebuffer Protocol*. RFC 6143. RFC Editor. URL: https://www.rfc-editor.org/rfc/rfc6143.txt.

Richardson, T., Q. Stafford-Fraser, K. R. Wood and A. Hopper (1998). »Virtual network computing«. In: *IEEE Internet Computing* 2.1, pp. 33–38. DOI: 10.1109/4236.656066.

Scheifler, R. W. (2004). *X window system protocol, X Version 11, Release 7.7*. Tech. rep. X Consortium. URL: https://www.x.org/archive/current/doc/xproto/x11protocol.pdf.

III Green IT and Energy Efficiency

Green IT in a University Environment: Promoting Sustainability through Transparency

Findings from the GAIT project and outlook for bwCloud3

Lena Ritzinger, Jan Münchenberg, Michael Schmidt

Institute for Sustainable Energy Systems (INES), Institute for Machine Learning and Analytics (IMLA), Offenburg University of Applied Sciences, Offenburg, Germany

Abstract

Legal requirements are increasingly demanding more sustainability in IT, including in the university sector. However, the implementation of green IT measures is often hampered by a lack of financial incentives, outdated technical structures, staff shortages, and acceptance problems. The project »Green Academic IT Potential (GAIT)« addresses these challenges by creating transparency about energy and resource consumption and promoting a change in awareness at all levels.

With the help of key figures and measurement systems, the ecological impact of IT decisions is to be visualised, and sustainable measures introduced in a targeted manner. The most important results include the prioritization of measures such as server virtualization, the introduction of video conferencing systems, and the use of energy-efficient hardware.

The follow-up project bwCloud 3 transfers these approaches to cloud services in order to tap into further savings potential and promote sustainable IT decisions. Transparency regarding the use of resources remains a key success factor, even if its implementation is sometimes time consuming.

1 Initial situation and motivation

1.1 Sustainability at universities

The discussion about sustainability has gained considerable importance in recent decades, and today legal requirements, regulations, and social expectations are present in almost all areas of life, including university IT.

Baden-Württemberg is aiming for a net greenhouse gas-neutral state administration by 2030 (§ 11 KlimaG BW, from 7.2.2023) and has obliged public institutions to take sustainability into account in tenders since 2018 (VwV-Beschaffung from 24 July 2018). Throughout Germany, the Energy Efficiency Act (§ 6 EnEfG, dated 13.11.2023) obliges data centres with a non-redundant nominal connected load of 300 kilowatts or more and public institutions with an annual final energy consumption of more than 1 GWh to save 2 % of their energy consumption each year. This means that not only large data centres are affected by the EnEfG, but also smaller IT infrastructures and workplace IT at universities. Accounting for just under a quarter of university electricity consumption, IT is a relevant factor in achieving the savings targets.

According to a recent Bitkom study, IT performance rose by 78 % between 2010 and 2020, while electricity consumption only increased by 52 % to around 16 billion kWh (0.6 % of total German energy consumption) due to technological advances and energy-saving measures (Hintemann et al., 2022). A further increase in performance is expected in future, while at the same time electricity consumption is to be reduced and IT security guaranteed.

However, as universities (Hochschulen) do not pay for their own electricity, investments in more efficient hardware are often unprofitable, and inefficient in-house data centres are often seen as the cheaper option. The IT sector is also under high pressure due to cyber security requirements, short innovation cycles and growing digitalisation, meaning that human resources are being used specifically to tackle these challenges. Even if these hurdles are overcome, acceptance problems or a lack of information often means that employees, students or university management do not provide sufficient support for implementation.

Universities have a special role model function when it comes to sustainability. Thus, despite the obstacles mentioned, numerous green IT measures must be implemented at universities. By implementing green IT measures, they can not only fulfil their ecological responsibility, but also act as a role model for other social actors. In addition, building a ›green‹ image helps to make the university more attractive to students and employees.

1.2 Green IT in literature

Green IT is little known outside of IT departments, although IT is omnipresent in the university environment.

Green IT encompasses various aspects: On the one hand, sustainability through IT (e.g. through online conferences instead of business trips), and on the other hand, the sustainable use of IT (e.g. energy-efficient hardware, green coding and virtualisation of servers).

There is already some research on green IT measures, such as the Baden-Württemberg state strategy Green IT (Ministerium für Umwelt, 2023) and the Borderstep study (Hintemann et al., 2020), which analyse the potential of various green IT measures. However, many of the measures listed in the literature are outdated, not directly applicable to universities or relate exclusively to data centres. There are also helpful sources on the topic of key figures: (Shao et al., 2022) provide an overview of the most important key figures for data centres, and standards such as the ISO 30134 series, the blue angel for Data Centres DE-UZ 228 and the Energy Efficiency Act (EnEfG) provide further information. In addition, projects such as LEAP (Harryvan et al., 2020), EcoRZ (EcoRZ, 2020), KPI4DCE (Schödwell et al., 2018) and GCC (Gröger et al., 2021) have developed key performance indicator systems for evaluating data centres or servers. However, this work focuses exclusively on data centres, meaning that workplace IT in universities is largely ignored.

The aim of this paper is to present a holistic approach to promoting and implementing green IT at universities. The focus is on creating transparency based on the results of the GAIT project.[1].

[1] The GAIT (Green Academic IT Potential) project at Offenburg (HSO) and Biberach (HBC) universities, funded by the Baden-Württemberg Ministry of the Environment, Climate Protection and the Energy Sector, aims to quantify the savings potential of information and communication technology (ICT) at universities with the help of sustainability indicators

1.3 Prioritisation of the measures

In GAIT around 50 measures were identified through literature research and discussions with IT employees at HSO and HBC. These measures were evaluated and prioritised by 9 IT experts from other universities in terms of their savings potential (benefits), feasibility and degree of implementation. The experts opinions were combined with the results of the literature in order to create a well-founded prioritisation of the measures (see Figure 1).

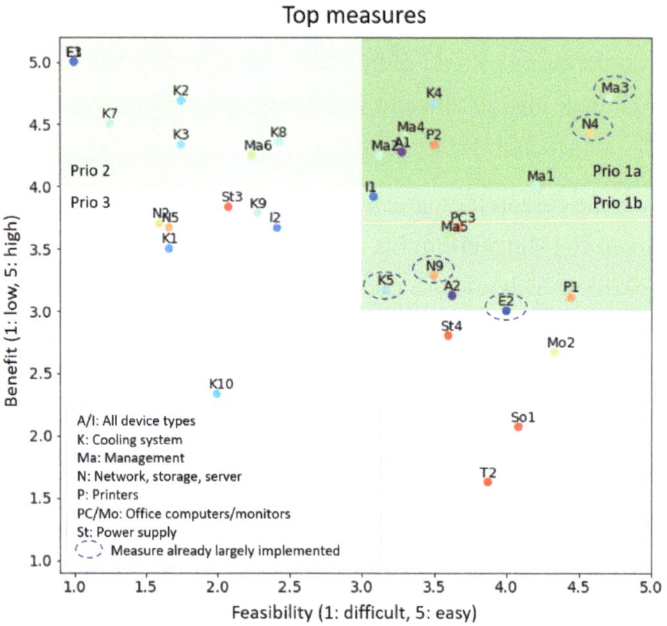

Figure 1: measure prioritisation by benefit and feasibility (Ritzinger et al., 2024)

The measures with the greatest potential that have not yet been fully implemented can be divided into the categories Priority 1a and 1b (see Table 1).

Measures such as server virtualisation (N4), introduction of a telephone and video conferencing system (Ma3), continuation of teleworking (E2), reduction of the difference between the maximum recommended and actual operating temperature in server rooms (K5) and use of modern storage media (N9) have already been largely implemented. Although these measures generally have a high benefit, they hardly offer any further savings potential at universities.

Table 1: Measures for green IT priority 1a and 1b

Prio1a	Prio1b
Ma1: Appointment of a green IT officer Ma2: Introduction and operation of an energy management system (EnMS) and integration into existing systems A1: Utilisation of energy-saving function (computers/peripherals) Ma4: Document management systems (DMS) for paperless working P2: Multi-user multifunctional devices instead of single-user printers/scanners/copiers K4: Dynamic power control of the cooling system	I1: Replacement of outdated devices with energy-saving ones, considering certifications PC3: Replacement of desktop PCs with mini PCs A2: Automatically disconnect unused devices from the mains P1: Paper/toner-saving settings (duplex, b/w printing), use of biotoners Ma5: Workflow management system (WfMS) for paper-saving work

What is striking about this prioritisation is that in Priority 1 (a+b), three out of four measures relating to the data centre have already been implemented. Therefore, the measures in priority 1 (medium to high benefit and easy to implement) mainly concern areas outside the data centre. In contrast, priority 2 (high benefit, but difficult to implement) measures mainly involve the optimisation of air conditioning (K).

This results in two central questions:

- Question 1: How can the implementation of measures outside the data centre be driven forward?
- Question 2: How can measures that are difficult to implement but potentially very useful be realised in the data centre?

2 Creating awareness at universities

Creating awareness of green IT at universities is crucial for the implementation of measures outside the data centre, as employees and, in some cases, students must participate or adapt their behaviour in order to realise potential savings. One example of this is reducing the number of office printers. If users are aware of the effects of their behaviour and are aware of options for action and possible savings, they are more likely to be prepared to leave their comfort zone and change their behaviour in order to use IT more sustainably.

Transparency can also be beneficial when it comes to the question of how costly measures can be implemented in the data centre. The university management often does not know how much energy is consumed in the data centre, what proportion of the university's total consumption it accounts for and how much energy could be saved through optimisation measures. A budget for more efficient hardware or optimisation measures is less likely to be approved if the decision-makers are not aware of the savings potential.

The most important measure for implementing Green IT as smoothly as possible is therefore to create awareness through transparency. However, transparency alone cannot solve all problems: In many university data centres, restrictions exist due to established structures, meaning that renewal and conversion measures are only possible to a limited extent. Greater optimisation potential can often only be realised through a new building. Fact-based communication of the existing problems (IT security gaps, inefficiencies, limited expandability, etc.) can encourage the decision to build a new building and help to plan the new data centre with a view to the future. [2]

In order to create transparency across the university and make IT more sustainable, the foundations must first be laid by selecting relevant key figures and recording them as part of a comprehensive inventory and setting up a monitoring system. In addition, a person responsible for raising awareness of green IT, prioritising and implementing measures and advising university management and staff must be appointed to take on these tasks as an integral part of their duties.

2.1 Key figures

Similar to the measures, an detailed literature review was also conducted for the key figures, and the identified indicators were evaluated particularly with regard to their relevance and availability.

2.1.1 Overall target figures – conveying the overall picture

Based on the literature review, the overall goal is to record the total values of the four expense categories carbon footprint (CF_{tot}), energy consumption (EnC_{tot}), raw mater-

[2] In this context, please refer to the guide from HIS-HE and TÜV Rheinland, which sets out relevant aspects for the construction of a new data centre: https://medien.his-he.de/fileadmin/user_upload/Forum_HIS-HE_Rechenzentren.pdf

ial consumption (RV_{tot}) and water consumption (WV_{tot}). As these values are difficult to record in relation to the entire life cycle of hardware, in GAIT target values were defined that mainly relate to the utilisation phase (see Table 2). These key figures are to be recorded for each university-category (see Figure 2) in order to evaluate the influence of the individual categories.

Table 2: Overview of key figures for university IT

abbrev.	key figure (target value)	[unit], range, target value	data collection	calculation basis/ source
CF	CO_2 emissions during the utilisation phase	[tCO_2eq], 0 - ∞, as small as possible	composed of the emissions from electricity and resource consumption	emission factors according to BICO2BW, consideration of scope 1 to 3
EnC	energy consumption of university IT during the utilisation phase	[kWh], 0 - ∞, as small as possible	–	data centre: measurement according to Blue Angel DE-UZ 228; user & campus infrastructure: extrapolation
RC	resource consumption of university IT during the utilisation phase	[m^3, kg, sheets, units], 0 - ∞, as small as possible	At least: resource consumption NEA, refrigerant/water consumption of the cooling system, paper consumption, ink/toner consumption	measurements/ information from technical department, IT department, finance department
$\#IT_{In}$	number of newly procured IT devices	[-], 0 - ∞, as small as possible	–	information from the finance department
$\#IT_{Out}$	number of IT devices decommissioned	[-], 0 - ∞, similar to $\#IT_{In}$ (input = output)	–	information from the finance department

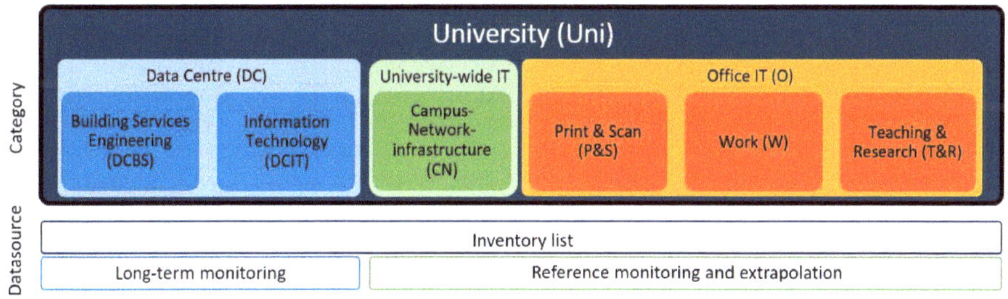

Figure 2: Categorisation of University-IT and datasources for key figures

Key figures can be used both for internal communication and for the public, but should be embedded in the overall context. For example, IT electricity consumption can be presented as a proportion of the university's total electricity consumption or over time.

In order to ensure comparability, it is recommended that the target figures are recorded relative to the number of university members (employees and students).

2.1.2 Optimisation indicators – uncovering potential for action

The aforementioned target figures can reveal weaknesses in the system, but are not suitable for identifying their causes. Additional key figures should therefore be recorded (see Table 3). These key figures are used to support decision-making, optimise target figures and communicate potential actions and the success of measures internally.

Table 3: Overview of key figures for optimising university IT.
Sources: DIN EN 50600-1:2019, ISO 30134-1:2016, Blue Angel DE-UZ 228, (Belady, 2008; EcoRZ, 2020; Erek, 2012; Harryvan et al., 2020; Lorenz et al., 2020; Schödwell et al., 2018; Zarnekow, 2013)

Key figure	[unit], range, target	Calculation (No. = Number of)	Relevance	Note
Uni: %nIT Share of sustainable IT hardware in newly procured hardware	[%], 0-100 %, max.	$\frac{\textit{No. new certified devices}}{\textit{No. new devices}}$	Evaluates the consideration of sustainability in procurement. Can be used to check the effectiveness of procurement guidelines.	It is recommended that the TCO-Certified, Blue Angel, EU Ecolabel or equivalent certificates are taken into account.
Uni: REF Renewable Energy Factor: Share of renewable electricity in total energy consumption	[%], 0-100 %, max.	$\frac{\textit{renewabel energies}}{\textit{total energy}}$	At HAWen only relevant for the rented buildings, as state-owned buildings are already supplied with 100 % green electricity. EnEfG: from 2027: REF=100 %	A high proportion of renewable electricity (self-generated and purchased green electricity with environmental attributes) is not synonymous with energy-efficient operation.
DC: PUE Power Usage Effectiveness	[-], 1-∞, min.	$\frac{EnC(DC)}{EnC(DCIT)}$ Measurement at... PUE1: UPS output, PUE2: PDU output, PUE3: IT hardware input	High PUE values indicate inefficient building technology (especially cooling). EnEfG: applies to existing data centres from 2027: ≤ 1.5 Required for Blue Angel DE-UZ 228 certification	The reciprocal value of the PUE, the DCiE, is easier to understand: it shows the share of IT energy in the total data centre energy. Caution: No statement about the necessity of IT hardware or the efficiency of IT utilisation.
DC: T(DC) Average, maximum and minimum data centre temperature	[°C], -, max.	Read/calculate from time series	Higher temperatures require less cooling and are therefore preferable as far as possible.	Attention: safe operation must still be guaranteed!

continued on next page

Table 3: (continued)

Key figure	**[unit], range, target**	**Calculation (No. = Number of)**	**Relevance**	**Note**
DC: ERF Energy Reuse Factor: Proportion of reused energy	[%], 0-100 %, max.	$\frac{\textit{Reused energy}}{EnC(DC)}$	Often not feasible in small data centres due to the small amount of waste heat, therefore optional. EnEfG: for new data centres from 2027: >=15 % Required for Blue Angel DE-UZ 228 certification	Caution: Do not see waste heat utilisation as heating (more heat requirement = more servers are left running unnecessarily)!
DC: %A Proportion of the occupied area in the total area	[%], 0-100 %	$\frac{\textit{occupied DC area}}{\textit{total DC area}}$	Efficiency of space utilisation: large, unused areas are usually cooled and illuminated and should therefore be avoided.	Attention: Structural conditions (power connection, cooling capacity) can be a limiting factor here.
DCIT: VIR_{SV} Server virtualisation level	[%], 0-100 %, max.	$\frac{\textit{No. VM hosts}}{\textit{No. physical servers}}$	Virtualisation is a basic prerequisite for efficient server operation, as servers can be better utilised and less hardware is required.	Attention: No savings are achieved through virtualisation per se. These are subsequently realised by avoiding new purchases and temporarily switching off or removing servers.
DCIT: $ITUE$ Hardware utilisation	[%], 0-100 %, max.	$\frac{\textit{Average}}{\textit{Installed}}$ Server: Clock frequency, Memory: Storage space, Network: Network bandwidth	Low values may indicate redundant hardware or zombie IT and therefore potential for consolidation. Required for Blue Angel DE-UZ 228 certification	Attention: No statement about the benefit of the performance provided, i.e. duplicate files also increase the utilisation of the storage.
DCIT: IEC Idle Energy Coefficient: proportion of ›wasted‹ idle energy	[%], 0-100 %, min.	$\frac{IT_{E,idle}}{EnC}$ With: $IT_{E,idle} = (100\% - \textit{ITUE}) \times \textit{Idle power} \times t$ Recording at least for servers.	Similar statement as ITUE therefore optional. High values indicate high power consumption due to partial load or idle operation. Improvements can be achieved through more efficient hardware (lower idle power), temporary shutdown or consolidation.	Optimisation limited by hardware-side idle consumption. Caution: No statement about the benefit, i.e. idle consumption is rated negatively, while energy consumption for duplicate calculations is rated positively.
DCBS: CER Cooling Efficiency Ratio: Annual performance factor of the cooling system	[%], 0-100 %, max.	$\frac{\textit{heat removed form DC}}{EnC(C)}$	Indicates the efficiency of the refrigeration system. It can be optimised in particular by a low proportion of time with partial load operation and a low temperature range. Required for Blue Angel DE-UZ 228 certification	The optimisation of the CER is limited by basic physical laws and the design of the system.
DCBS: FCF Free Cooling Factor: Proportion of free cooling	[%], 0-100 %, max.	$\frac{\textit{hours with free cooling}}{\textit{total cooling hours}}$	Free cooling saves energy for ›cold production‹. A high proportion should therefore be aimed for.	Limited by outdoor temperature

continued on next page

Table 3: (continued)

Key figure	[unit], range, target	Calculation (No. = Number of)	Relevance	Note
DCBS: C_{LD} Cooling Load Density: Installed cooling capacity in relation to the DC area	[kW/m²], 0-∞, min.	$\frac{\textit{installed thermal output}}{\textit{DC area}}$	Similar to PUE, therefore optional. Provides information about the efficiency of the cooling: If, for example, only the cold aisle is cooled, the CLD is lower than if the entire data centre room is cooled	Attention: safe operation must continue to be guaranteed
O: WP_{Em} Equipment per employee/student workplace	[devices/workstation]	Average number of devices from the inventory list, an inspection or survey	The average number of devices provides valuable information on redundancies and also serves as a basis for extrapolating energy consumption.	Ideally, in addition to the equipment at the university, the equipment of the employees in the home office is also recorded.
O: $WP_{\%DPC}$ Proportion of desktop PCs to user computers	[%], 0-100 %, min.	$\frac{\textit{No. desktop PCs}}{\textit{No. computers}}$	Desktop PCs should only be used in exceptional cases, which is why their share should be as low as possible.	A share of 0 % is not realistic, as desktop PCs are required for computing-intensive tasks.
O: $WP_{\%SD}$ Share of shared desktops	[%], 0-100 %, max.	$\frac{\textit{No. shared workstations}}{\textit{No. workstations}}$	Improve workplace utilisation through desk sharing, especially with a high proportion of employees working from home, to save resources and energy.	Desk sharing is not a sensible option for all employees.
O: WP_U Average utilisation of workplaces	[%], 0-x %, max.	bwLehrpool statistics evaluation or survey values	basis for the extrapolation of energy consumption. High ›unused time‹: Optimisation through automatic activation of standby mode or automatic shutdown after a defined time High ›off time‹: Optimisation through reduction of workstations/desk sharing	Utilisation is defined as the proportions of ›unused‹ (idle/standby mode), ›occupied‹ (on mode) and ›offline‹ (off mode) The ›occupied time‹ is limited by the maximum working hours of the employees or the closing times of the university for student workstations.
O: $PS_{\%O}$ Proportion of office printers (printers, multifunctional devices)	[%], 0-100 %, min.	$\frac{\textit{No. office printers}}{\textit{total No. printers}}$	Office printers consume a lot of space, resources and energy. This key figure is used to identify potential savings and to monitor measures to reduce the number of printers	Office printers are defined by a limited group of people <20 people
O: $PS_{\%RP}$ Share of recycled paper in total paper consumption	[%], 0-100 %, max.	$\frac{\textit{recycled paper used}}{\textit{total paper used}}$	According to VwV Beschaffung, recycled paper should be used. This key figure is used to check target achievement	–

A graphical representation, for example in the form of network diagrams or levels, is a good way of communicating the key figures more effectively (see Belady (2008), EcoRZ (2020) and Jeong et al. (2014)). This makes it possible not only to compare the indicators with each other, but also to make them directly understandable for people outside the field.

2.1.3 Indicators for measures – communicate specific savings potential

In order to support the implementation of specific measures in the area of user IT, it is important to communicate concrete savings potential of measures in a target group-specific and application-oriented manner. Extensive information materials were created for this purpose, based on literature research and own measurements. These documents are publicly accessible[3] in order to raise awareness of green IT and facilitate the implementation of measures. The provision of such practical information is crucial to increasing the acceptance of green IT and bringing about sustainable behavioural changes among university members.

2.2 Inventory

For the inventory and later categorisation and calculation of the key figures, some basic data is required that applies to the entire university:

- Total electricity consumption of the university [kWh_{el}/a] (measurement)
- CO_2 emission factor of the German electricity mix in tCO_{2eq}/kWh_{el}
- Time series ambient temperature in °C (hourly measurement)
- Number of students and employees
- Number of student and employee workplaces at the university
- Hardware inventory per category including at least the following data
  - active use or storage
  - Idle, standby, off and average operating power in W
  - certifications (e.g. TCO-Certified)
  - optional: energy, resource and water consumption as well as CO_2 emissions from production, distribution and disposal (manufacturer's specifications)

[3] https://sites.google.com/hs-offenburg.de/green-academic-it/startseite

Precise knowledge of the hardware inventory, in particular the number of devices per category, is essential for calculating the target values in the area of user IT and the campus network infrastructure, as energy consumption in these areas cannot be fully measured due to their decentralised nature. For the data centre, on the other hand, consumption can be recorded through long-term monitoring, meaning that a complete and up-to-date inventory list is of less importance here. Nevertheless, precise data, such as idle power, is also required for various calculations in the data centre if no direct measurement is carried out.

During the project, considerable gaps were identified in the inventory lists at some of the pilot universities. Often, only hardware and software above a certain threshold is recorded in the inventory lists, which means that low-investment hardware, such as telephones or some monitors, is often not included in the lists. In addition, complicated internal processes for inventory and disposal can make it difficult to update the lists. Further gaps arise because data relevant to sustainability considerations, such as performance values, are not recorded in the inventory lists as standard. In addition, only a few manufacturers provide the necessary technical data.

These experiences from the project show possible challenges that can also occur at other universities, but do not necessarily have to. In order to create a solid database, the existing inventory list of the finance department should first be cleaned up and supplemented with an additional database for recording technical data. Internal processes should also be optimised to ensure that the inventory list remains up-to-date and complete.

2.3 Energy monitoring

Annual consumption in the data centre should be recorded by means of comprehensive long-term monitoring based on the Blue Angel DE-UZ 228 measurement concept. For the decentralised infrastructure, such as the campus-wide network and user IT, energy consumption is determined by reference measurements and extrapolations (see Figure 2). It is important to integrate IT monitoring into the university's general energy management system.

As part of the GAIT project, an additional software module for the Smart Energy Box (SEB) used for energy management was developed in close collaboration with the EnMa HAW project (Energy Management at Universities of Applied Sciences). This module enables IT consumption data to be recorded directly from the internal measured values of the IT devices themselves via SNMP queries (Simple Network Management Protocol) without the installation of additional meters, thus integrating the energy values into the energy management system.

The analysis of the recorded time series can reveal further optimisation potential, for example the reduction of peak loads and idle times or the shifting of workloads to less busy times. This allows both efficiency increases and improved system stability.

The calculation of the energy consumption of the decentralised infrastructure, in particular the workstation computers, was realised in the GAIT project using Excel-based extrapolations. These are based on the hardware inventory, the average utilisation profile and the power consumption in various operating modes.

At the two pilot universities, IT power consumption was determined to be 17% of total power consumption at HBC and 24% at HSO. The computer centre accounted for the largest share of this consumption.

3 Conclusion and outlook

The »Green Academic IT Potential (GAIT)« project has demonstrated the important role that transparency regarding energy and resource consumption plays in the implementation of green IT measures at universities. A targeted key performance indicator and monitoring system makes it possible to visualise the ecological impact of IT decisions and make well-founded decisions on the sustainable design of the IT landscape. Transparency creates awareness at all levels, from IT departments and university management to employees and students.

In work package 2 (»bwCloud goes green«) of the »bwCloud 3« project, the GAIT approach is transferred to the bwCloud-OS in order to create new opportunities for scaling green IT measures and reducing CO_2 emissions. One major challenge is that universities often do not directly pay for their electricity consumption, which can make operating their own servers more economically attractive. There is also a lack of clear guidelines on accounting for CO_2 emissions for cloud services. This is because outsourcing IT processes reduces the university's energy consumption, but at the same time increases consumption in the cloud provider's data centre. A holistic view or allocation of consumption to the originators is therefore necessary.

Furthermore, it is difficult to directly compare the CO_2 emissions of IT services between different universities and the bwCloud-OS, as there are institutional differences. Specific key figures such as Power Usage Effectiveness (PUE) and server utilisation provide a better basis for evaluation. As part of work package 2, comparable measurement data and key figures are to be collected for the bwCloud-OS and made available in a dashboard. This should enable users to compare their ecological footprint through cloud use with the values of their own data centre. This allows them to take ecological aspects into account in addition to monetary aspects when deciding to use the cloud.

Funding

The »Green Academic IT Potential (GAIT)« project was funded by the state of Baden-Württemberg, which was approved by the state parliament. The project ran under the funding code BWND21105-21106 and was carried out in cooperation between Offenburg University of Applied Sciences and Biberach University of Applied Sciences from September 2021 to September 2024.

Corresponding Author

Lena Ritzinger: lena.ritzinger@hs-offenburg.de
Offenburg University of Applied Sciences,
Institute for Sustainable Energy Systems (INES),
Badstr. 24a, 77652 Offenburg, Germany

ORCID

Lena Ritzinger https://orcid.org/0009-0008-8567-7163
Jan Münchenberg https://orcid.org/0009-0005-1727-6323
Michael Schmidt https://orcid.org/0000-0002-5615-6069

References

Belady, C. (2008). *The green grid productivity indicator*. White Paper WP #15. The Green Grid. URL: https://www.thegreengrid.org/en/resources/library-and-tools/395-WP.

EcoRZ, F. N. R. B.-W. (2020). *Nachhaltige Rechenzentren Leitfaden*. Tech. rep. Stuttgart: EcoRZ. URL: https://www.nachhaltige-rechenzentren.de/wp-content/uploads/2020/06/2020-06_Nachhaltige-Rechenzentren_Leitfaden_BF.pdf.

Erek, K. (2012). *Nachhaltiges Informationsmanagement: Gestaltungsansätze und Handlungsempfehlungen für IT-Organisationen*. Vol. 2. Schriftenreihe Informations- und Kommunikationsmanagement der Technischen Universität Berlin. Univ.-Verl. der TU. ISBN: 978-3-7983-2413-8.

Gröger, J., R. Liu, L. Stobbe, J. Druschke and N. Richter (2021). *Green Cloud Computing: Lebenszyklusbasierte Datenerhebung zu Umweltwirkungen des Cloud Computing*. Tech. rep. Umweltbundesamt. URL: https://www.umweltbundesamt.de/sites/default/files/medien/5750/publikationen/2021-06-17_texte_94-2021_green-cloud-computing.pdf.

Harryvan, D., M. Verzijl, M. Amzarakov and N. E. Agency (2020). *LEAP-Track-1-Powermanagement-Pilot-analysis*. Tech. rep. Certios/WCoolIT. URL: https://amsterdameconomicboard.com/app/uploads/2020/10/LEAP-Track-1-%E2%80%98Powermanagement-Pilot-analysis.pdf.

Hintemann, R., S. Hinterholzer and J. Clausen (2020). *Rechenzentren in Europa - Chancen für eine nachhaltige Digitalisierung: Teil 2*. Tech. rep. Berlin: Borderstep Institut. URL: https://www.eco.de/wp-content/uploads/dlm_uploads/2020/11/di_studie_rechenzentren_teil2_201110.pdf.

Hintemann, R., S. Hinterholzer, M. Graß, T. Grothey and T. u. n. M. e. V. Bundesverband Informationswirtschaft (2022). *Bitkom-Studie: Rechenzentren in Deutschland 2021 – Aktuelle Marktentwicklungen*. Tech. rep. Bitkom.

Jeong, S. and Y.-W. Kim (2014). »A holistic investigation method for data center resource efficiency«. In: *2014 International Conference on Information and Communication Technology Convergence (ICTC)*. IEEE, pp. 548–551. ISBN: 978-1-4799-6786-5. DOI: 10.1109/ICTC.2014.6983207. URL: https://ieeexplore.ieee.org/document/6983207.

Lorenz, B.-M., M. Wiedmann, N. Conrad and M. Brodbeck (2020). *Praxisleitfaden Nachhaltigkeit in Rechenzentren*. Tech. rep. Höchstleistungsrechenzentrum der Universität Stuttgart. URL: https://www.hlrs.de/fileadmin/about/social_responsibility/Sustainability/HLRS_NHK_Praxisleitfaden-2020.pdf.

Ministerium für Umwelt, K. u. E. B.-W. U. M. (2023). *Landesstrategie Green IT*. URL: https://um.baden-wuerttemberg.de/de/klima-energie/klimaschutz/klimaneutrale-landesverwaltung/green-it/kompetenzstelle-green-it/die-landesstrategie.

Ritzinger, L. and S. Wagner (2024). *Abschlussbericht Green Academic IT Potential*. Tech. rep. Hochschule Offenburg and Hochschule Biberach. URL: https://bwsyncandshare.kit.edu/s/yjKP78Xz4gDfnWr.

Schödwell, B., R. Zarnekow, R. Liu, J. Gröger and M. Wilkens (2018). *Kennzahlen und Indikatoren für die Beurteilung der Ressourceneffizienz von Rechenzentren und Prüfung der praktischen Anwendbarkeit: KPI4DCE*. Tech. rep. Umweltbundesamt. URL: https://www.umweltbundesamt.

de / sites / default / files / medien / 1410 / publikationen / 2018 - 02 - 23 _ texte _ 19 - 2018 _ ressourceneffizienz-rechenzentren.pdf.

Shao, X., Z. Zhang, P. Song, Y. Feng and X. Wang (2022). »A review of energy efficiency evaluation metrics for data centers«. In: *Energy and Buildings* 271. ISSN: 0378-7788. DOI: 10.1016/j.enbuild.2022.112308. URL: https://www.sciencedirect.com/science/article/pii/S0378778822004790.

Zarnekow, R. (2013). *Green IT: Erkenntnisse und Best Practices Aus Fallstudien*. 1st ed. Berlin, Heidelberg: Springer Berlin / Heidelberg. ISBN: 978-3-642-36151-7. URL: https://ebookcentral.proquest.com/lib/kxp/detail.action?docID=1206108.

GreenIT for cooperative Services

Findings from the bwCloud3 project

Jan Münchenberg, Lena Ritzinger

Institute for Machine Learning and Analytics (IMLA), Institute for Sustainable Energy Systems (INES), Offenburg University of Applied Sciences, Offenburg, Germany

Abstract

Cooperative IT services are becoming increasingly important for higher education and research institutions. So far, the focus has mostly been on the fair distribution of financial costs, personnel expenses and risks among the participating institutions – primarily from the perspective of the service providers and customers. However, new legal regulations and sustainability objectives, such as the UN Sustainable Development Goals (SDGs[1]) and GreenIT initiatives, now require that additional aspects of ecological considerations are also taken into account in cooperations. Currently, few established concepts address this need. This paper explores which existing concepts of the financial perspective can be transferred to ecological load sharing from the perspective of established IT service management. It identifies key challenges and underscores the necessity for cultural shifts in decision-making processes, where traditional financial frameworks prove insufficient. While cooperative arrangements may pose difficulties for providers, they offer significant benefits for customers. The statewide service bwCloud-OS serves as a practical example of an initial approach. The ongoing project aims to refine these ecological burden-sharing models further, providing a foundational framework for sim-

[1] Sustainable Development Goals of United Nations

ilar initiatives in other statewide services, thereby contributing to Baden-Württemberg's goal of achieving climate-neutral universities.

1 Motivation

Cooperative IT services in higher education are becoming increasingly essential, as evidenced by their growing number and adoption. In Baden-Württemberg alone, numerous statewide services exist – such as bwHPC, bwCloud-OS, bwLehrpool, bwIDM, bwFDM, among others. The participating institutions aim to jointly address the escalating challenges posed by limited financial and human resources through collaboration. This necessitates a partnership-oriented relationship between provider and client institutions, with fair sharing of costs and risks. To date, financial considerations – particularly investment and operating costs – have been the primary focus.

Looking ahead, institutions must also integrate sustainability aspects, including the United Nations Sustainable Development Goals (SDGs), into their strategic planning and mandatory reporting. For instance, the Energy Efficiency Act (EnEfG, effective 13 November 2023) mandates that public institutions with an annual final energy consumption exceeding 1 GWh implement an energy management system and achieve annual energy savings of at least 2%. Since most universities surpass this consumption threshold, they are required to comply with these regulations and demonstrate ongoing progress. Additionally, universities must develop qualified energy and climate protection concepts (EuKK), as stipulated by the circular issued by Economics Minister Bauer on 26 July 2022, contributing to the target of net greenhouse gas neutrality for state administration by 2030 (§ 11 of the Baden-Württemberg Climate Protection and Climate Change Adaptation Act (KlimaG BW), dated 7 February 2023).

This evolving regulatory landscape creates an urgent need to create ecological balances – such as energy and CO_2-balances – and to equitably allocate resource consumption and environmental impacts (hereafter referred to as "burdens") among the participating institutions. To support this, the Ministry for the Environment, Climate and Energy Sector provides an Excel-based tool enabling universities to compile greenhouse gas inventories, from which energy balances can be readily derived. However, suitable implementation concepts for ecological burden sharing in the area of IT service management are still lacking.

This paper examines the extent to which established IT service management models for monetary cost-sharing among cooperation partners can be adapted to ecological balancing, highlighting the challenges that must be addressed to achieve effective implementation.

2 Methods

ITIL[2] is the de facto standard for IT service management. In this paper, its definitions and principles (*ITIL 4* 2020), which primarily cover financial aspects, are expanded to include aspects of environmental accounting (*DIN EN ISO 14044* n.d.).

2.1 Fundamentals

Service is at the centre of ITIL and is defined as »a way to commonly create value by facilitating the achievement of customers' desired outcomes without the customer having to manage certain costs and risks.« This paper focuses on the dimensions of value, costs and risks, including both financial and environmental aspects.

In IT service management, delivering **value** to customers and their users – such as employees – is always the top priority. Value is created from the customer or user's perspective when they can enhance their efficiency, for example, by increasing the likelihood of achieving their desired outcomes, or when barriers are removed, such as by improving information security, data protection, legal compliance and more. This approach is especially relevant for universities in meeting these critical requirements effectively.

ITIL primarily takes into account the procurement and operating **costs** (investment, staff, resources (electricity, consumables etc.), project costs etc.) in the service lifecycle. In the following, the term »costs« is used to refer to both financial and environmental indicators such as CO_2-consumption. As a result, the disposal phase in the lifecycle also becomes more important, for example, especially when divergent financial and ecological amortisation periods (terms) have to be weighed against each other.

[2] Information Technology Infrastructure Library

In terms of **risks**, the main focus to date has been on financial and personnel aspects such as a shortage of skilled labour and staff turnover, as well as information security. Ecological accounting expands the risk assessment, particularly those caused by constantly changing legal limits and new measurement methods and calculation formulas. This is due to the still inadequate standardisation of ecological indicators and processes, particularly in the IT sector. Large IT groups such as Google, Amazon and HP develop their own IT environmental indicators for their services. In addition, there are already numerous national standardisation efforts, e.g. (IT-Planungsrat, 2023). However, there are no globally applicable standards.

In order to view decision-making processes in IT service management from different perspectives, the following stakeholders must be distinguished:

- **Users**: The actual users of the service, with which they want to achieve added value in their work. In the university context, these are primarily people from the areas of research and teaching, supported by people from the administration.
- **Customers**: The contractual contact persons of the institutions, usually the management level. They are responsible for strategy, finances and compliance, including, more recently, the ecological balances. They are the top decision makers and providers of money and resources. They prioritise and must weigh up financial and ecological facts. Each institution must decide whether to allow individual users or sub-organisations (e.g. individual researchers or institutes) as independent customers in parallel, although their costs must be included in the university's overall CO_2-balance.
- **Provider**: The service provider who ensures the reliable provision of the service. Entrepreneurial risk is not permitted in the university environment. Therefore, all costs and risks and, more recently, the ecological burdens of a service should be shared fairly between the partners within the framework of a cooperation.

2.2 Analysis – decision-making process

Institutions must decide whether they want to operate services independently or outsource them externally and, in the latter case, to whom. A cost-benefit analysis is common practice. The most important decision criteria from the customer's point of view are (Figure 1):

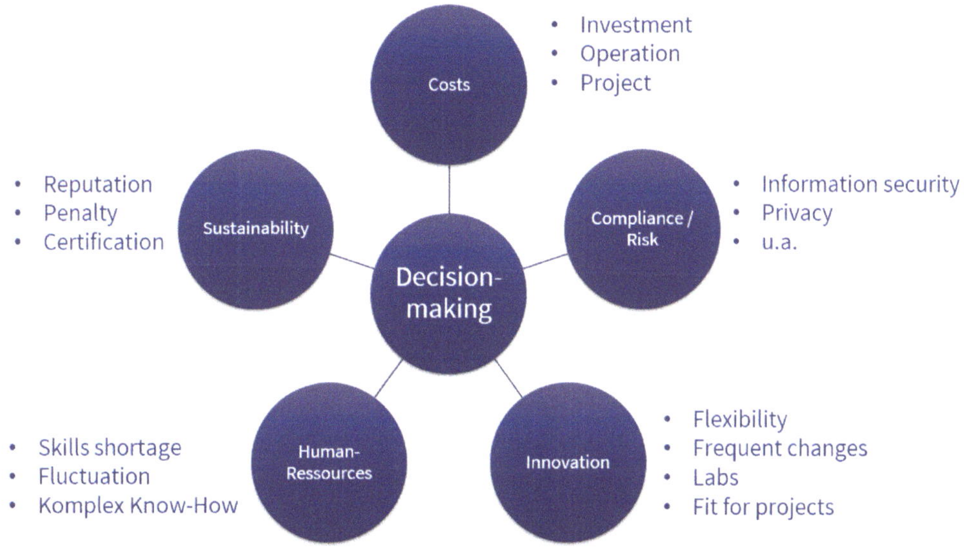

Figure 1: Decision criteria in the cost-benefit analysis

In order to develop a common understanding for decisions within a university, there is usually an IT strategy to which all departments and university members should orientate themselves. This is the only way to efficiently procure, operate and further develop central IT infrastructures and services for research and teaching and to utilise synergies. In reality, however, departments such as institutes and faculties or research projects often procure and operate their own IT infrastructures. While this was still practicable and acceptable in the past due to the purely cost-orientated approach, the increasingly complex decision-making dimensions (see Figure 2) require evaluation in the context of the entire university.

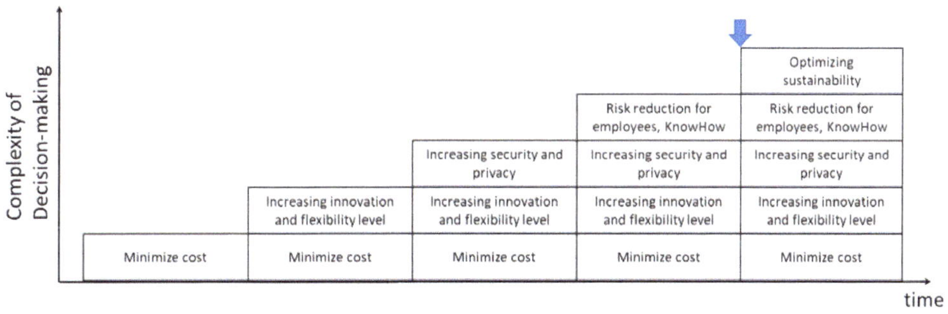

Figure 2: Increasing complexity due to growing number of decision dimensions

For example, in matters of information security and data protection, the weakest link – such as a project infrastructure procured by a researcher – always determines the risk for the entire institution. The situation is similar with the ecological balance sheet. The sum of all consumption, including the dedicated server systems, is included in the overall assessment, even if a more ecologically favourable central VM cluster is actually available and centrally financed.

While there is a widespread understanding of costs and usually also of security, many users are not yet aware of the need for Green IT. Decision-makers must therefore develop a communication strategy to make it clear to all stakeholders why sustainability plays a role in IT and why the ecological balance sheet of their own institution depends on the commitment of each individual. It is often difficult to emphasise the benefits to users. If necessary, guidelines on ecological aspects should be drawn up, similar to those for data protection, information security and procurement.

This poses further challenges for university management, as they are usually responsible for finance, compliance and risk management as the top decision-makers. However, IT topics such as AI, high-performance computing (HPC) or research data management (RDM) are often very complex and difficult for management to fully grasp, making it difficult for them to make the right decisions. Another complicating factor for the strategy of centralised structures is that technological progress and requirements in the various research domains move at different speeds. In order to be at the forefront of research and teaching as an institution, this often means entering grey areas and taking risks. It is also sometimes a challenge to reconcile the different interests of researchers and teaching staff. Transparency and a common understanding of the ecological and economic goals must be created among users so that decisions can be understood in the following cases:

1. Replacement of existing solutions: Reasons include end of life, cost savings, increased costs (e.g. due to new licence models, electricity costs), shortage of skilled workers, staff changes (e.g. due to retirements), data protection or security issues, strategic developments (e.g. digital sovereignty) or the realisation of sustainability goals.
2. Opening up new areas: Promotion of new research and teaching areas through suitable IT infrastructures such as for AI, HPC or FDM.

While in the first case the users (researchers and teachers) are already familiar with the solutions offered as well as experience and key figures on utilisation are available, this is lacking in the second case. This is more of a »bet on the future«, as success cannot yet be assessed and user acceptance is uncertain. The benefits often only become apparent after several years, as users first have to be convinced of the new solution and have to integrate the new potential into their everyday work. Centralisation can also be a step backwards from the perspective of the individual user, as functionality may be reduced or flexibility lost. In return, however, sustainable financing and support for the solution are guaranteed.

Decision-makers must find the right solutions for their own institution and for the individual subject areas. A decision must be made between:

- independently: The costs and risks are borne entirely by the institution itself. Ecological costs remain local.
- commercial: Customers lose digital sovereignty and pay for usage. Ecological costs are an entrepreneurial risk for the service provider. In the medium term, however, customers will very probably have to include some of these costs in their own ecological balance. In the case of scientific publications, there are already initial approaches that, for example, the ecological footprint must be stated as part of the research. Service providers can often achieve better ecological results by utilising synergy effects.
- cooperative: A service is provided jointly with like-minded institutions, with one institution usually taking the lead. Risks as well as financial and ecological costs are shared fairly.
- hybrid: Different solutions are combined. For example, the cooperative bwCloud-OS service can be used as IaaS, while own virtual machines or software packages are operated on it. In this case, the ecological costs of all individual components must be added together.

2.3 Cooperations

The aim of cooperation is to create added value for all institutions by involving all partners in decision-making processes on an equal footing. Costs, risks and ecological burdens are shared fairly. While the free market has a regulating effect in the commercial sector and only the best providers will prevail in terms of costbenefit analysis, the core of collaborations in the higher education landscape is mutual trust and the common goal of maintaining or regaining digital sovereignty.

A common understanding is a prerequisite for cooperation. Specifically, the common basis is the definition of goals, key figures, measurement methods and their interpretation, which must be understood and applied by all stakeholders. In the example of the higher education landscape in Baden-Württemberg, the largest common denominator is the regulations and strategies of the MWK[3], which are incorporated into the individual institutions' own (IT) strategies and regulations.

Many cooperative approaches are still in the development phase. For example, there are still no standardised evaluation methods and suitable key figures at the institutions. In order to facilitate cooperation, the currently emerging bwIT-Alliance is attempting to harmonise strategies in certain areas. Accordingly, an IT framework cooperation agreement is being created, which will be signed by all universities in the alliance. It is intended to create a common understanding among all institutions as a basis for cooperation and to be used for decision-making processes. This is to be implemented in the statewide service bwCloud-OS as the first cooperation – a major challenge in order to establish the service in the university landscape in the long term.

For example, when it comes to sustainability, it is crucial to first determine what constitutes a climate-neutral university and which ecological indicators are relevant. Binding guidelines from the Ministry of the Environment or the MWK are also necessary, especially if a malus model is to be introduced later. This creates standardised goals in the university landscape, on the basis of which the individual institutions can align their own strategies.

A decision in favour of cooperation is fundamental and usually difficult to reverse, especially for smaller institutions. Customers therefore become dependent, as they themselves have little influence on the costs and burdens of the service, which is the responsibility of the provider. In turn, the provider must try to pass these on in full, which from the customer's point of view cannot and must not be an automatic process, as they expect the provider to do everything possible to carry out an optimal cost-benefit analysis from everyone's point of view. This is a major challenge which, as is usual in a demo-

[3] Ministry of Science, Research and Arts Baden-Württemberg

cracy, brings greater added value for some and less or even negative added value for others. Solidarity is required.

Cooperations can be topic/service-related locally (within an institution, e.g. the institutes, faculties and the computer centre), between individual universities or centrally under the umbrella of the bwIT-Alliance, e.g. within the framework of statewide services. A typical classification of services provided in the cloud is (Figure 3):

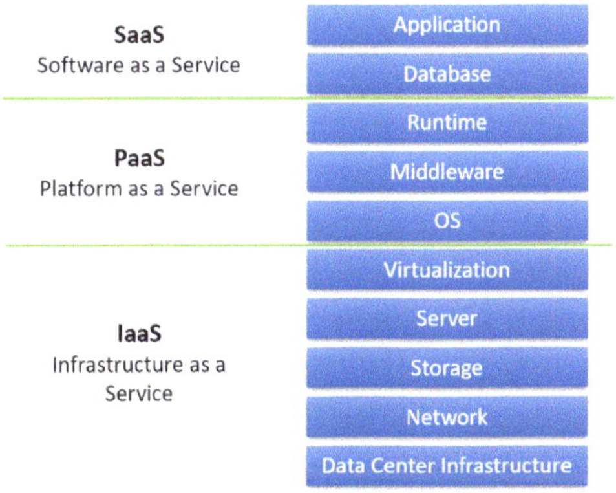

Figure 3: Types of services provided in the cloud

2.4 Billing models

As already mentioned several times, all financial and ecological costs and risks must be distributed fairly among each other in collaborations:

$$costs, risks[Prov] = levy[Inst_1] + levy[Inst_2] + \ldots + levy[Inst_n]$$

In the case of existing bwServices of the universities, such as bwLehrpool, it has become established that the service providers disclose a full cost calculation for the purpose of transparency and, in the event of significant changes, e.g. the number of customers or costs, look for new distribution options together with the customers.

There are already numerous billing models within cooperations for services or the billing of software licences. The following approaches have been established to determine the cost shares between all participating institutions:

1. **Flat-rate**: The costs are distributed among the customers according to a fixed formula. An established example of a distribution key is the categorisation according to company size (turnover, number of employees etc.) or, in the university context, the number of students, FTEs (full-time equivalents) etc. The distribution key is multiplied by the respective costs.

2. **Source-related**: Costs that can be charged directly to a customer through the use of a service. The prerequisite for this is the measurability of the necessary key figures. Established examples are the number of transactions or tokens, consumption of computing time, storage space, etc.

3. **Hybrid**: Combination of both

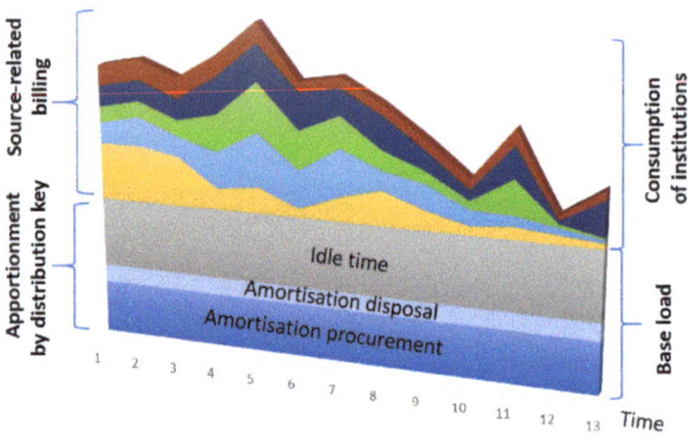

Figure 4: Fair distribution of costs and risks between providers and institutions for an IaaS-type service

There are different challenges depending on the type of service. For the hybrid approach, Figure 4 shows the allocation of costs arising from the base load and the institution-specific consumption. A decisive factor for the level of amortisation costs is the determination of the term of server infrastructures, which in the industry is usually 5 years. For this period, the potential development of utilisation rate must be taken into account at the procurement stage, although this often cannot be predicted clearly as is the case with current AI development, for example. Buffers must be procured and put into operation accordingly. In the industrial sector, this is precisely the entrepreneurial risk, which is not possible in the university landscape and must therefore be distributed among all customers from both a financial and an ecological perspective. A distinction must be made between:

1. **Base load**: Amortisation of the costs arising from procurement and disposal as well as idle time. These costs cannot be allocated according to causation. Idle operating costs include rent, air conditioning, data centre infrastructure (hardware, software, staff), consumption (electricity, ...), ... As a rule, billing can only be mapped by means of an apportionment using a distribution key.

2. **Consumption of the individual institutions**: Costs caused by the utilisation of the users of an individual institution. For example, increased electricity and air conditioning costs are incurred during computing times compared to idle times, ... These can usually be allocated to customers using definable logics and can therefore be charged directly. In the best case scenario, the user can be shown a cost forecast for the intended activity in advance so that the need for billing can be weighed up.

2.5 Components of cost and burden allocation

ITIL already proposes several building blocks for the billing and pricing of a service. All costs incurred during the entire lifecycle of a service must be taken into account. Depending on the phase (procurement, operation, disposal), these must be priced differently (see above: flat rate, cost-by-cause or hybrid). As shown in Figure 5, the costs are made up of one-off investment costs (procurement and project costs) and ongoing operating costs (consumables, rent, licences, electricity etc.). Disposal is often overlooked in the overall cost analysis.

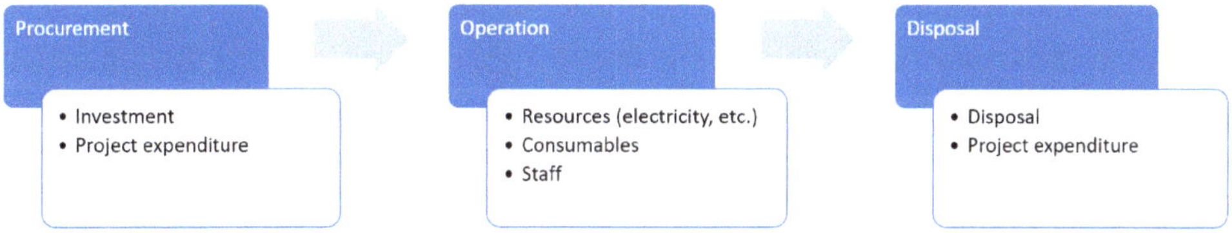

Figure 5: Cost types over the entire service lifecycle

If this idea is transferred to the ecological balance sheets, there is a similar breakdown. The production and transport costs must also be taken into account in procurement. As with the financial view, a decision must be made here as to whether a one-off balance sheet or amortisation over several years should be made.

In the university sector it is common practice to operate system components for longer than is usual in industry in order to save costs – which usually automatically has a positive effect on the ecological balance sheet.

Every customer is aware that the service provider wants to cover these costs in full, including a profit or risk premium. Software and staff costs are eliminated from the ecological balance sheet. Essentially, only areas of IaaS (infrastructure as a service) are relevant.

2.6 Key figures and measurement methods

The basic key figures for billing must be measurable, understandable and comprehensible for all stakeholders. This is the only way to achieve acceptance of billing. Reporting and measurement methods should be pragmatic and not cause a great deal of effort. Customers should have the feeling that they can influence a reduction in costs or an improvement in the ecological balance themselves by reducing consumption. There are already numerous approaches for the calculations, which were analysed in the GAIT project and further developed in a system of key figures (Ritzinger et al., 2024). The results there are being applied in the bwCloud3 project. The KPI4DCI model of the Federal Environment Agency (Wilkens et al., 2024) and the Green IT Strategy of the IT Planning Council (IT-Planungsrat, 2023) are leading the way, particularly in the public sector.

The implementation of Green IT in cooperations requires standardised models that are applicable and established throughout the state or among the cooperation partners. Changes in the system of key figures, e.g. due to legal changes, must be determined in regular coordination meetings between the cooperation partners. Annual cycles have proven their worth here. It makes sense for billing to be centralised. This is the only way to ensure the required transparency for all partners. It is also the only way to react quickly and appropriately to unexpected events such as sudden increases in electricity prices.

3 Results and discussion

The *bwCloud3* project, particularly in its *Green IT* work package, is intended to demonstrate how both financial and ecological benefits can be achieved within the Baden-Württemberg university landscape through targeted collaboration and strategic billing models. The integration of GreenIT aspects into the billing model not only offers the possibility of mapping ecological costs according to their source, but also supports the strategic orientation of individual institutions, which can thus make financial and ecological optimisations at the same time. This creates an advantage for providers and users of statewide services alike, which forms a sustainable basis for further cooperation.

Nevertheless, the challenge remains to create adequate incentives for both the providers and users of such services. The financial evaluation of the cost-benefit analysis, which has dominated up to now, often works in favour of the owner-operator, which has so far limited the willingness to cooperate. An innovative billing model that allows for both financial and ecological incentives is essential in order to fully utilise the added value of joint solutions.

The bwIT-Alliance represents a promising approach to establishing a statewide standard that is scalable to all statewide services. The example of bwCloud-OS illustrates the potential of such a standard as a central building block for GreenIT initiatives and as a multiplier for other services such as bwLehrpool, bwSync, bwFDM or bwHPC. The overarching agreement of all stakeholders on the benefits of cooperation is a strong foundation, but this must be supplemented by concrete incentive systems in order to ensure both ecological and financial sustainability in the long term. Politicians must create precisely such incentives in order to reduce the ecological costs in the country and achieve the declared climate targets.

Corresponding Author

Prof. Dr. Jan Münchenberg: jan.muenchenberg@hs-offenburg.de
Offenburg University of Applied Sciences, Badstr. 24, 77652 Offenburg, Germany

ORCID

Jan Münchenberg https://orcid.org/0009-0005-1727-6323
Lena Ritzinger https://orcid.org/0009-0008-8567-7163

References

DIN EN ISO 14044 (n.d.). *DIN EN ISO 14044:2021-02, Umweltmanagement_- Ökobilanz_- Anforderungen und Anleitungen (ISO_14044:2006_+ Amd_1:2017_+ Amd_2:2020); Deutsche Fassung EN_ISO_14044:2006_+ A1:2018_+ A2:2020.* DOI: 10.31030/3179656. URL: https://www.dinmedia.de/de/-/-/325953813.

ITIL 4 (2020). *ITIL 4: digital and IT Strategy*. First edition. OCLC: 1241092143. Norwich, United Kingdom: TSO. ISBN: 978-0-11-331650-2.

IT-Planungsrat (2023). *Handlungsleitfaden zur Green-IT-Strategie des IT-Planungsrates für die Ziele 1, 4 und 7*. Accessed: 2024-10-03. URL: https://www.it-planungsrat.de/fileadmin/it-planungsrat/aktuelles_pressemitteilungen/GreenIT_Handlungsleitfaden_IT-Standorte.pdf.

Ritzinger, L. and S. Wagner (2024). *Abschlussbericht Green Academic IT Potential*. Tech. rep. Hochschule Offenburg and Hochschule Biberach. URL: https://bwsyncandshare.kit.edu/s/yjKP78Xz4gDfnWr.

Wilkens, M., F. Neubauer, R. Hellwig, L. Ackermann and F. Chwoyka (2024). *Abschschlussbericht: KPI4DCE im Feld: Umweltbewertung ausgewählter Rechenzentren und Best Practices*. Tech. rep. TEXTE 43/2024. Umweltbundesamt, p. 50. URL: https://www.umweltbundesamt.de/sites/default/files/medien/11850/publikationen/43_2024_texte_kpi4dce_im_feld.pdf.

Energy-Efficient Scientific Computing and AI in Freiburg

A Comprehensive Approach to Weighting Demand and Sustainability

Armin Saur, Dirk von Suchodoletz, Bernd Wiebelt, Björn Grüning

eScience, University of Freiburg, Freiburg, Germany

Abstract

The growing adoption of Artificial Intelligence (AI) across scientific disciplines, education and administration adds a new and substantial dimension to global energy demand, complementing the already significant requirements of traditional high-performance computing (HPC). These developments unfold against the backdrop of profound transformations in energy supply, driven by the imperatives of climate change as well as societal and geopolitical challenges.

Universities invest a considerable share of their budgets in IT infrastructure and the necessary energy to run them, creating a significant environmental impact. As publicly funded institutions they should contribute to its mitigation. This paper provides an overview of ongoing experiments, implemented measures, and potential directions for further optimization. Supported by current infrastructure projects on different layers of the IT operations stack, we explore various strategic options. The planning of new foundational infrastructure, such as data centers, and the definition of research and development agendas, create unique opportunities to shape sustainable future developments.

1 Motivation

Universities, owing to their central role in identifying and explaining key societal developments, carry a particular responsibility for promoting the sustainability of modern societies. Consequently, a critical assessment of their resource consumption, especially in the field of IT and scientific computing, is inevitable. This calls for an intensified focus on sustainability in long-term infrastructure planning and IT modernization. Such considerations must become integral to institutional strategy, fostering a cultural shift toward sustainable and energy-efficient scientific computing in a broader sense.

In 2022, data centers, cryptocurrencies, and artificial intelligence (AI) together accounted for almost 2 % of global electricity consumption. Between 2025 and 2027, electrical energy demand in Europe is projected to grow by approximately 1.9 % annually (IEA, 2024, 2025). This expansion in computational power requirements increasingly faces justified scrutiny regarding its sustainability and societal benefit. Rising energy demands thus create strong incentives for optimization, prompting a fundamental rethinking across disciplines – from research design and software development to workflow execution.

»Free lunch ist over (again).« For decades, in the public sector only investment costs were seriously considered when acquiring new high-performance compute hardware. The mantra used to be »the most bang for the buck«. Running costs, if considered at all, played only a minor role. If anything, human resources were the limiting factor, while energy consumption was not, regarding power supply, cooling and energy costs. In the context of scientific computing, long-standing paradigms must be revisited and adapted to the realities of today and tomorrow. The following points thus formulate the core research problems.

- The prevailing focus on peak performance alone may be suboptimal. We need to determine whether a *performance-energy sweet spot* exists that yields comparable scientific output while significantly reducing energy consumption, rather than insisting on a 10 % reduction in runtime at the cost of a 20 % increase in energy use (Kocot et al., 2023).
- The conventional mantra of maintaining permanent 100 % utilization of an HPC system is increasingly questionable from an economic standpoint. When operational expenditures approach or exceed the initial capital investment, the justific-

ation for scheduling jobs from users who have already exceeded a fair share – and who do not optimize their workloads – must be critically examined.

- Emerging technologies such as AI and Quantum Computing cannot be ignored in discussions of economical and ecological resource consumption. Despite the »fear-of-missing-out« narrative and the long-term promise of these technologies, there is a pressing need to develop and adopt energy-efficient methods for their execution already in the present.
- The energy balance of compute systems cannot be assessed solely by looking at its operational power draw. A substantial, often-overlooked component of the total carbon footprint is the embodied energy, which is the amount of primary energy that is consumed in the entire supply chain of the hardware, from raw-material extraction to various steps of production and the final disposal of obsolete components.

The purpose of this paper is to delineate the current challenges faced by the computer center and to outline possible pathways toward a more sustainable and efficient campus-wide computing ecosystem. We do not claim to provide a complete solution; rather, we present an overview of measures that have already been implemented, an inventory of ongoing initiatives, and a forward-looking description of development scenarios that are aligned with regional digital-infrastructure strategies (Suchodoletz et al., 2026b).

2 Status Quo and Legal Obligations

Today, and for a long time into the future, energy requirements will be the economical and ecological drive for change and innovation (IEA, 2023). While regional strategies like Baden-Württemberg's Green-IT initiative[1] have been in place, concrete actions have been catalyzed by the escalating climate crisis. Consequently, policy responses such as the Energy Efficiency legislation[2] have brought IT-driven energy demands into sharper focus.[3] At the state level, there are regulations concerning sustainability and resource

1 See https://www.baden-wuerttemberg.de/fileadmin/redaktion/m-um/intern/Dateien/Dokumente/1_Ministerium/Aufgaben_und_Organization/Green-IT/191122-Kurzbericht-Landesstrategie-Green-IT.pdf, visited on 07.07.2025

2 Enacted in late 2023: https://www.gesetze-im-internet.de/enefg/BJNR1350B0023.html, visited on 07.07.2025

3 The University of Freiburg as a whole accounts for emissions of $30500-47000$ t CO_2 and a projected energy consumption of 50 GWh/a in 2022 (Krieglstein, 2021).

consumption, such as the Green IT Strategy (July 2014). The Climate Protection Act (February 7, 2023) aims for a net-zero greenhouse gas emissions state administration by 2030. For this purpose, there is a greenhouse gas accounting tool (BICO2Land-BW), which considers annual energy and resource consumption, as well as the emissions from newly acquired items in the reference year.

To address the problem, several key concepts and mitigation measures must first be clarified. One of the most widely used indicators of data-center energy performance is the Power Usage Effectiveness (PUE). It quantifies how efficiently a facility converts electrical power into useful computing work and is defined as

$$\mathrm{PUE} = \frac{\text{Total Facility Energy}}{\text{IT Equipment Energy}}$$

as per DIN EN 50600-4-2, August 2019 edition (DIN, 2019). A PUE value of 1.0 indicates perfect efficiency – meaning all consumed energy is used directly for computing. Higher values reflect additional energy overhead for cooling, power distribution, and other infrastructure systems.

Energy Reuse Factor (ERF) is a metric that quantifies how much of a data center's energy consumption is reused outside the data center itself. It is defined as the ratio of reused energy to the total energy consumed by the facility:

$$\mathrm{ERF} = \frac{\text{Reused Energy}}{\text{Total Facility Energy}}$$

An ERF of 0 means no energy is reused, while an ERF nearing 1 indicates that most of the consumed energy, such as waste heat, is effectively recovered and used for other purposes (e.g. for heating nearby buildings). The Renewable Energy Factor (REF) is a metric that measures the proportion of a data center's total energy consumption that is supplied from renewable sources, with:

$$\mathrm{REF} = \frac{\text{Renewable Energy Used}}{\text{Total Energy Consumed}}$$

An REF of 0 indicates that no renewable energy is used, while an REF of 1 (or 100%) means the data center is fully powered by renewable energy sources.

The *EnEfG* (2023) enacted to promote sustainable developments defines threshold values for energy key performance indicators (KPIs) for data centers, including PUE, ERF, and REF. Legacy data centers which started operations before 01.07.2026 will be allowed a maximum PUE of 1.5 starting from 01.07.2027 and a maximum PUE of 1.3 starting from 01.07.2030. Additionally, institutions with an average annual energy consumption exceeding 3 GWh in 2021-2023 have to establish a certified energy management system.[4]

Continuous measurements of electrical power and energy consumption of the data center's essential components are required. Measures must be taken to steadily improve the data center's energy efficiency (PUE). For institutions that surpass the 2.5 GWh threshold per year, this includes the general obligation to either avoid or reuse waste heat by application of state-of-the-art methods. Additionally, there is a disclosure obligation to operators of district heating networks and a reporting obligation to the Federal Agency for Energy Efficiency by 31.03.2025.

The law defines annual energy savings of 2 % for the university as a whole, which must be realized annually (subject to penalties) until 2045. While these specifications will need to be concretized in the context of the further development of scientific computing, the general requirement for energy-saving measures is clearly defined by the law and thus becomes the responsibility of the respective institution.

3 Campus Infrastructure and Energy Demands

The Freiburg University Computing Center has been providing computing services since 1971. Today it hosts a heterogeneous portfolio of large scale IT services like bwCloud-OS[5] and the storage sytem bwSFS (Suchodoletz et al., 2026a) for research data. Additionally, it offers extensive support for scientific computing via the federated bwHPC initiative. The central HPC system NEMO1 (Janczyk et al., 2019) entered operation in 2016 and, after eight years of service, was replaced by a new generation of resources (NEMO2) that became available in 2024–2025 (Wiebelt et al., 2026).

[4] According to http://data.europa.eu/eli/reg/2009/1221/oj/deu, and an environmental management system, according to https://www.iso.org/standard/69426.html by 30.07.2026, both visited on 07.07.2025

[5] A Baden-Württemberg state-wide OpenStack cloud service for higher education and research; see https://bwcloud-os.de/, visited on 07.07.2025. The University of Freiburg is one of the four hosting sites.

The central server rooms on the University of Freiburg campus are integral to the central infrastructure, utilized by various institutions and faculties for hosting machines dedicated to research, teaching, and administration. The whole infrastructure at the main site requires a peak cooling capacity of approximately 400 kW (Speck, 2007). A new server room is being planned on the Freiburg university campus, designed to offer additional 600 kW of capacity. However, just adding new capacity is not sufficient, particularly given the reality of climate change. Sustainable solutions have to consider the entire IT operations stack, from hardware planning and procurement to the design of efficient code and workflows. The deliberate and intelligent application of human expertise, the hallmark of research institutions, combined with technical innovation and efficiency improvements, may prove decisive in effectively managing both energy and cost expenditures. Planning considerations involve three key capacity parameters: power supply, cooling, and available space in terms of rack units. Typically, one of these parameters reaches a limit, preventing the accommodation of additional systems. Historically, space (rack units) was the limiting factor, but increasingly, cooling requirements pose a significant challenge. The construction of new server rooms or the upgrade of existing ones is associated with high costs and requires extensive planning. Within a data center, the energy demand comprises the following components:[6]

- Primary Demand: The main energy consumption is attributed to the systems supporting various applications, including diverse services for research, teaching, and administration, as well as computing and storage of large datasets. This constitutes the lion's share of the data center's operational energy use.
- Network Connectivity: Energy is required for communication between components, across the campus, and with the global internet. Network components such as Ethernet switches consume approximately 0.3 kW for 10 Gigabit/s+ (about 50 ports) and 0.15 kW for 1 Gigabit/s (about 50 ports), while routers add at least 0.5 kW per installation. Even when multiple Gigabit/s and 100 Gigabit/s Ethernet, as well as 100 Gigabit/s Omni-Path, are present, their contribution is marginal.
- Server Racks: The racks housing the machines have an average energy demand of nearly 1 kW per rack for fans, control, and monitoring electronics. Just considering the main server room of the data center, this adds an additional 40 kW to power consumption.

[6] Various forms of measurement were used: Ranging from individual instruments to rack internal PDUs and individual servers via IPMI.

- Cooling Efforts: Cooling the aforementioned components is crucial. Conservative estimates for relatively recent installations suggest a ratio of at least 1:10, meaning that for every kilowatt-hour of electrical power supplied, an additional 0.1 kWh is used for cooling. The older main site of the Freiburg University Computing Center currently achieves a ratio of around 1:6 with its cooling system.

Complementary to these issues, the effects of climate change are evident in the increasing frequency of hot summers, demanding greater cooling efforts. The common practice of releasing waste heat into the surrounding air contributes to further warming an already heated area over prolonged periods. Cooling aggregates and fans must operate more intensively on hot days, producing more noise that can become a nuisance to nearby residents. Addressing these energy demands by optimizing the infrastructure will be a crucial goal for the University of Freiburg in the future: Satisfy growing computational needs in a sustainable fashion.

4 Typical Power Demands of Scientific Computing

The recently decommissioned HPC system NEMO1 (Janczyk et al., 2019) serves as a concrete example to illustrate the scale of requirements and energy expenditures. The cluster occupied 11 out of the 40 available server racks, comprising approximately 1000 individual nodes, necessary peripherals such as network components, fast interconnects and a high performance parallel file system. NEMO1 had a total operational lifespan of precisely eight years, up to August 2024. The average continuous power consumption was around 160 kW. With an estimated average electricity price of € 0.22 per kWh, the total electricity cost for the system amounted to € 2.4 million. This was paid out of the university budget.[7] Overall, the energy costs over the eight-year lifespan of NEMO1 added up to approximately two-thirds of the system's initial acquisition cost.

Unlike NEMO1, which was mostly a traditional CPU-based HPC system, its successor NEMO2 in its initial procurement already included a significant amount of specialized nodes with GPUs/APUs. This partition was further extended by the state's AI funding (Wiebelt et al., 2026). This follows the current global trend to complement general

[7] Excluding later expansions and reductions in operation due to the 2022 energy crisis. Additional expenditures for cooling, server racks, and network components accounted for roughly 20 % of the total.

purpose CPU nodes with special purpose GPU nodes, in particular for AI use cases. Typically, GPU hardware has higher energy demands, but in turn produces faster results for the targeted problems.

5 Implementation Options and Building Blocks

Approaches to reducing energy demand encompass all aspects necessary for system operation, ranging from the basic infrastructure with energy supply and dissipation, to the machines and the individual compute services running on them for scientific computing and AI training.

The energy demands of electrical components vary significantly, with the largest share attributable to compute nodes. Savings in computations and the shutdown of unneeded machines have the most substantial effect. Since cooling runs effectively around the clock throughout the year, even minor optimizations in this area have financial and ecological impacts. Additionally, future legal requirements regarding the utilization of waste heat must be met.

Unlike modern mobile architectures designed for power optimization, servers exhibit significant energy demand even under low utilization. Batch systems, such as the HPC cluster or the compute portion of the de.NBI-Cloud, are designed for more or less full load operation. Other operational models may experience more fluctuating utilization patterns. Understanding the power consumption characteristics of different server configurations is crucial for optimizing the overall energy efficiency of data centers (PUE).

Optimization of Scientific Computing: One key metric for user satisfaction is the wait time from job submission to job start. Depending on the expertise of the user, the perceived quality of the system might depend more on its perceived responsiveness than on its actual throughput. One traditional strategy to cope with this cognitive distortion has been the provision of as much computational power as possible. This was the primary focus in acquiring systems for scientific computing for a long time. However, with operating costs becoming more important, both financially (energy) and socially (climate), this simple strategy needs significant rework.

The diversity of research approaches and projects makes straightforward comparability challenging. Similarly, typical operating system statistics on system utilization, such as CPU, RAM, storage, and network usage, make it difficult to estimate how well code and workflows actually perform. The following points should therefore be addressed:

- A main approach to further reducing energy demand lies in optimizing the applications themselves. Metrics need to be established to assess optimization potentials. »Low hanging fruits« should be identified and targeted first.
- Close exchange with users helps in understanding needs and optimization potentials. A general scientific support approach, as partly implemented through bwHPC-S5 or research data management for handling large data sets, can be beneficial. Experience shows that focusing on the user group with the least experience often achieves significant progress.
- A Single Point of Contact can ensure sensible routing of requests so that applications are executed on the most suitable infrastructure.
- For selecting the appropriate platform, a much more holistic approach should be adopted, allowing further routing to external third parties outside the bwHPC network, such as the bwCloud-OS or suitable commercial clouds, e.g. under the OCRE framework agreement. Strategic offloading of certain computations to external infrastructures can reduce wait times without creating long-term dependencies.
- Despite increasing demands for interactive and ad-hoc use of compute resources, a relatively uniform non-interactive usage pattern can be achieved via cross-system meta-scheduling, as already used by some services (e.g., Galaxy) and groups (e.g., particle physics).
- To promote sustainability awareness, projects could be required to apply for a defined energy budget rather than a fixed number of CPU/GPU hours. Shifting proposals from estimating compute time to estimating energy demand would encourage greater attention to energy efficiency.

These considerations should be supported by appropriate incentives. Initial ideas, such as awarding prizes for related research at conferences like the HPC Symposium, have already been implemented. Similarly, funding priorities can be realigned to emphasize optimization over a pure focus on hardware. The goal must be to initiate a cultural change that recognizes activities in scientific computing for optimizing workflows and code as independent scientific achievements. Furthermore, it should be possible to apply for compensation for consulting and support services aimed at energetic optimization.

Future Design of HPC systems and Operational Models: The rapid progress and frequent changes of GPU technologies should be addressed through timed renewal cycles. Instead of a single large-scale procurement, it is more sensible to replace the hardware in staged batches to yield sensible lot sizes for tender procedures, and allow data centers to provide researchers with up-to-date hardware on a regular basis. Consequently, the total capacity for scientific computing and AI can be adjusted more closely and more quickly to the actual demand. This matches an operational model that foresees dynamic, demand-driven financing (Wesner et al., 2016), e.g. funding that follows the creation of new professorships or project grants. For older equipment an on-demand model can be employed: the hardware is powered down and only switched on when a short-term, high-intensity need arises (e.g., an interactive job or a large teaching event with a brief runtime). A further degree of flexibility can be achieved by moving hardware between different operational paradigms, such as the traditionally batch-oriented HPC model and a more dynamic, cloud-like model (Lafayette et al., 2019).

With the idea of a continuously running HPC system abandoned, new opportunities lie ahead: Together with suitable energy suppliers it should be investigated whether a cost-optimizing control of the system is economically justified. The concept is to disconnect a defined part of the compute systems from the power grid for a pre-planned interval, thereby relieving the grid during peak-load periods. Key research questions are:

- How can an efficient *hibernate* of part of the HPC system be realised?
- How large is the lost computational capacity during the off-period, and how does it compare with the monetary savings on the electricity bill?
- At which price differential does the approach become financially viable, given the initial investment costs, operational costs and computational throughput?

Operating scientific-computing and AI infrastructures in this way poses particular challenges when large loads have to be switched on or off simultaneously. The local power grid must be capable of handling such steep changes, or the control system must implement a staged ramp-up/ramp-down. The latter requires appropriate control primitives (e.g., command-and-control frameworks) for the affected server groups and racks.

A further variant is a cold-standby concept: Older server hardware is kept in reserve for ad-hoc events such as massive cloud-based courses, or de-commissioned HPC clusters are powered up only when exceptionally cheap, green electricity is available. Implementation is straightforward provided sufficient rack space and network connectivity exist; however, it reduces the available »re-routing« area for future upgrades. Moreover, a trade-off emerges between the baseline cost of maintaining these spare racks and the potential savings obtained by postponing hardware replacement.

Long-running jobs are particularly costly in terms of energy. Therefore, optimizing the workload is a precondition for most of the measures discussed above: Partition (or compartmentalise) large jobs so that they can be executed in shorter, more manageable chunks. Ensure that jobs are suspend-resume safe, enabling rapid pre-emptive shutdown of idle resources without loss of progress.

Planning New Server Rooms for the University: At the level of physical infrastructure, the buildings and server rooms, the pursuit of energy-efficiency is strongly shaped by organizational aspects. This includes the implications for planning that stem from the rectorates and the university units that are responsible for implementation. Numerous studies on the concrete design of climate-neutral data centers already exist (Köddering et al., 2021), but their applicability to our specific context still has to be verified. Server rooms must be certified according to legal requirements; aiming for a high-level certification forces the adoption of measures that improve energy efficiency.

Due to the physical limits of semiconductor scaling, performance gains in modern GPUs and CPUs are increasingly accompanied by higher energy consumption. Higher performance entails greater power draw and, consequently, increased heat dissipation requirements. As device dimensions continue to shrink, ever-higher thermal loads must be removed through only marginally larger chip packages. Conventional air-cooled systems are approaching practical limits in fan speed and airflow, which has driven the growing adoption of hot-water cooling (HWC). Compared with air cooling, HWC operates at substantially higher coolant temperatures, often enabling the elimination of compressor-based chillers. Air-cooled solutions that rely on inlet temperatures of 8–12 °C are becoming increasingly costly, as the temperature differential to ambient conditions continues to grow. Although HWC systems typically involve higher initial capital costs, they are more compact and frequently more energy-efficient in operation. As power densities in scientific computing and AI architectures continue to rise, system availability is increasingly shifting toward HWC. Accordingly, hot-water cooling is planned for approximately half of the rack capacity at the new site currently under design, with a focus on compute-intensive and energy-demanding workloads. From a long-term strategic perspective, this trend also informs state-wide infrastructure planning. In particular, the option of a joint Tier-3 data center at a single location is under consideration, where access to renewable energy sources and the effective reuse of waste heat could provide significant advantages.

Energy-Sensitive Procurement: The topic has been addressed in a broader sense and already incorporates optimization of the entire IT-infrastructure operation. In previous tenders for large numbers of desktop PCs and for the predecessor HPC cluster, the energy demand was already taken into account, but turned out to not be critical for the final decision. Today, the energy efficiency of IT components is a central tender criterion – it was a decisive factor in the procurement of NEMO2 (Wiebelt et al., 2026). Suppliers therefore had to steer clear of the long-standing peak-performance paradigm: the last few percentage points of a system's speed often cost a disproportionate amount of additional energy for a marginal gain in computational throughput.

This focus alone is insufficient though. Demands that are not covered yet by joint infrastructures such as HPC or cloud should be considered as well. To enforce both energy sensitivity and consolidation, the university's IT-procurement processes need to be restructured. Early alignment of requirements with state-wide and campus-wide consolidated offers would allow better scaling. The incentive grows when a transparent cost accounting for all aspects of operation is available; this accounting also serves as input for further optimization.

Energy and System Monitoring: Certain requirements for energy monitoring already arise from the Energy Efficiency Act. For resource-monitoring reasons, the central data centers on campus have recorded real-time and aggregated energy consumption, broken down by individual infrastructures such as the HPC cluster, AI infrastructure, cloud and storage systems. By linking usage to the inventory data of the server rooms, it is possible to translate utilization shares into energy costs allocated to faculties, institutes or research groups. This provides transparency regarding the effort and utilization of the respective infrastructures and would enable a charge-back of electricity costs – a practice already established at other HPC sites, e.g. for the bwUniCluster. The organizational framework for this is the bwIT Alliance[8] that has been created recently.

Consolidation of Basic IT Building Blocks: Consolidation can achieve significant resource savings. Server and storage virtualization increase utilization and make the holding of reserve capacity far cheaper, because not every project or service operates at 100 % utilization all the time, yet they are required to plan for that worst-case scenario. Central virtualization structures (hypervisor stacks, cloud platforms and HPC services) have been available for a long time. Numerous concrete steps have already been taken and the amount of decentralized server installations has been reduced markedly over the past decade. Further savings can be realized by exploiting temporal load fluctuations:

- Consolidate virtual machines onto fewer hosts when the load is (significantly) lower, e.g. during night-time, weekends, or when interactive sessions are idle.
- Migrate VMs so that hosts are better utilized and VMs are packed more tightly.
- Apply suspend-resume for low-priority workloads.
- Run a watchdog/monitoring service that identifies suitable VMs for migration, empties hosts, and switches those hosts off.

Campus-wide server-room consolidation should be continued. In long-term strategic planning the university is even considering locating the next generation of compute resources at a site with a significantly more favourable energy and climate profile than Germany's warmest metropolis.

Training and Software Development: Effective measures for improving efficiency in scientific computing and AI are not self-explanatory because they involve several layers and entry points. Consequently, they must be supported by training and education. This should accompany the cultural change toward a stronger awareness of energy costs in scientific computing and AI usage. Enhanced qualification of early-career researchers can help them use HPC systems or new technologies such as AI much more efficiently. A possible model is provided by the SIM-Labs at other research support organizations (e.g. KIT, HLRS), which focus on code development and optimization (Suchodoletz et al., 2026b). A certification could serve as proof of competence in using these systems

[8] See https://uni-tuebingen.de/it/einrichtungen/zentrum-fuer-datenverarbeitung/bwit-aw/, visited on 07.07.2025

efficiently. Higher-tier concepts, such as scientific peer review of large compute-time requests, could also be considered. First concrete consequences have already been drawn for the current HPC and DIC framework concept (Suchodoletz et al., 2026b), which aim to realise HPC and cloud support for scientific computing in a more integrated way, thereby enabling energy-efficient routing of compute jobs.

Heat-Recovery and Additional Measures: The two data center sites for scientific computing of Freiburg University – both the existing campus data center and the new building currently in planning – are subject to the aforementioned Energy-Efficiency Act (*EnEfG* 2023). The existing main data-center location could already benefit from a feasibility study carried out in 2023 that examined the utilization of waste heat by a local district-heating provider. The study concluded that, especially when the computer center waste-heat is combined with further heat contributors in the cooling distribution infrastructure of the institute quarter, the overall heat-recovery potential becomes even more attractive. Moreover, the study identified optimization options that can raise cooling efficiency and thereby modestly expand the usable cooling capacity. Exploiting these options could alleviate bottlenecks that are expected to arise from the massive expansion of AI workloads and from the delayed commissioning of the new site. During the planning phase of the new location, heat-recovery was already incorporated into the technical design. In this context, hot-water cooling is advantageous because the higher temperature levels in the supply and return lines simplify the extraction and integration of waste heat into the district-heating network.

Given the continuously high power demand, on-site photovoltaic (PV) generation is a natural complement as a local source of renewable electricity. The data center is housed in a building that offers a large, flat roof free of other installations, providing ample area for PV modules (Ministerium für Finanzen Baden-Württemberg, 2023). As an additional measure to mitigate the increasingly hot summer conditions – and the resulting deterioration of working conditions in the strongly illuminated offices – shading of the façade with PV-integrated louvres should be considered. A comparable solution has already been implemented on the sister building in Heidelberg.

6 Conclusion and Outlook

Scientific computing and AI account for a large share of the university's total electricity bill. The associated costs should be invested wisely – primarily through workflow- and code-optimization – while the ecological footprint must be reduced. Obvious levers are on-site PV and waste-heat recovery, yet only a tiny fraction of university roofs and parking-lot areas are equipped with PV; the implementation process is slow and often never even starts in contrast to the stated goals of the state (Ministerium für Finanzen Baden-Württemberg, 2023). The necessary »green-science« steps are tangled in the responsibilities of three ministries (Environment, Science, research and culture, Finance), with building-related decisions being the heaviest burden for any sustainability project. A feasibility study conducted two-plus years ago showed that waste heat from the data center and laboratory cooling could be fed into a forthcoming district-heating network, but the project has not progressed. Besides the environmental conscience of today's and future student generations, the university incurs tangible financial losses from untapped potential. Addressing this requires coordinated action among the university, the city, the state, and energy utilities.

The research community can help by taking several concrete steps: the legacy HPC system was tuned primarily for peak performance, which allowed its replacement to be delayed, whereas the new system has been procured with future electricity prices and efficiency criteria already built in. Dynamic service operation was first applied to the deep-learning cluster of the technical faculty, which is switched off during periods of low demand. This mode of operating will be progressively extended to the bwCloud-OS infrastructure and the Galaxy workflow system. Additional funding for code optimization, which was previously postponed because of high staff costs and a lack of expertise, should be paired with targeted training programs. Monitoring is being expanded so that transparent, per-job kWh usage can be reported for individual systems, institutes and research groups. By aligning job characteristics with these flexible, energy-aware operational models, the HPC center can markedly reduce both its financial and ecological footprint while still fulfilling the scientific and educational needs of its user community. Ongoing work on the HPC-DIC concept (Suchodoletz et al., 2026b) and forthcoming strategy papers will formalize this vision, giving the state of Baden-Württemberg another opportunity to assume a pioneering role in sustainable high-performance computing.

Acknowledgments

We thank the Ministry of Science, Research and Arts Baden-Württemberg for the support of the bwHPC-S5, de.NBI and bwCloud 3 projects and the Ministry of the Environment for supporting the referenced Study on the Use of Waste Heat (UM15-0272-36/5/4).

Corresponding Author

Armin Saur: armin.saur@rz.uni-freiburg.de
eScience Department, Computer Center Albert-Ludwigs university,
Hermann-Herder-Str. 10, 79104 Freiburg, Deutschland

ORCID

Armin Saur https://orcid.org/0009-0003-8037-7288
Dirk von Suchodoletz https://orcid.org/0000-0002-4382-5104
Bernd Wiebelt https://orcid.org/0000-0003-2771-4524
Björn Grüning https://orcid.org/0000-0002-3079-6586

References

DIN (2019). *DIN EN 50600-4-2: Data centre facilities and infrastructure — Part 4-2: Energy efficiency — Energy efficiency assessment methodology*. Standard EN 50600-4-2. August 2019 edition. Deutsches Institut für Normung (DIN). URL: https://www.din.de/en.

EnEfG (2023). *Gesetz zur Steigerung der Energieeffizienz in Deutschland*. URL: https://www.gesetze-im-internet.de/enefg/BJNR1350B0023.html.

IEA (2023). *World Energy Outlook 2023*. Report 2023/WEO. Accessed: 2025-12-17. Paris, France: International Energy Agency. DOI: 10.18186/2023-WEO.

– (2024). *Electricity 2024 – Analysis*. IEA. URL: https://www.iea.org/reports/electricity-2024 (visited on 19. 08. 2025).

– (2025). *Electricity 2025 – Analysis*. IEA. URL: https://www.iea.org/reports/electricity-2025 (visited on 19. 08. 2025).

Janczyk, M., D. von Suchodoletz and B. Wiebelt (2019). »bwForCluster NEMO. Forschungscluster für die Wissenschaft«. In: *Proceedings of the 5th bwHPC Symposium. HPC Activities in Baden-Württemberg*. Freiburg, September 2018. 5th bwHPC Symposium. Ed. by M. Janczyk, D. von Suchodoletz and B. Wiebelt. TLP, Tübingen, pp. 29–50. DOI: 10.15496/publikation-29041.

Kocot, B., P. Czarnul and J. Proficz (2023). »Energy-Aware Scheduling for High-Performance Computing Systems: A Survey«. In: *Energies* 16.2. ISSN: 1996-1073. DOI: 10.3390/en16020890.

Köddering, K., A. Gruber, J. Peters and N. L. Kranich (2021). »Climate-neutral data-center design – concepts, challenges and roadmap«. In: *Sustainable Computing: Informatics and Systems* 33, p. 100658. DOI: 10.1016/j.suscom.2021.100658.

Krieglstein, K. (2021). *Klimaschutzkonzept der Albert-Ludwigs-Universität Freiburg*. Universität Freiburg, Arbeitskreis Nachhaltige Universität Freiburg. URL: https://www.nachhaltige.uni-freiburg.de/de/laufende-projekte/klimaschutzkonzept-uni-freiburg.

Lafayette, L. et al. (2019). »The Chimera and the Cyborg«. In: *Advances in Science, Technology and Engineering Systems Journal* 4.2, pp. 1–7. DOI: 10.25046/aj040201.

Ministerium für Finanzen Baden-Württemberg, ed. (2023). *Energie- und Klimaschutzkonzept für Landesliegenschaften 2030*. URL: https://fm.baden-wuerttemberg.de/fileadmin/redaktion/m-fm/intern/Publikationen/230711_EuK.pdf.

Speck, D., ed. (2007). *550 Jahre Albert-Ludwigs-Universität Freiburg: Festschrift*. Originalausg. Freiburg: Alber. 5 pp.

Suchodoletz, D. von et al. (2026a). »bwSFS – A Federated Storage Backbone for Research Data Management. A Foundational Infrastructure for RDM Services«. In: *Proceedings of the 10th bwHPC Symposium. HPC Activities in Baden-Württemberg*. Freiburg, September 2024. 10th bwHPC Symposium. Ed. by M. Janczyk, D. von Suchodoletz, B. Wiebelt and M. Frank. KIT Scientific Publishing, Karlsruhe, pp. 247–263. DOI: 10.58895/ksp/1000169488-16.

Suchodoletz, D. von et al. (2026b). »Framework Concept of the Universities in the State of Baden-Württemberg. High-Performance Computing (HPC) and Data-Intensive Computing (DIC) in the Period 2025–2032«. In: *Proceedings of the 10th bwHPC Symposium. HPC Activities in Baden-Württemberg*. Freiburg, September 2024. 10th bwHPC Symposium. Ed. by M. Janczyk, D. von Suchodoletz, B. Wiebelt and M. Frank. KIT Scientific Publishing, Karlsruhe, pp. 195–211. DOI: 10.58895/ksp/1000169488-13.

Wesner, S., D. von Suchodoletz and G. Schneider (2016). »Überlegungen zu laufenden Cluster-Erweiterungen in bwHPC«. In: *Kooperation von Rechenzentren, Governance und Steuerung - Organisation, Rechtsgrundlagen, Politik*. Ed. by D. von Suchodoletz, J. C. Schulz, J. Leendertse, H. Hotzel and M. Wimmer. Berlin, Boston: De Gruyter Oldenbourg, pp. 331–342. DOI: 10.1515/9783110459753-028.

Wiebelt, B., D. von Suchodoletz and M. Janczyk (2026). »bwForCluster NEMO 2: Sustainable Tier-3 HPC Infrastructure. Finding DORIE: Diskless Architecture enabling Optimized, Reproducible,

Integrated, and Efficient HPC Operations«. In: *Proceedings of the 10th bwHPC Symposium. HPC Activities in Baden-Württemberg*. Freiburg, September 2024. 10th bwHPC Symposium. Ed. by M. Janczyk, D. von Suchodoletz, B. Wiebelt and M. Frank. KIT Scientific Publishing, Karlsruhe, pp. 213–228. DOI: 10.58895/ksp/1000169488-14.

IV Infrastructure and Data Management

Framework Concept of the Universities in the State of Baden-Württemberg[1]

High-Performance Computing (HPC) and Data-Intensive Computing (DIC) in the Period 2025–2032

Dirk von Suchodoletz[†], Bernhard Neumair[†], Martin Frank[*],
Vincent Heuveline[*], Thomas Walter[*], Steffen Wendzel[*], Oliver Kohl-Frey[*],
Stefan Farrenkopf[*], Alexander Pfister[*], Jörn Beutner[*], Michael Resch[*],
Raphael Dorn[‡], Thomas Nau[†]

[*]Member of the Directors of the Computing (or Information) Centers of the Universities of the State of Baden-Württemberg Working Group (ALWR-BW)
[†]Member at the time of writing of the document, left committee since then
[‡]Ministry of Science, Research and Arts Baden-Württemberg (MWK)

1 Strategic Objectives

Digital infrastructures and associated services have become the backbone of scientific research across nearly all disciplines. Therefore, a high-performance computing (HPC) concept must address a multitude of challenges, including the increasing digitization of workflows, advancements in natural sciences instrumentation, new research approaches in digital humanities, enhanced resolution in imaging techniques, and the growing application of artificial intelligence (AI). Publicly funded and operated research infrastructures are crucial in this context. Federated structures generate synergies and offer clear strategic advantages over isolated solutions, particularly in HPC and data-

[1] This paper is a translated and slightly shortened version of the German publication (Suchodoletz et al., 2023) reviewed and recommended by the German Science Foundation (DFG).

intensive computing (DIC). To benefit users, these structures must be reliably, sustainably, and future-proof developed based on long-established foundations. In line with Baden-Württemberg's scientific and economic standing, they should promote human-centric digitalization, co-shape modern technological developments, unleash additional creativity, and support the broad distribution of competencies. Based on international standards, digital services must be suitably networked at all levels (local, regional, national, and international). To enhance Baden-Württemberg's attractivity, and to transform universities into attractive employers for IT professionals, the following strategic objectives have been established:

- Ensuring globally competitive hardware and software provision for the entire scientific community in the state in the field of HPC/DIC
- Integration into European and national HPC/DIC strategies, as manifested in the EuroHPC Joint Undertaking,[2] the Gauss Centre for Supercomputing (GCS),[3] National High-Performance Computing (NHR),[4] and the National Research Data Infrastructure (NFDI)[5]
- Transfer of knowledge and skills gained in HPC/DIC to society and industry

Alongside scientific challenges in high and highest-performance computing, operational challenges are increasingly emerging. In light of climate change risks, data centers must align more closely with sustainability criteria, meet future legal requirements, and contribute to reducing CO_2 emissions. A central task for the coming years is to achieve genuine climate neutrality in high and highest-performance computing centers. Key areas of action include:

- Optimizing energy efficiency with the goal of climate neutrality and certification; exploring and implementing new operational models and system designs for using (volatile) renewable energy sources; retrofitting existing buildings and further consolidating sites to create a climate-positive data center; raising user awareness.
- Focusing on the sustainable development of scientific software, particularly to enhance energy efficiency; improving the qualification of young scientists to utilize HPC/DIC systems or new technologies like AI more efficiently.

[2] See https://eurohpc-ju.europa.eu/index_en, visited on 14.08.2025
[3] See http://www.gauss-centre.eu, visited on 14.08.2025
[4] See http://www.nhr-verein.de/, visited on 14.08.2025
[5] See http://www.nfdi.de/, visited on 14.08.2025

Beyond these general objectives, the strategy for 2025-2032, as before, includes flexibly responding to current challenges to swiftly and effectively support and promote new scientific developments through necessary digital infrastructure. Expected new challenges include: Research data management (RDM), the rapid growth in AI research and its application across all scientific disciplines as well as exploration and utilization of new hardware concepts in HPC/DIC, particularly quantum computing.

2 Status Quo

Over the past 40 years, Baden-Württemberg has strategically positioned itself in the HPC/DIC environment. Since the 1980s, HPC systems have been procured at various locations within the state, and the necessary connectivity has been provided through the BelWü science network. This foundation has been continuously developed both strategically and technically, and has been intertwined with (inter)national advancements. This has strengthened knowledge transfer within partner networks, as well as to users and industry. External scientific experts have repeatedly emphasized that the solutions established in Baden-Württemberg serve as a model for (inter)national infrastructures. During the term of the current concept, both the HPC described in section 2.1 and the storage systems in section 2.2 will be continuously renewed and expanded accordingly.

2.1 HPC Performance Pyramid in Baden-Württemberg

At the European level *(Tier-0)*, the GCS, with its partners LRZ (Garching), HLRS (Stuttgart), and JSC (Jülich), serves as a leading European Exaflop provider, with the Jülich site playing a pivotal role. Funding is provided through the SiVeGCS/SiVeGCS+ projects and the EuroHPC Joint Undertaking. Within GCS, HLRS coordinates major European projects for the Exascale domain of EuroHPC, currently leading the EuroCC and CASTIEL projects. At the German level *(Tier-1)*, the HLRS at the University of Stuttgart functions as a national and European high-performance computing center. Under the SiVeGCS project, funded by the Federal Ministry of Education and Research and the three state ministries for science, a Tier-1 system was commissioned at HLRS in 2020. The SiVeGCS+ extension, approved in 2021, realized a transition system in 2024 and plans an Exascale system to commence operations at HLRS in 2026/2027 to be available for national high-performance computing until 2032.

At *Tier-2*, the Scientific Computing Center (SCC) at the Karlsruhe Institute of Technology (KIT) operates as a high-performance computing center and a hub for data-intensive computing. Within the National High-Performance Computing alliance, SCC manages the Tier-2 system HoreKa, which supports various scientific disciplines, including materials science, earth system sciences, energy and mobility research in engineering, and particle and astroparticle physics. SCC leads the support for Research Software Engineering and significantly contributes to numerical methods and libraries within the NHR alliance. During the period covered by this paper, major computer procurements are planned at the beginning and end of the timeline.

At *Tier-3*, based on experiences from bwGRiD (2007-2012), the state-wide Tier-3 computing cluster infrastructure was reorganized under the bwHPC implementation concept. Clusters for selected disciplines are operated at four locations (Freiburg, Heidelberg, Tübingen, Ulm) under the bwForCluster initiative. Additionally, a shared cluster for all universities in the state (bwUniCluster) was established as an entry-level resource for HPC and to provide basic computing power for all scientific disciplines not directly represented in the bwForClusters. Independent of this concept, there may be specific local computing capacities below the Tier-3 systems, which are not further considered here.

Tier-3 assignments are based on the DFG subject classification system.[6] This assignment can be adjusted and expanded, which will be addressed in the extended accompanying project. In particular, when expanding and renewing the bwForClusters, the subject-specific dedication will be adapted considering the previous usage of the systems. Engineering sciences have a special role in this assignment due to the long-standing experience in HPC usage in this field. In addition to the basic provision on the bwUniCluster, further demand is directly covered by the systems at Tier-2 and Tier-1. Therefore, the competence center for engineering sciences is also aligned across levels, benefiting from the experiences in Karlsruhe and Stuttgart.

2.2 Data Management and Storage Systems

The implementation concept of the state for data-intensive services – bwDATA (Hartenstein et al., 2013) and the HPC/DIC concept for the years 2018-2024 (Schneider et al.,

[6] See Figure 1 in (Suchodoletz et al., 2023) and http://www.dfg.de/dfg_profil/gremien/fachkollegien/faecher/, visited on 14.08.2025

2019) aimed to provide outstanding storage and data management systems for all scientific disciplines represented in the state. These systems support the entire scientific data life cycle, from data generation in HPC systems or experiments, through data evaluation, to storage in repositories and archive systems. To ensure seamless integration and easy data migration between all systems for users, the systems are federated and connected, among other things, through the results of the accompanying project bwHPC-S5. In addition to the storage systems of the HPC systems, whose assignment follows the subject classification of the HPC systems, and a general archive system at KIT (bwDataArchive), the following storage and data management systems are currently in user operation: The LSDF of Heidelberg and Karlsruhe and the bwSFS primarily of Tübingen and Freiburg, later extended by Stuttgart and Hohenheim universities (Suchodoletz et al., 2026).

2.3 Science Data Network BelWü

The BelWü science network provides a high-performance, highly available infrastructure in the state as a basis for accessing HPC systems and networking HPC systems with data management and storage systems. This infrastructure is continuously developed with state funding. The predominantly exclusively used fiber optic infrastructure (dark fiber) and the proprietary IP system platform based on it provide great flexibility for further development and high future security regarding increasing bandwidth requirements and new network functionality. High-performance transitions to other science networks such as X-WiN and Switch, as well as to commercial networks, ensure that internationally networked researchers in Baden-Württemberg find optimal conditions for technical networking.

2.4 Scientific Support and Governance

These hardware structures have been complemented by shared, synergistic operational frameworks within the accompanying project *bwHPC-S5*, system- and cross-layer software provisioning, an excellent coordinated multi-level user support infrastructure as well as IT security operations. All supporting structures contribute significantly to the consolidation of computing resources, leading to a more sustainable and efficient use of funds and personnel. Accompanying projects have also established structures for the technological advancement of systems, where – through initiatives such as technology sprints – new HPC developments are evaluated for their applicability, and ensure highly efficient use of research infrastructure and its continuous optimization – including in terms of Green IT. Organizationally, a layered support model is represented through the following teams:

- The *Cluster Allocation Team (CAT)* assists in assigning new HPC and DIC projects to the most suitable cluster sites in the state, ensuring optimal working conditions while maximizing resource efficiency.
- The seven *bwHPC Competence Centers* provide domain-specific expertise in scientific fields with high HPC/DIC demands to the research community: (1) Bioinformatics, Pharmacy, Medical Informatics, and Astrophysics; (2) Computational Chemistry and Quantum Sciences; (3) Geosciences; (4) Global Systems Science; (5) Engineering Sciences, (6) Particle Physics, Neuroscience, Microsystems Engineering, and Materials Science, (7) Structural and Systems Biology, Medical Science, Soft Matter, and Computational Humanities.
- *Tiger Teams* have successfully addressed well-defined research challenges for years by temporarily assembling researchers with the necessary experts (e.g., in hardware, software, or system operations) for focused sprints.[7]

Beyond these technical-scientific support layers, *governance* – understood as overarching steering bodies – is primarily carried out by three key groups: (1) Strategic decisions regarding the development of Tier-3 state clusters and state-wide data infrastructure are made by the *Working Group of Heads of Scientific Computing and Information Centers in Baden-Württemberg (ALWR-BW)*, established by the State Rectors' Conference (LRK). Requirements from other steering bodies are coordinated through the ALWR-BW and project leaders. (2) The *State User Committee (LNA-BW)* is responsible for scientific oversight of the operation and development of defined digital research infrastructures. It articulates scientific user requirements, evaluates the effectiveness of mechanisms for resource allocation and infrastructure utilization, proposes improvements to allocation and load-balancing mechanisms, and issues recommendations for enhancing the scientific alignment of projects and concepts within the HPC/DIC state strategy. (3) The *Steering Committee for Digital Research Infrastructure Baden-Württemberg* serves as the

[7] Examples of recent success stories are documented on the bwHPC project pages (Suchodoletz et al., 2023).

overarching authority, representing both operators and users of digital research infrastructures within the HPC/DIC state strategy.

2.5 Knowledge Transfer into Industry and Society

The transfer of knowledge and skills from university research to industry and society has a long-standing tradition in the state of Baden-Württemberg. Initial steps were already taken in 1986, with a significant milestone achieved in 1995 through the founding of the »High-Performance Computing for Science and Industry Ltd.«,[8] which facilitated knowledge transfer between academia and industry. From 2008 onward, Solution Centers were established to address specific challenges, bringing together industry and public research under one roof for collaborative HPC and DIC research and development. Today, the following centers are active: Automotive Solution Center for Simulation,[9] Smart Data Solution Center,[10] and Media Solution Center.[11] A Medical Solution Center got established a little bit later. To specifically support small and medium-sized enterprises (SMEs), the state of Baden-Württemberg, in collaboration with KIT and the University of Stuttgart, founded SICOS BW in 2011.[12]

3 Challenges and Domains of Action

The state strategy must address diverse challenges, including significant technological shifts, the growing role of AI, and the increasing integration of digital methods across scientific disciplines. To meet these challenges, comprehensive application support is essential to achieve goals in energy efficiency, sustainability, utilization of new hardware architectures, development of high-performance research software, efficient data management, and handling of sensitive data. Digital sovereignty must be a central consideration in all actions under this state strategy, permeating all identified areas of focus.

[8] HWW, see https://www.hww.de/, visited on 13.08.2025
[9] ASCS, see https://www.asc-s.de/, visited on 13.08.2025
[10] SDSC-BW, see https://www.sdsc-bw.de/, visited on 13.08.2025
[11] MSC-BW, see https://www.msc-bw.com/, visited on 13.08.2025
[12] See https://www.sicos-bw.de/, visited on 13.08.2025

3.1 Scientific Requirements

Historically, simulation applications have consistently used available computing power, and this trend will continue as they balance system size and computational capacity. The demands for both data volume and computing power are expected to grow super-exponentially: Climate simulations at kilometer-scale resolution are expected to significantly enhance predictive accuracy by resolving effects previously represented through parameterization. Digital twins of real systems can become increasingly realistic by incorporating more and smaller subsystems. Scientific experiments and observations will soon generate exponentially growing data volumes in ever-shorter timeframes (»data avalanche«). Breakthroughs in machine learning (ML) and AI rely on increasingly large models that require successful training.

The digital transformation in research also reaches new communities beyond traditonal HPC and DIC users, such as those in the humanities and economics, which require both capacity and support to get started. The diversification of research areas necessitates specific methodological approaches in HPC and DIC, e.g. Machine learning requires close integration of high-performance computing and data management resources. Additionally, the close integration of measurement devices – such as high-throughput microscopes – with HPC and DIC systems across different locations is essential.

Finally, scientific activities are now highly interdisciplinary, requiring collaborative solutions across communities. This is reflected in decentralized IT solutions that must meet compatibility requirements to enable data exchange. Participation and mechanisms for permeability across institutions and national borders must be considered to meet research needs. The goal is to provide science with sustainable (in terms of reliability and resource conservation) and extensive HPC/DIC capacities (both hardware and support) tailored to their needs.

The further development of support structures is of particular importance within the new strategy, as they form the basis for the efficient use of HPC/DIC infrastructure by a large and growing number of researchers and scientific communities. In addition to classic HPC consulting, onboarding for the use of scientific IT infrastructures is becoming increasingly important. This requires a holistic assessment of the individual needs of a research project and, in the next step, appropriate mapping to a local, statewide, or higher-level research infrastructure. In principle, the previous path of creating synergies through statewide cooperation should continue to be pursued. In particular, sites without HPC/DIC systems should continue to be included in statewide user support. Significant parts of user support should continue to be provided by the accompanying project bwHPC-S5.

To meet new challenges and requirements, the following developments and additions are specifically planned for support structures and the bwHPC-S5 project: Further development of the subject structure, e.g., with regard to the Excellence Strategy of the DFG and BMBF; addressing the special needs of medicine and economics; further development of competence centers, e.g., with regard to supporting AI/ML methods. Intensified collaboration between scientific users, methodological research, and computing centers can be achieved by establishing Simulation & Data Labs for scientific fields of particular importance in Baden-Württemberg. Overall, high-quality and reliably plannable support for researchers in the long term will only be achievable if sustainable personnel development also takes place in the support and operating centers. Personnel recruitment is already a very serious problem today, given the high proportion of fixed-term positions.

3.2 Energy Efficiency and Sustainability

Ensuring the supply of globally competitive HPC/DIC systems to the entire scientific community in Baden-Württemberg increasingly presents challenges in terms of energy efficiency and sustainability. The energy demand of high-performance and supercomputers has increased approximately tenfold over the past 20 years, accompanied by rising cooling requirements and their associated consequences.

HPC/DIC systems face a fundamental cost shift as Moore's Law and Dennard scaling reach their limits. Performance gains now depend on larger, more power-hungry chips rather than efficiency improvements. Before 2022's energy price surges, a system's five-year electricity costs already matched its purchase price. By the end of this strategy's timeline, operating costs may far exceed acquisition costs, making energy efficiency a critical priority.

Climate protection and sustainability also require that energy efficiency becomes a key criterion in the procurement and operation of systems. To increase energy efficiency, the consistent use of advanced cooling techniques, utilization of waste heat, and integration of HPC/DIC system supply into combined heat, power, and cooling systems on campus are targeted. The goal is to maximize scientific knowledge gain per unit of energy consumed. To strengthen a consistently sustainable setup at all operator sites following the Green IT state strategy, certification of all centers according to EMAS or a comparable standard is planned. Where not already done, the switch to renewable energy sources should be considered. Through the practiced decoupling of broad scientific support and the actual location of discipline-specific equipment, a central approach could be the consolidation of Tier-3 hardware at an optimal operating site. New operating models must also be examined and implemented like considering energy consumption rather than computing time to creates incentives to make codes energy-efficient, for example through porting them to accelerators. Future system designs and operation could be more closely aligned with the availability of renewable energy, e.g. through dynamic load adjustments. Further objectives include close user support to (energetically) improve their workflows and select the optimal software for their research questions. All measures affecting users should be preceded by awareness-raising and preparatory actions within the accompanying project.

3.3 System Components and Architectures

An effective HPC/DIC strategy requires balancing innovation with stability – avoiding both premature adoption of unproven architectures and over-reliance on outdated systems. GPUs and accelerators now offer higher performance for specialized tasks but demand greater programming effort. Future »fused« chips integrating GPU and CPU cores may simplify programming, though economic viability, energy efficiency, and physical limits remain challenges. Energy-efficient hardware development will prioritize new CPU architectures and accelerators. Collaborative innovation labs – linking HPC centers and research institutions – will explore emerging technologies like quantum computing and AI, testing hardware, algorithms, software, and applications. While quantum computing's scientific utility remains uncertain, disruptive technologies (e.g., tensor processing units, monolithic chips) must be monitored and evaluated for integration. Cloud providers now offer HPC/DIC resources, raising questions about public vs. private provision. Hybrid models like cloud bursting, offloading excess jobs to cloud data centers, could optimize capacity, but data sovereignty and protection must guide decisions. System evolution will also emphasize interactive, cloud-like access – via dedicated HPC partitions, expanded OS support (e.g., Windows), and virtualization/containers. These changes aim to engage new communities (e.g., economics) and enable in-situ computing to minimize data transfers. Flexibility and energy efficiency will drive hardware and software co-design.

3.4 Software

Software has become a key component of scientific work, and there is hardly any research discipline today that does not require the use of software. Algorithms and knowledge are encoded in software. While open-source software allows direct co-development and further development by the scientific community, proprietary software carries risks due to regularly changing price and license models. The challenge is to set new standards for the development of outstanding research software and to lead research software engineering into a new era. This is particularly important in the context of increasing energy efficiency and sustainability, especially of HPC systems. If the goal is not only to achieve »more HPC cycles per kWh« but also »more knowledge gain per kWh,« energy-optimized research software is a crucial component.

Large-scale equipment, services, and other resources related to research software are ubiquitously used by the scientific community. Therefore, research software must meet the same stringent requirements that researchers place on their data, samples, equipment, and infrastructures. Software must – like any other infrastructure – be continuously developed, maintained, and supported, sometimes over decades. Successful and sustainable software projects often rely on strong, thriving, and usually international communities and always require long-term funding. For example, the Dutch eScience Centre states in its strategy paper: »Research software must be treated on a par with research data and publications at the political level and in practice«.[13] The British Software Sustainability Institute simply states: »Better Software, Better Research«.[14]

At the state level, research software must also be sustainably treated as a vital infrastructure for the needs of modern science to secure scientific insights and breakthroughs. Excellent research software can also develop into successful services. In particular, open-source software offers numerous approaches to increasing computational efficiency and continuous adaptation to new hardware architectures and operating models. The (further) development of open research software and algorithms deepens researchers' un-

[13] See https://doi.org/10.5281/zenodo.3378572, visited on 13.08.2025

[14] See https://www.software.ac.uk/resources/publications/better-software-better-research, visited on 13.08.2025

derstanding and creates a broad basis for knowledge transfer to industry and society. This can set further impulses for all our research disciplines and maintain and expand Baden-Württemberg's leading role in scientific computing in Germany and beyond. The challenges are:

- Creating awareness that research software is an essential part of the state research infrastructure that must be implemented and operated accordingly;
- Recognizing research software as a legitimate research output;
- Creating a sustainable and professional approach to the development and management of energy-optimized research software through appropriate support structures and services, as well as motivated and adequately compensated research software engineers;
- Supporting communities in creating optimized software, particularly regarding energy requirements, for their research work and offering this support to all partners and stakeholders. Support is particularly needed for highly scalable parallel software, adaptation to modern computer architecture (e.g., GPU), optimized numerical methods for simulation, software sustainability and performance engineering, continuous integration services, and continuous development.

Experience in the HPC field has clearly shown that considering the underlying hardware alone is not sufficient for successful use in research. Software development plays a decisive role, not only for performance gains but also for energy efficiency. The underlying computer architectures of HPC systems are increasingly heterogeneous, leading to high complexity, e.g. reflected in the use of accelerators such as GPUs and FPGAs, which must work in coordination with CPUs. Multicore technology, now ubiquitous in computer architectures, requires specific concepts for optimal use. Thus, the greatest potential for performance gains lies in software development; optimally with the involvement of researchers.

Significant software adaptations are often required, becoming an increasingly important part of research activities. If not done sustainably, the result is often unmaintainable software and non-reproducible science. This is due to a lack of software engineering training for researchers, limited funds for further development and maintenance of existing software, and few permanent software developer positions. The intended strategy aims to promote and thereby improve the development of scientific software to ensure reproducible science and software sustainability. The planned measures should serve as a link between different scientific disciplines and thus enable collaboration and interdisciplinary research. A three-pillar concept should be implemented for the software strategy, focusing on development, teaching, and public relations.

According to the UK Research Software Survey 2014 (Goble, 2014), 69 % of researchers state that their research would no longer be feasible without research software. 56 % of the 417 surveyed researchers develop their own research software. Accordingly, the present concept provides for the strong promotion and support of software development for scientific research activities on HPC systems. This applies both to the development of open-source numerical building blocks adapted to the respective systems and to the adaptation of existing software to the available computer architecture. These activities will not only be carried out by the HPC centers but will also draw on the competencies of the respective universities in the field of scientific computing and software development. Furthermore, courses on all aspects of sustainable software development as well as mentoring programs should be offered, particularly for pre- and postdocs at the universities of Baden-Württemberg. The same applies to experienced researchers who should be able to take advantage of corresponding advanced training and conferences in the domain of software development.

A statewide format should be initiated with the aim of promoting initiatives in the field of software development and teaching and a corresponding HPC software ecosystem with high visibility should be established statewide through concrete projects. These should focus on long-term software solutions. Through these measures, a competence should be further developed that can be utilized by all researchers on the HPC systems of Baden-Württemberg. The focus should initially be on the areas of AI, machine learning, and data analytics.

3.5 Data Management and Storage Systems

Data volumes produced in future measurements, observations, or simulations most probably will grow exponentially. However, significant energy consumption only occurs when data is processed or analyzed. The discipline-specific specialization of compute and post-processing and data analysis systems, as well as research data management, require increasingly better integration of digital research infrastructures throughout the entire data lifecycle (see Sect. 2.2). Researchers collect or receive data from sources that, like further processing, visualization, and subsequent provision to third parties, no longer need to be located at their own site. With the increasing expansion of statewide storage systems, their use is growing. Here, the researchers' ideas of easily integrable workflows with direct data access must be aligned with the possibilities of distributed systems.

The challenges in the area of research data are addressed through the consistent further development of data management and storage systems in the BW Data Federation. While the basics are laid here by a uniform authentication and authorization structure, many workflows require copying data to the respectively optimized storage area, for example, of an HPC system or for later secure storage in a data publication repository. Such a »copy« data federation should be extended to a »mount« one for suitable use cases, allowing data to be loaded in one place and directly used in another. The rapid movement of large data volumes requires both the availability of fast data networks and integration into future scheduling and staging systems. Another step is the increased establishment of an object storage federation, which, on the one hand, significantly simplifies remote data access compared to network file systems but requires a rethink on the application and workflow side. In the medium and long term, repositories for data publication and long-term archiving must support research data management through both generic and community-specific metadata provision via intelligent search functions and well-defined APIs.

3.6 Handling Sensitive Data

Researchers in bioinformatics, neuroscience, medical science, and computational humanities frequently process sensitive data – including genetic, biometric, health, and socio-economic data – all governed by EU GDPR. While research purposes often justify data use, explicit consent and ethics committee approvals remain mandatory. HPC operators, acting as GDPR processors, must establish data processing agreements or documented SOPs. Concepts are needed that enable the storage and processing of such personal data at other operator sites within the group of state universities. Some sites, particularly those with a strong biomedical focus, have addressed this issue through certification. All operators are implementing ISMS (ISO 27001/BSI-C5 certification recommended) to ensure verifiable data security and strengthen researcher trust in bwHPC infrastructure as current bwForClusters have limited suitability for high-protection sensitive data due to insufficient data/execution environment separation in distributed file systems. Future systems must incorporate robust data separation (encryption-at-rest, fine-grained ACLs, VLAN isolation) aligned with operational requirements. This requires the often personnel-intensive strengthening of expertise among all stakeholders orchestrated e.g. through tiger-teams.

3.7 Digital Sovereignty

For universities and research institutions, digital souvereignty is the foundation of free research, making transparency, capacity for action, and unrestricted choice of tools their guiding principles and thus the state HPC/DIC strategy. In a globalized world, not all necessary components are usually in one hand, inevitably leading to a balancing process between available digital components (chips, networks, software), suppliers (geopolitical considerations), and forms of provision (HPC on-premises, cloud). The openness of scientific results and, specifically, codes (Open Science, Open Source) represents an important criterion in the scientific field. Joint strategy development with partner institutions for coordinated action and cross-university cooperation is important to achieve synergies. Regular impact assessments are to be carried out, the necessary and accepted degree of independence to be negotiated, and the cost-effectiveness and user-friendliness of IT solutions to be evaluated. Maintaining and developing the competencies of those responsible, operators, as well as junior and senior researchers is central to making sovereign decisions. The promotion of open science and open source create the necessary prerequisites for digital sovereignty in the areas of HPC/DIC. Publicly funded science can take a pioneering role here, fulfilling its role model function for application in business and civil society.

3.8 Structures and Organization

HPC/DIC in Baden-Württemberg is integrated into international, European, and German structures. These include the GCS and NHR in Germany. At the European level, a new additional structure is developing with the EuroHPC Joint Undertaking.[15] From the users' perspective, this results in four organizational levels: the local university level, the state level BW (Tier-3 bwHPC), the federal level (Tier-1 GCS and Tier-2 NHR), and

[15] See https://eurohpc-ju.europa.eu/, visited on 13.08.2025

the European level (EuroHPC). The challenge for the university location BW and its operating institutions is to make the consistent use of these levels available to science in the state. The continuation of previous state concepts for HPC and DIC faces the challenge of further integration with new structures such as NHR and the establishment of new and deeper interfaces to specific communities, as has already been successfully implemented by de.NBI for bioinformatics.

With the NFDI, nationwide associations of individual subject communities are being created for cross-cutting standardization and further development of research data management. Many HPC communities and HPC providers in Baden-Württemberg and beyond will use NFDI services and contribute to them. This requires, on the one hand, coordination of strategies to avoid duplicate developments and, on the other hand, offers the opportunity to provide the established DIC services nationwide based on overarching AAI structures but also secured operating models, and the possibility of billing these services. In 2023, the universities and colleges of Baden-Württemberg formalized their IT cooperations of providing and using services through a framework agreement, the IT Alliance for Science based on the State Higher Education Act (LHG §6 Paragraph 1). The IT Alliance provides researchers at Baden-Württemberg's universities with a formal framework for accessing research infrastructure services outlined in this concept. It also establishes cost models and ensures legal clarity on key issues.

Remarks

We thank the Ministry of Science, Research and Arts Baden-Württemberg for the support of the bwHPC-S5 and bwCloud3 projects and the ongoing support for the renewal of the Tier-3 HPC as well as the storage infrastructures. We gratefully acknowledge the input of Caroline Ruiner, Gerhard Schneider, and Stefan Wesner.

Corresponding Author

Martin Frank: martin.frank@kit.edu
Scientific Computing Center, Hermann-von-Helmholtz-Platz 1
76344 Eggenstein-Leopoldshafen, Germany

ORCID

Dirk von Suchodoletz https://orcid.org/0000-0002-4382-5104
Martin Frank https://orcid.org/0000-0001-8562-6982
Vincent Heuveline https://orcid.org/0000-0002-2217-7558
Thomas Walter https://orcid.org/0000-0002-8656-2340
Steffen Wendzel https://orcid.org/0000-0002-1913-5912
Oliver Kohl-Frey https://orcid.org/0000-0001-7050-3701
Stefan Farrenkopf https://orcid.org/0000-0003-2640-4444
Jörn Beutner https://orcid.org/0009-0007-6648-3833
Michael Resch https://orcid.org/0000-0002-7159-9634

References

Goble, C. (2014). »Better software, better research«. In: *IEEE Internet Computing* 18.5, pp. 4–8. URL: https://www.software.ac.uk/publication/better-software-better-research.

Hartenstein, H., T. Walter and P. Castellaz (2013). »Aktuelle Umsetzungskonzepte der Universitäten des Landes Baden-Württemberg für Hochleistungsrechnen und datenintensive Dienste«. In: *PIK-Praxis der Informationsverarbeitung und Kommunikation* 36.2, pp. 99–108. DOI: 10.1515/pik-2013-0007.

Schneider, G. et al. (2019). »Umsetzungskonzept der Universitäten des Landes Baden-Württemberg für das High Performance Computing (HPC), Data Intensive Computing (DIC) und Large Scale Scientific Data Management (LS^{2}DM)«. Gekürzte Fassung. In: *Proceedings of the 5th bwHPC Symposium. HPC Activities in Baden-Württemberg*. Freiburg, September 2018. 5th bwHPC Symposium. Ed. by M. Janczyk, D. von Suchodoletz and B. Wiebelt. TLP, Tübingen, pp. 3–16. DOI: 10.15496/publikation-29040.

Suchodoletz, D. von et al. (2023). »Rahmenkonzept der Universitäten des Landes Baden-Württemberg für das High-Performance Computing (HPC) und Data-Intensive Computing (DIC) für den Zeitraum 2025 bis 2032«. In: DOI: 10.15496/publikation-90185.

Suchodoletz, D. von et al. (2026). »bwSFS – A Federated Storage Backbone for Research Data Management. A Foundational Infrastructure for RDM Services«. In: *Proceedings of the 10th bwHPC Symposium. HPC Activities in Baden-Württemberg*. Freiburg, September 2024. 10th bwHPC Symposium. Ed. by M. Janczyk, D. von Suchodoletz, B. Wiebelt and M. Frank. KIT Scientific Publishing, Karlsruhe, pp. 247–263. DOI: 10.58895/ksp/1000169488-16.

bwForCluster NEMO 2: Sustainable Tier-3 HPC Infrastructure

Finding DORIE: Diskless Architecture enabling Optimized, Reproducible, Integrated, and Efficient HPC Operations

Bernd Wiebelt, Dirk von Suchodoletz, Michael Janczyk

eScience, University of Freiburg, Freiburg, Germany

Abstract

The bwForCluster NEMO 2 is a Tier-3 HPC system at the University of Freiburg with 260 stateless provisioned compute nodes. The comprehensive renewal was completed in 2024 with heterogeneous partitions featuring AMD EPYC Milan and Genoa CPUs, NVIDIA GPUs, and AMD MI300A APUs supporting research in particle physics, neuroscience, microsystems engineering, and materials science. The system offers a full flash parallel filesystem (one Petabyte) and high performance network interconnects with 100 Gbit/s Ethernet and optional Omni-Path for MPI workloads. All nodes boot from network via GitLab CI/CD generated immutable images streamed through DNBD3, enabling versioned deployments with immediate rollback. The procurement prioritized total cost of ownership and energy efficiency. The shareholder model, established with the previous HPC system in 2016, enables research groups to acquire extended usage rights while promoting IT consolidation. The evolved security concept includes self-encrypting disks for the shared parallel file system, encrypted local NVMe drives on the compute nodes, two-tier network segmentation, and multi-factor authentication through bwIDM federated login. Administrative access requires FIDO2 SSH keys through dedicated jump hosts reducing the amount of possible attack vectors.

1 bwForCluster NEMO 2

The bwForCluster NEMO 2 is a Tier-3 high-performance-computing (HPC) system hosted at the University of Freiburg. It is an integral element of the Baden-Württemberg state-wide scientific-support infrastructure and operates under the HPC-DIC concept, a service and operational model that has been refined and expanded over almost two decades (Barthel et al., 2019; Hartenstein et al., 2013; Suchodoletz et al., 2023, 2026c). After operating the NEMO1 system, which was commissioned in August 2016 for eight years (Janczyk et al., 2019), the complete renewal was completed by the end of 2024. The system supports university research groups in the state of Baden-Württemberg, serving the domains of particle physics, neuroscience, microsystems engineering, and materials science.

User support and operations are provided by the eScience department of the University of Freiburg data center as part of bwHPC-S5 (Barthel et al., 2019). The bwHPC competence center offers consulting, support, and onboarding for researchers. NEMO2 is further an important component of the university's IT strategy for providing compute and AI capacity.[1]

1.1 Design Decisions

During the renewal process, key design decisions were made in consultation with the user community. The transition from a pure CPU platform to one supporting accelerators followed two paths. First, traditional NVIDIA CUDA GPUs were added for established workflows. Second, AMD MI300A APUs provide an innovative CPU-GPU combination with unified memory architecture, eliminating memory copies between CPU and GPU. This simplifies programming for memory-intensive scientific workloads including molecular dynamics simulations, large language model inference, and applications requiring frequent data exchange between processing units.

For MPI workloads, the Milan partition was equipped with repurposed Omni-Path hardware from NEMO1 alongside 100 GbE networking with RoCEv2 capability.[2] This dual-

[1] IT Infrastructure Concept of the University: https://uni-freiburg.de/frs/wp-content/uploads/sites/11/IT-Infrastrukturkonzept-fuer-die-Forschung.pdf, visited on 25.09.2024

[2] Remote Direct Memory Access over Converged Ethernet (Version 2) allows low latency, high-bandwidth communication between nodes like InfiniBand and Omni-Path.

network approach enables practical performance comparisons between Omni-Path and RoCEv2 for various MPI workloads, especially for latency-sensitive tightly coupled simulations.

The Genoa partition foregoes dedicated MPI networking since its high core count per node provides sufficient intra-node parallelism for Tier-3 workloads. Mellanox cards with Infiniband and Ethernet support preserve flexibility for future adaptations.

The BeeGFS parallel filesystem was replaced with Weka full flash storage, providing approximately 90 GB/s performance with redundancy through erasure coding. Technical details are described in Section 4.

NEMO2 minimizes self-operated infrastructure by utilizing university services for S3, GitLab CI/CD, and network management (Infoblox). The NEMO2 operation team focuses primarily on the aspects of core HPC operations and thus operates only boot infrastructure, Slurm controller, and monitoring systems.

System images are generated through a GitLab CI/CD pipeline combining Packer and Ansible (over 25 roles for Slurm, GPU drivers, container runtimes). Images are versioned, stored in S3, and streamed to nodes via DNBD3 with caching proxies, enabling immediate rollback. The local disk is used for write operations on the shared root filesystem provided through the block device, as scratch space and for local Slurm job directory. Implementation details can be found in Janczyk et al. (2026).

1.2 Technical Platform

NEMO2 is a traditional x86 based HPC system with 260 compute nodes across four specialized partitions that address different workload profiles (Table 1 and Figure 1).

CPU Partition 1 (AMD Milan): 137 nodes each with two AMD EPYC 7763 processors offering 64 cores at 2.45 GHz base frequency, 512 GiB RAM, and 1.92 TB of NVMe storage. Networking uses 100 GbE with RoCEv2 capability via Mellanox plus »Omni-Path 100« repurposed from NEMO1 for MPI workloads. This configuration was selected based on total cost of ownership considerations at 170 kW total power consumption. This partition provides 17,536 cores total.

Table 1: NEMO2 hardware overview (260 diskless nodes total)

Type	Configuration	Count
AMD EPYC Milan	4-in-1 chassis, racks 31–35	137
AMD EPYC Genoa	1U chassis, racks 41–46	106
AMD MI300A APU	rack 36	4
NVIDIA L40S	racks 35–36	9
NVIDIA H200	rack 44	2
Login nodes	rack 43	2
Infrastructure	rack 43, local disks (Slurm, storage, etc.)	20

CPU Partition 2 (AMD Genoa): 106 nodes each with two AMD EPYC 9654 processors offering 96 cores at 2.4 GHz base frequency, 768 GiB RAM, and 3.84 TB of NVMe storage. Networking is similar to Partition 1 but without Omni-Path since 192 cores per node provide sufficient intra-node parallelism for Tier-3 workloads. This partition was procured in a second tender round with stronger weighting of operating costs and especially energy efficiency. It provides 20,352 cores total.

APU Partition (AMD MI300A): Four nodes each with four AMD Instinct MI300A APUs providing 512 GB HBM3 per node.[3] The unified memory architecture enables seamless data access without PCI Express bottlenecks, particularly for memory-intensive scientific workloads. The MI300A APU architecture is already deployed in large Tier-1 systems such as Hunter at HLRS Stuttgart.[4] The four nodes were procured together with CPU Partition 2.

GPU Partitions (NVIDIA): Nine nodes each with four NVIDIA L40S GPUs providing 48 GB GDDR6 per GPU, and two nodes each with eight NVIDIA H200 SXM GPUs providing 141 GB HBM3e per GPU.[5] NVIDIA offers a proven software ecosystem with broad support for scientific applications. The H200 nodes were procured in 2025 with additional AI-dedicated funding from the Ministry of Science, Research and Arts Baden-Württemberg. This funding, along with additional resources from future shareholder contributions, enables flexible expansion of AI hardware as demand evolves.

[3] High Bandwidth Memory (HBM) is used in high-performance data center accelerators.
[4] See https://www.hlrs.de/de/loesungen/systeme/hunter, visited on 25.09.2024
[5] Using »Server PCI Express Module« (SXM), a high-bandwidth socket for Nvidia GPUs.

Storage (Weka Filesystem): One Petabyte of full flash storage with 13 nodes and one hot-standby node (AMD EPYC 7542P, 256 GiB RAM, eight 15.36 TB NVMe drives per node, 200 GbE uplink). The 10+2 erasure coding tolerates failure of two drives per node or two complete nodes. Performance is approximately 90 GB/s.

Boot Infrastructure: Primary server as ESXi VM with two physical proxy servers for DNBD3 caching. Complete rebuild of the deployment infrastructure is possible in approximately 30 minutes using Ansible, excluding the setup of the operating system. Details can be found in Janczyk et al. (2026).

NVIDIA versus AMD: The decision to deploy both GPU architectures reflects different strategies. NVIDIA GPUs represent the proven choice with a mature software ecosystem where CUDA is the de facto standard, broad support from scientific software, and extensive community experience. The challenges lie in rather steep pricing, limited availability and long lead times of up to one year, requiring flexible procurement strategies such as framework contracts and bank guarantees.

AMD represents an exciting alternative for HPC workloads with excellent availability, native support for LLM frameworks including TensorFlow and PyTorch, and the innovative MI300A APU architecture with unified memory. The combination of both architectures gives the community choice, where CUDA based workloads run on NVIDIA hardware while AMD native applications can leverage the APU advantages.

2 System Security

HPC clusters are attractive attack targets both for their computing power and for the sensitive research data they process. Unlike web frontends or VM based systems, users on NEMO2 have non-privileged but direct access via SSH to the bare-metal operating system of the login nodes and the compute nodes. Network segmentation and security were therefore central considerations from the start when designing NEMO2 (Figure 1). The lingering threat of yet undisclosed local root exploits necessitated special security measures including strict network separation, minimal attack surface through stateless operation, and rapid patching via the CI/CD pipeline. The original security concept had to be evolved further (Suchodoletz et al., 2021).

Stateless Operation as Security Feature: Compute nodes have no local operating system installation, preventing persistent storage of sensitive data. The system images

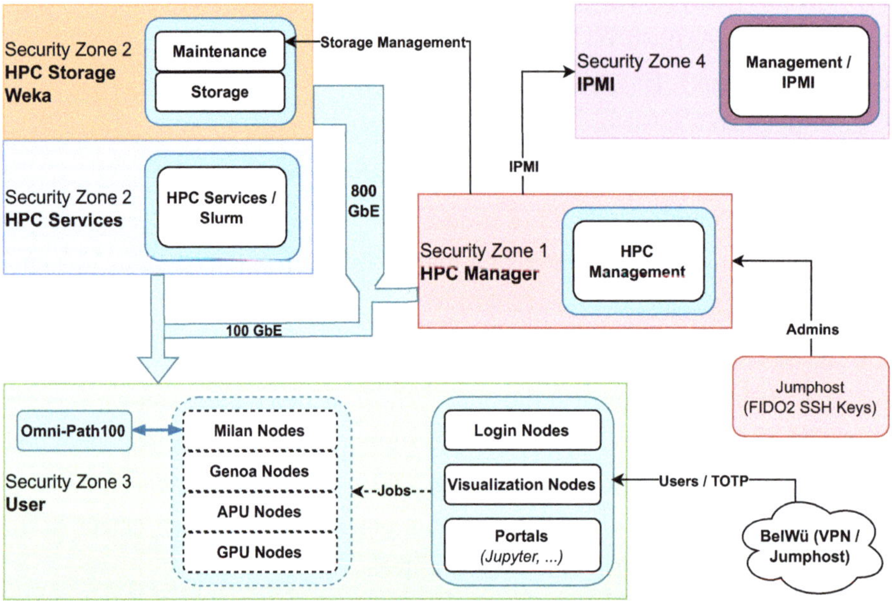

Figure 1: The system design and structure of the renewed NEMO system with its relevant building blocks and network security zones.

streamed via DNBD3 are mounted read-only at the block device level. Writes are captured by a copy-on-write layer backed by encrypted local NVMe storage. A separate encrypted partition serves as `$TMPDIR` for Slurm jobs. Both partitions are discarded on every reboot. This immutability prevents attackers from deploying persistend malware in the system image or affecting other nodes, even with root access. Details are provided in Janczyk et al. (2026).

Network Segmentation: The entire infrastructure resides in internal `10.x` networks and is strictly separated from campus and other central IT infrastructures. Two physically separated network tiers exist.

- **IPMI/Management Network:** Physically separated cabling for administrative access to IPMI controllers and management interfaces of Weka storage nodes. Administrative access is allowed exclusively through dedicated jump hosts using FIDO2 SSH keys. A special management node, itself only reachable through jump hosts, runs no services except SSH.

- **Compute Network:** User jobs, storage access via 100 GbE, and infrastructure servers including DNBD3, Slurm controller, and monitoring reside here. Omni-Path is used exclusively for MPI workloads on the Milan partition. Services provided by infrastructure servers are accessible from the compute network, while SSH access to the servers themselves is exclusively available through jump hosts, protected by FIDO2 SSH keys.

DMZ Concept: Servers requiring public accessibility such as login nodes do not receive public IP addresses. Instead, only specific ports are made accessible via port forwarding or reverse NAT. Inbound SSH access is restricted to the BelWü network, implementing a geofencing approach that limits potential attack vectors to the academic network infrastructure. Outbound connections are permitted through the DMZ using NAT, limiting the access to other network segments on campus. This allows for simple but restrictive firewall and switch configurations.

Multi-Factor Authentication: User access occurs exclusively through bwIDM, the Baden-Württemberg Identity Management system, with two factor authentication using TOTP or FIDO2 SSH keys.[6] KIT RegApp serves as the service provider.[7] Administrative access to servers and jump hosts require FIDO2 SSH keys. User acceptance of this security concept is achieved through multiple available options for the second factor and clear communication of necessity.

Storage Encryption: Weka storage is configured to use the self-encrypting abilities of the underlying NVMe drives. Home directories include snapshot functionality for protection against accidental deletion, as described in Section 4.

3 Operating Model

The operating model of NEMO2 is further evolved from previous approaches (Janczyk et al., 2019) and based on consistent automation, containerization, and a diskless approach that enables rapid deployment and rollback.

[6] Federated identity management for universities in Baden-Württemberg: https://www.bwidm.de/, visited on 10.03.2025

[7] KIT Registration Service: https://www.scc.kit.edu/en/services/regapp.php, visited on 10.03.2025

3.1 Diskless Network Boot and CI/CD Pipeline

All 260 compute nodes remote boot their root filesystem via images provide by a dedicated boot server and generated by a GitLab CI/CD pipeline. Packer creates Rocky Linux 9.x images in QEMU/KVM, while Ansible applies over 25 roles covering Slurm, GPU drivers, and container runtimes. Images are versioned with GitLab job IDs, stored in S3, and streamed via DNBD3 through two proxy servers with local SSD caches. A local storage device inside the compute node is no mandatory requirement. Therefore, the boot process is literally diskless. However, since local drives are present in all compute nodes, they are used as the complementary write layer for the network served (immutable) initial OS image. The local drives hold the ephemeral data which is discarded on every reboot.

A central CSV file maps MAC addresses to boot files enabling per-node control. Individual nodes can be switched to test images while others remain on stable versions. When problems occur, immediate rollback is possible by changing the default boot menu entry to point to an older revision. No image conversion or file copying is needed. Turnaround time is minutes rather than hours. Detailed technical description can be found in Janczyk et al. (2026).

bwHPC-S5 decided to switch from Moab Scheduler to Slurm with Pyxis for container integration. This allows flexible research environments using Apptainer or Enroot and facilitates migration of existing workflows.[8] The smooth transition from the old system was enabled by parallel operation of both clusters. The staged procurement allowed replacing only part of the hardware initially. Since NEMO2 had to be installed in the same racks as NEMO1, only half of the NEMO1 nodes were initially removed and replaced with NEMO2 hardware. Both systems ran in parallel for a time until NEMO1 could be fully decommissioned.

3.2 Remote Visualization

NEMO2 implements a flexible visualization concept covering various usage scenarios. The infrastructure is based on consolidated resources where login nodes can simultan-

[8] Earlier implementations were published in Bauer et al. (2019) and Janczyk et al. (2018).

eously be used for interactive visualization, while compute intensive 3D visualization runs on dedicated GPU nodes including L40S and H200 through Slurm jobs.

Technical implementation is container based. Xpra and VirGL run in Apptainer or Enroot containers and enable persistent remote desktop sessions with hardware accelerated GPU support. Users can disconnect from visualization sessions and reconnect later without interrupting the rendering process. Container images for visualization are provided through GitLab CI/CD pipelines, ensuring consistent software versions and simplifying maintenance.

Future plans include expansion with additional visualization options such as Virtual Desktop Infrastructure for more complex desktop requirements profiting from ongoing developments in the bwCloud 3 project (Bentele et al., 2022; Scherle et al., 2026). Further options are web based interfaces like JupyterLab for browser based workflows without client installation.

4 Data Management and Storage Systems

NEMO2 implements a two tier storage strategy for the initial part of the research data lifecycle. On the one hand, the Weka parallel filesystem handles actively processed data including HPC jobs, home directories, and workspaces. On the other hand, inactive data considered for further processing can be moved to the S3 object storage system bwSFS (Suchodoletz et al., 2026b). This architecture functionally separates the expensive high performance parallel file system storage from the more cost effective S3 object storage. Users can choose to transfer important research results to further university storage systems dedicated to long term preservation and research data management.

4.1 Weka Parallel Filesystem

The Weka full flash filesystem with one Petabyte NVMe is the central storage system for all active data on NEMO2. With approximately 90 GB/s bandwidth, it provides the performance needed for parallel HPC jobs and AI workloads.

Home directories reside on Weka and benefit from high performance and integrated snapshot functionality. Automatic snapshots capture previous states hourly from 9:00 to 18:00 on weekdays with 10 snapshots retained, daily with 7 snapshots, and weekly with 4 snapshots. The snapshots are transparently available under `/home/.snapshots/` and provide read-only access to older versions, protecting against accidental deletion or ransomware. However, snapshots do not protect against total storage system failure, so users should copy important non-recoverable or hard-to-reproduce data regularly to external storage destinations.

Workspaces are designed as scratch areas and currently exclusively use the Weka parallel file system for time-limited storage areas.[9] A future extension to additionally offer workspaces in the S3 object space is under development. Users reserve workspaces with defined lifetime, with a maximum of 100 days and up to 100 extensions. After expiration, a grace period of 30 days precedes final deletion. Quota is 5 TiB per workspace without inode limits, important for machine learning with millions of small files.

Workspaces are allocated with `ws_allocate`, extended with `ws_extend`, and released with `ws_release`. Automatic email reminders warn before expiration. Group workspaces for team collaboration are created with the `-G` flag. During the grace period, workspaces are recoverable with `ws_restore`. The time limitation promotes active data management and prevents uncontrolled data growth on expensive flash storage. Workspaces have no snapshots, so important results must be copied to home directories or S3 before expiration.

On NEMO1, the high performance parallel file system used servers with NVMe flash drives for metadata storage and servers with spinning Nearline SAS disks for data storage. However, metadata intensive workloads from single users, e.g., heavily reading and writing directory contents or operating on thousands of small files in parallel, could significantly affect the file system performance for all other users. Since flash drives became more affordable and the NVMe protocol replaced the outdated Nearline SAS protocol for data storage, a full-flash architecture using NVMe was chosen to boost performance and better accommodate metadata-heavy workloads.

[9] Github repository for HPC Workspace tools: https://github.com/holgerBerger/hpc-workspace, visited on 10.03.2025

4.2 Object Storage (S3)

The university S3 service provides intermediate storage for medium term data retention and external data sharing (Suchodoletz et al., 2026a). For long term backup and archival, users should utilize their respective institutional backup services. S3 is designed for flexible data access via token-based authentication and serves the following purposes.

- **Intermediate Storage:** Medium term data storage between active work and final archival
- **External Data Sharing:** Data access via access tokens, enabling worldwide data access and distribution to third parties
- **Project Collaboration:** Data exchange between research groups and institutions
- **CI/CD Artifacts:** Boot images for NEMO2, see Janczyk et al. (2026)
- **Staging Area:** Import of external datasets before processing on Weka

Data transfer is currently supported via HTTPS, `rclone`, and AWS CLI. More convenient access methods are planned in the future. The workflow follows the principle of active data on Weka for performance, intermediate data on S3 for flexibility, and completed research data in institutional long term archival systems.

5 Optimization Approaches

NEMO2 optimization targets a balanced relationship between computing power, energy efficiency, and operating costs (Saur et al., 2026).

TCO Oriented Processor Selection: Procurement chose CPUs with moderate base clock rates: AMD EPYC 7763 Milan at 2.45 GHz (boost to 3.5 GHz) and AMD EPYC 9654 Genoa at 2.4 GHz (boost to 3.7 GHz). These optimize computing power to energy consumption. Dynamic power consumption of CMOS circuits scales with $P_{dyn} = \alpha C V^2 f$, making higher frequencies disproportionately expensive in energy.

Operating costs for power and cooling over five years were heavily weighted in the evaluation. The 170 kW limitation for the Milan partition was dictated by available cooling capacity.

Energy Aware Scheduling: NEMO2 prepares for dynamic resource management. When the job queue is low, nodes can be excluded from scheduling after completing running jobs and powered down through node draining. With rising demand, nodes are powered up as needed. This significantly reduces power consumption since even underutilized servers consume considerable energy. Looking forward, dynamic energy pricing could be exploited for time flexible workloads, though this requires job hibernation technology with checkpointing to storage and later restart without compute cycle loss, currently still a research topic.

Mixed Mode Operations: NEMO2 supports simultaneous operation of different job types. Batch jobs and interactive jobs for development and debugging run in parallel. Slurm with Pyxis enables fine grained resource allocation at the core level rather than node level, increasing resource efficiency. Container based workloads simplify this coexistence through isolation between jobs.

Monitoring and Transparency: SERT values, the Server Efficiency Rating Tool, document hardware energy efficiency and create transparency toward funding agencies. Further planned optimizations include continuous monitoring of power consumption, cooling capacity, and job efficiency. Telemetry data via Telegraf and InfluxDB will provide the foundation for data driven decisions on cluster optimization.

6 Sustainability and Shareholder Model

NEMO2 addresses sustainability through TCO oriented procurement focused on energy efficiency, modular design for longer service life, and diskless operation that does not rely on local storage but benefits from it. SERT values transparently document energy efficiency.

The shareholder model allows research groups to acquire extended usage rights through financial participation including guaranteed resources and priority access, while simultaneously promoting IT consolidation (Wesner et al., 2016). Groups do not procure their own departmental systems but instead participate in centrally operated infrastructures with professional support. This reduces total operating costs through shared infrastructure for cooling, power, and personnel while preventing decentralized resource silos. The substantial expansion of NEMO1 and NEMO2 through shareholders demonstrates community confidence. Local governance through scientific and technical advisory boards and close exchange at the bwHPC symposiums promote continuous improvement.

7 Conclusion and Outlook

NEMO2 demonstrates successful integration of modern HPC concepts with practical operational requirements. Three central success factors characterize the system: TCO oriented procurement prioritizing energy efficiency over peak performance, diskless CI/CD operation eliminating configuration drift with rapid rollback capability, and the shareholder model promoting IT consolidation while providing guaranteed resources.

Quantitative Improvements: NEMO2 offers substantial capacity increases compared to NEMO1. Core count increased from approximately 18,400 to 37,888, representing a 106 percent increase. Weka full flash replaced BeeGFS over Omni-Path 100, providing a 4 to 5 times performance improvement. The system uses 100 GbE throughout for compute and storage, compared to NEMO1 which used 1 GbE for management and boot, Omni-Path 100 for MPI and storage, and 10 to 40 GbE for login and server nodes. New GPU and APU resources enable diverse computational workloads including AI, scientific visualization, molecular dynamics, and other GPU-accelerated applications.

Lessons Learned for Future HPC Projects: The staged procurement process across two tenders proved strategically advantageous. The initial cooling capacity limitation of 170 kW led to prioritizing energy-efficient systems in the first tender and resulted in the acquisition of the Milan partition. After creating additional cooling capacity and recalculating available power, the second tender resulted in the acquisition of the Genoa and APU partition and benefited from improved performance-per-watt values and more favorable pricing with the newer processor generation. The staged procurement process enabled experience transfer from the first to the second tender and a qualified response to market developments.

Infrastructure planning required intensive coordination with the technical server room management staff. Power supply, PDU configuration, and cooling connections needed more coordination effort than initially expected. Developing the CI/CD pipeline required substantial initial investment but delivers significant operational efficiency gains. Network segmentation should be designed from project start, as subsequent changes to network architecture are complex and disruptive.

Outlook: User-encrypted volumes for enhanced data security are under evaluation. Energy aware scheduling with dynamic node draining during low utilization is in preparation. Looking forward, job hibernation technology could enable time flexible workloads with dynamic energy pricing. The hardware concept for NEMO3 is already under discussion with expected deployment around 2030. Focus topics include further GPU integration, expanded visualization options including VDI and web based interfaces, and evaluation of other CPU architectures with respect to energy efficiency.

The combination of proven concepts including the shareholder model (Wesner et al., 2016), workspaces, object storage, and Slurm scheduling with innovations including diskless boot using CI/CD, Weka full flash, and AMD MI300A APUs positions NEMO2 as a modern, flexible Tier-3 research infrastructure. The system addresses current trends including rising energy costs, sustainability requirements, AI workloads, and container based scientific software, providing a blueprint for similar mid-scale HPC systems.

Acknowledgments

The authors would like to thank the state of Baden-Württemberg for its support of bwHPC and the German Research Foundation (DFG) for funding under »Project number 455622343« (bwForCluster NEMO 2). Parts of the developments presented in this paper were made possible through the contributions provided by the projects bwLehrpool, bwCloud3 and bwHPC-S5 that are supported by the Ministry of Science, Research and Arts Baden-Württemberg.

Corresponding Author

Bernd Wiebelt: bernd.wiebelt@rz.uni-freiburg.de
eScience Department, Computer Center, University of Freiburg,
Hermann-Herder-Str. 10, 79104 Freiburg, Germany

ORCID

Bernd Wiebelt https://orcid.org/0000-0003-2771-4524
Dirk von Suchodoletz https://orcid.org/0000-0002-4382-5104
Michael Janczyk https://orcid.org/0000-0003-4886-736X

References

Barthel, R. and J. Salk (2019). »bwHPC-S5: Scientific Simulation and Storage Support Services. Unterstützung von Wissenschaft und Forschung beim leistungsstarken und datenintensiven Rechnen sowie großskaligem Forschungsdatenmanagement«. In: *Proceedings of the 5th bwHPC Symposium. HPC Activities in Baden-Württemberg*. Freiburg, September 2018. 5th bwHPC Symposium. Ed. by M. Janczyk, D. von Suchodoletz and B. Wiebelt. TLP, Tübingen, pp. 17–28. DOI: 10.15496/publikation-29039.

Bauer, J., D. von Suchodoletz, J. Vollmer and H. Rasche (2019). »Game of Templates. Deploying and (re-)using Virtualized Research Environments in High-Performance and High-Throughput Computing«. In: *Proceedings of the 5th bwHPC Symposium. HPC Activities in Baden-Württemberg*. Freiburg, September 2018. 5th bwHPC Symposium. Ed. by M. Janczyk, D. von Suchodoletz and B. Wiebelt. TLP, Tübingen, pp. 245–262. DOI: 10.15496/publikation-29057.

Bentele, M., D. von Suchodoletz, M. Messner and S. Rettberg (2022). »Towards a GPU-Accelerated Open Source VDI for OpenStack«. In: *Cloud Computing*. Ed. by M. R. Khosravi, Q. He and H. Dai. Cham: Springer International Publishing, pp. 149–164. ISBN: 978-3-030-99191-3. DOI: 10.1007/978-3-030-99191-3_12.

Hartenstein, H., T. Walter and P. Castellaz (2013). »Aktuelle Umsetzungskonzepte der Universitäten des Landes Baden-Württemberg für Hochleistungsrechnen und datenintensive Dienste«. In: *PIK-Praxis der Informationsverarbeitung und Kommunikation* 36.2, pp. 99–108. DOI: 10.1515/pik-2013-0007.

Janczyk, M. and J. Bauer (2026). »Automated Infrastructure Provisioning for Heterogeneous High-Performance Computing Environments. A Multi-Stage CI/CD Framework with Network Boot Integration«. In: *Proceedings of the 10th bwHPC Symposium. HPC Activities in Baden-Württemberg*. Freiburg, September 2024. 10th bwHPC Symposium. Ed. by M. Janczyk, D. von Suchodoletz, B. Wiebelt and M. Frank. KIT Scientific Publishing, Karlsruhe, pp. 229–246. DOI: 10.58895/ksp/1000169488-15.

Janczyk, M., D. von Suchodoletz and B. Wiebelt (2019). »bwForCluster NEMO. Forschungscluster für die Wissenschaft«. In: *Proceedings of the 5th bwHPC Symposium. HPC Activities in Baden-Württemberg*. Freiburg, September 2018. 5th bwHPC Symposium. Ed. by M. Janczyk, D. von Suchodoletz and B. Wiebelt. TLP, Tübingen, pp. 29–50. DOI: 10.15496/publikation-29041.

Janczyk, M., B. Wiebelt and D. von Suchodoletz (2018). »Virtualized research environments on the bwForCluster NEMO«. In: *Proceedings of the 4th bwHPC symposium*. Universitätsbibliothek Tübingen, pp. 37–40. DOI: 10.15496/publikation-25195.

Saur, A., D. von Suchodoletz, B. Wiebelt and B. Grüning (2026). »Energy-Efficient Scientific Computing and AI in Freiburg. A Comprehensive Approach to Weighting Demand and Sustainability«. In: *Proceedings of the 10th bwHPC Symposium. HPC Activities in Baden-Württemberg*.

Freiburg, September 2024. 10th bwHPC Symposium. Ed. by M. Janczyk, D. von Suchodoletz, B. Wiebelt and M. Frank. KIT Scientific Publishing, Karlsruhe, pp. 175–192. DOI: 10.58895/ksp/1000169488-12.

Scherle, M., A. Saur, V. Kasireddy, R. Gieschke and D. von Suchodoletz (2026). »SPICE for hardware accelerated remote desktop access. Central building Block of an open source VDI«. In: *Proceedings of the 10th bwHPC Symposium. HPC Activities in Baden-Württemberg*. Freiburg, September 2024. 10th bwHPC Symposium. Ed. by M. Janczyk, D. von Suchodoletz, B. Wiebelt and M. Frank. KIT Scientific Publishing, Karlsruhe, pp. 127–141. DOI: 10.58895/ksp/1000169488-9.

Suchodoletz, D. von, K. Glogowski, M. Seifert, M. Quandt and U. Hahn (2026a). »Technical Foundations and Service Integration in the bwSFS Storage Infrastructure. Research Data Management Practice«. In: *Proceedings of the 10th bwHPC Symposium. HPC Activities in Baden-Württemberg*. Freiburg, September 2024. 10th bwHPC Symposium. Ed. by M. Janczyk, D. von Suchodoletz, B. Wiebelt and M. Frank. KIT Scientific Publishing, Karlsruhe, pp. 265–282. DOI: 10.58895/ksp/1000169488-17.

Suchodoletz, D. von, J. Leendertse, B. Wiebelt, M. J. Messner and M. Janczyk (2021). »Stateless System Remote-Boot als Business-Continuity-Konzept«. In: *Sicherheit in Vernetzten Systemen 28. DFN-Konferenz*. Ed. by A. Ude. Hamburg: Books on Demand, F1–F21. ISBN: 978-3-7528-9805-7. DOI: 10.6094/UNIFR/218386.

Suchodoletz, D. von et al. (2023). *Rahmenkonzept der Universitäten des Landes Baden-Württemberg für das High-Performance Computing (HPC) und Data-Intensive Computing (DIC) für den Zeitraum 2025 bis 2032*. DOI: 10.15496/publikation-90185.

Suchodoletz, D. von et al. (2026b). »bwSFS – A Federated Storage Backbone for Research Data Management. A Foundational Infrastructure for RDM Services«. In: *Proceedings of the 10th bwHPC Symposium. HPC Activities in Baden-Württemberg*. Freiburg, September 2024. 10th bwHPC Symposium. Ed. by M. Janczyk, D. von Suchodoletz, B. Wiebelt and M. Frank. KIT Scientific Publishing, Karlsruhe, pp. 247–263. DOI: 10.58895/ksp/1000169488-16.

Suchodoletz, D. von et al. (2026c). »Framework Concept of the Universities in the State of Baden-Württemberg. High-Performance Computing (HPC) and Data-Intensive Computing (DIC) in the Period 2025–2032«. In: *Proceedings of the 10th bwHPC Symposium. HPC Activities in Baden-Württemberg*. Freiburg, September 2024. 10th bwHPC Symposium. Ed. by M. Janczyk, D. von Suchodoletz, B. Wiebelt and M. Frank. KIT Scientific Publishing, Karlsruhe, pp. 195–211. DOI: 10.58895/ksp/1000169488-13.

Wesner, S., D. von Suchodoletz and G. Schneider (2016). »Überlegungen zu laufenden Cluster-Erweiterungen in bwHPC«. In: *Kooperation von Rechenzentren, Governance und Steuerung - Organisation, Rechtsgrundlagen, Politik*. Ed. by D. von Suchodoletz, J. C. Schulz, J. Leendertse, H. Hotzel and M. Wimmer. De Gruyter Oldenbourg, pp. 331–342. ISBN: 9783110459753. DOI: 10.1515/9783110459753-028.

Automated Infrastructure Provisioning for Heterogeneous High-Performance Computing Environments

A Multi-Stage CI/CD Framework with Network Boot Integration

Michael Janczyk, Jonathan Bauer

eScience, University of Freiburg, Freiburg, Germany

Abstract

This paper describes the provisioning workflow for the 260 diskless compute nodes of bwForCluster NEMO 2 at the University of Freiburg. We combine a CI/CD pipeline using PACKER and ANSIBLE with DNBD3 network boot and S3 storage. A multi-stage approach separates base image creation from flavor specialization and runtime configuration, implementing the immutable infrastructure pattern. The heterogeneous hardware includes AMD EPYC Milan and Genoa CPUs, NVIDIA H200 and L40S GPUs, and AMD MI300A APUs. A two-tier DNBD3 architecture with caching proxies scales beyond 900 nodes. Four deployment channels enable staged rollouts and instant rollback through pointer files rather than image copies. By leveraging institutional services for S3 object storage, GITLAB, and DHCP, the only boot infrastructure maintained is three DNBD3 servers.

1 Introduction

The bwForCluster NEMO 2 at the University of Freiburg comprises 260 diskless compute nodes across heterogeneous hardware partitions (AMD EPYC Milan and Genoa CPUs, NVIDIA GPUs, AMD MI300A APUs) serving research in neuroscience, elementary particle physics, materials science, and microsystems engineering. Comprehensive hardware and architectural details are documented in Wiebelt et al. (2026).

Traditional HPC cluster management relies on local disks and manual provisioning, which leads to configuration drift and complicates software updates. In bwForCluster NEMO 2, all compute nodes boot from the network, always starting from the same centrally managed system image. This guarantees a consistent, known-good software environment across all nodes and eliminates per-node installation and maintenance. Since the shared system image is read-only on the nodes, NEMO2 uses a local block device as a temporary write layer to store file system changes during runtime. Therefore, the nodes can be restored to their original state by a reboot. The DNBD3 boot infrastructure delivers images over a dedicated network via two caching proxy and one primary servers, providing the bandwidth required for concurrent node boots.

This paper presents this diskless approach applied to bwForCluster NEMO 2 (Wiebelt et al., 2026): a fully stateless architecture where all 260 compute nodes boot from the network. A CI/CD pipeline builds and versions system images automatically, delivering them via DNBD3 (Rettberg et al., 2019) and enabling reproducible deployments with instant rollback capability.

2 Background

The HPC community has traditionally relied on proven system software designs, making incremental changes between system generations. Allen et al. (2020) argue that modern approaches focusing on manageability, scalability, and security can benefit the entire community. Our setup follows this philosophy by combining established technologies with modern CI/CD practices and Infrastructure as Code principles (Morris, 2020). This approach builds on our experience with NEMO1, deployed in 2015 (Janczyk et al., 2019; Suchodoletz et al., 2021; Wiebelt et al., 2016), while adopting deployment patterns suited to heterogeneous hardware and evolving demands.

For configuration management, we use ANSIBLE[1], which suits HPC environments since it requires no agents on target systems. Alternatives include xCAT, WAREWULF, and GRENDEL (Bruno et al., 2020). We preferred a tighter integration with modern CI/CD workflows. In previous work, we presented the »Sorting Hat« approach (Bauer et al., 2019) to dynamically assign compute nodes to different cluster environments. The approach presented here is simpler: instead of dynamic reassignment at runtime, we use static per-node boot file assignments that can be changed in a Git repository and take effect on the next reboot.

Container runtimes play an important role on NEMO2. We support APPTAINER[2], a Linux Foundation fork of Singularity (Kurtzer et al., 2017), and ENROOT[3], the latter integrated with SLURM via PYXIS[4]. For diskless booting, use the OPENSLX framework[5] that combines IPXE[6], custom DRACUT modules and DNBD3/`xloop` technologies[7] (see Section 3).

3 System Architecture

Our architecture separates three tasks: image building, image delivery, and runtime configuration. System images are built in a CI/CD pipeline (Section 4) in four stages: base image creation, flavor specialization, IPXE boot binary compilation, and runtime override preparation. The resulting artifacts are stored centrally in S3 object storage and streamed to compute nodes on demand via DNBD3 (Rettberg et al., 2019). DNBD3 is a distributed network block device protocol similar to NBD[8] but optimized for read-only image distribution. It supports on-demand block streaming with client-side failover, caching proxies, and CRC-based integrity verification. Runtime configuration resides in a separate Git repository and is distributed as a tarball fetched directly via the GITLAB API[9] that is extracted onto the copy-on-write layer during boot, allowing arbitrary file

[1] Ansible Documentation: https://docs.ansible.com/, visited on 07.04.2025
[2] Apptainer container runtime: https://apptainer.org/, visited on 07.04.2025
[3] NVIDIA Enroot: https://github.com/NVIDIA/enroot, visited on 07.04.2025
[4] Pyxis SLURM plugin: https://github.com/NVIDIA/pyxis, visited on 07.04.2025
[5] OpenSLX repositories: https://git.openslx.org, visited on 07.04.2025
[6] iPXE network boot: https://ipxe.org/, visited on 07.04.2025
[7] DNBD3 repository: https://github.com/bwLehrpool/dnbd3, visited on 07.04.2025, and xloop kernel module: https://github.com/bwLehrpool/xloop, visited on 07.04.2025, from the bwLehrpool project: https://www.bwlehrpool.de/wiki, visited on 07.04.2025
[8] NBD protocol reference: https://github.com/NetworkBlockDevice/nbd, visited on 07.04.2025
[9] GitLab repository archive API documentation: https://docs.gitlab.com/api/repositories/#get-file-archive, visited on 07.04.2025

additions or modifications without touching the immutable system image. This implements the *immutable infrastructure* pattern (Morris, 2020): system images are never modified in place but replaced with new versions. Section 7 discusses the security implications.

3.1 Technology Stack

We use PACKER[10] with QEMU as the build backend, producing compressed qcow2 images. ANSIBLE is used in the image build process to apply all system configuration through modular roles covering SLURM, GPU drivers, container runtimes, and scientific libraries. Changes to the ANSIBLE playbooks trigger automated rebuilds in GITLAB CI. The resulting images are uploaded to S3.

For network boot, the initial PXE boot via DHCP/TFTP fetches a custom IPXE binary that retrieves boot menus, kernel, and initramfs from S3 over HTTPS. DNBD3 streams the root filesystem as a block device. OPENSLX provides the integration layer through custom DRACUT[11] modules that handle network configuration, DNBD3 client setup, and a block device-based copy-on-write overlay using device mapper thin provisioning[12]. The `xloop` kernel module extends the standard Linux loop device with a file format subsystem, enabling direct use of qcow2 images as block devices without conversion to raw format.

A key design decision was separating boot infrastructure configuration from the images themselves. A dedicated Git repository maps MAC addresses to hostnames and boot files, controls which we call a *deployment channel* each node uses, and provides runtime configuration overrides for specific node types applied during boot. Four deployment channels point to specific image revisions: `stable` for production, `last` for the previous production revision (enabling instant rollback), `test` for pre-release validation on reserved nodes, and `latest` for the most recent CI build. Switching channels updates a pointer, not the image itself (see Subsection 4.4). These overrides can modify any system file and are organized into hardware and service-specific variants, allowing nodes to be reassigned to different images or configurations without triggering image rebuilds.

[10] HashiCorp Packer version 1.9.5: https://developer.hashicorp.com/packer/docs/v1.9.x, visited on 07.04.2025
[11] dracut-ng initramfs generator: https://github.com/dracut-ng/dracut-ng, visited on 07.04.2025
[12] `device-mapper` Documentation: https://www.kernel.org/doc/Documentation/device-mapper/thin-provisioning.txt, visited on 07.04.2025

3.2 Infrastructure Dependencies

A deliberate design goal was minimizing self-managed infrastructure by leveraging existing university services. The institutional storage team provides S3 object storage with versioning and high availability; accessible through bucket credentials and a custom endpoint URL. The eScience services team runs the GitLab instance that hosts our repositories, executes CI/CD pipelines, and serves the runtime configuration via API. GitLab spawns runners on-demand in bwCloud[13]. The network team operates Infoblox for DNS and DHCP; a script reads CSV configuration files and writes the corresponding entries (hostnames, IP addresses, PXE configuration) to Infoblox via its API.

The only boot infrastructure we deploy and maintain ourselves consists of one primary and two proxy DNBD3 servers. The three DNBD3 boot servers are configured by a single Ansible playbook with different parameters for proxy mode. The complete setup deploys from scratch in about 30 minutes (excluding base OS installation). Since the playbooks are version-controlled, any server can be rebuilt identically. Section 5 describes the server architecture.

4 Implementation

All image building and artifact generation is automated through GitLab CI/CD. The pipeline is structured into the four stages introduced in Section 3 and shown in Figure 1. The CI job definitions (`base`, `flavor`, `ipxe`) are maintained centrally. For NEMO2, we maintain multiple base images: the stable base with standard kernel versions, and a separate base for testing newer kernels with the Weka client for our parallel storage system. We build two primary flavors that can be derived from any of these base images: `worker` for production nodes and `worker-test` for validating new features before production rollout. The architecture is flexible enough to support additional custom flavors for other use cases (diskless infrastructure servers such as DNBD3 proxies, Slurm controllers, or monitoring nodes) or hardware-specific configurations (e.g., separate images optimized for different GPU families). For NEMO2, we currently use a single `worker` image

[13] bwCloud-OS: The state-wide OpenStack cloud platform service, https://bwcloud-os.de/, visited on 19.12.2025

across all compute hardware and apply hardware-specific settings at runtime through configuration overrides.

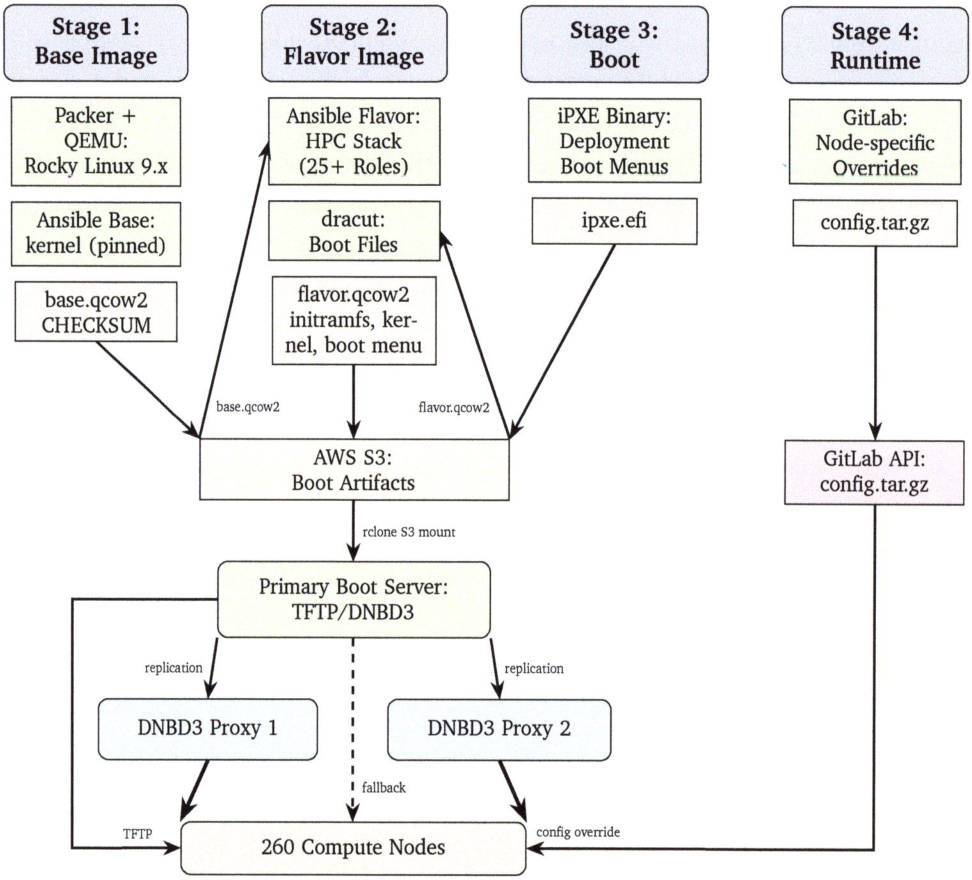

Figure 1: Four-stage build pipeline with deployment infrastructure. Stages 1–3 produce artifacts uploaded to S3. Stage 4 (runtime config) is managed via GitLab. Primary server provides TFTP and DNBD3 via S3 mount; DNBD3 proxies cache blocks locally.

The CI/CD pipeline definitions are reusable and can be included in other projects. Other teams can adopt them with minimal effort. A new project only needs to provide S3 bucket credentials, and its own Ansible roles; the pipeline then builds, versions, and uploads images automatically. Each project group can define its own base images with different kernel versions and derive multiple flavors from each base.

4.1 Base Image Pipeline

The base image pipeline runs in GitLab CI/CD using Packer inside a privileged Docker container with KVM access. Starting from a Rocky Linux 9.x ISO, Packer uses a minimal Kickstart file[14] to create a minimal VM using the QEMU builder. Ansible then applies basic configuration required for our cluster: a specific kernel version pinned for Weka client compatibility[15], `chronyd` for time synchronization, and other essential tools. To optimize the resulting image size and transfer times during CI/CD steps, we use qcow2 images which are sparsified in a last step. This base image typically only changes for kernel updates or security patches and serves as input for »flavored« images.

4.2 Flavor Pipeline

The flavor pipeline takes a base image and adds role-specific software. In NEMO2 Slurm client with container integration via Pyxis, GPU drivers for NVIDIA and AMD hardware, MPI implementations, and scientific libraries are set up. Changes in the Ansible playbooks trigger automated rebuilds in GitLab CI. Each build produces a complete, self-contained image suffixed with the GitLab CI job ID. This creates a direct mapping between Git commit, CI job, and deployed image. The Packer templates for both base and flavored images are maintained in a central repository[16].

After building the qcow2 image, the same pipeline extracts boot artifacts created using custom dracut modules. This ensures that the kernel and kernel modules within the image are compatible. This step is triggered using a separate Ansible playbook[17]. The output includes the kernel (`vmlinuz`) and an initramfs containing the DNBD3 client, `xloop` with qcow2 support, network drivers, and custom boot scripts. All artifacts and the corresponding iPXE boot menu are uploaded to S3 in revision-specific folders (e.g., `9752/`), establishing a direct mapping between GitLab commit, CI job, and deployed image (see Section 6, Listing 5, lines 1, 2 and 4). The boot menu pointing to the latest deployment is also updated.

[14] Packer templates with minimal Kickstart configuration: https://git.openslx.org/openslx-ng/packer-templates.git/tree/rocky-9-x86_64/http?h=hcl2, visited on 07.04.2025

[15] Weka compatibility matrix: https://docs.weka.io/4.2/install/prerequisites-and-compatibility#backends, visited on 15.04.2025

[16] OpenSLX Packer templates: https://git.openslx.org/openslx-ng/packer-templates.git/, visited on 07.04.2025

[17] ansible-dracut integration: https://git.openslx.org/openslx-ng/ansible-dracut.git/, visited on 07.04.2025

The iPXE binaries are built once per flavor and contain embedded HTTPS URLs pointing to a standard boot menu entry stored on S3 (see Section 6, Listing 5, lines 14–15). Once compiled, they work with any image revision without modification. They only need to be rebuilt when changes to the iPXE source, boot configuration, or PXE chain are required. See Subsection 5.2 for more details.

4.3 Runtime Configuration

To maintain flexibility and avoid frequent image rebuilds, we manage node-specific and frequently-changing settings in a separate Git repository that are applied during boot time instead of being configured in the images themselves. This repository serves three purposes: runtime override configuration (this section), boot file assignments and deployment channel management, and external infrastructure configuration for Infoblox DHCP/DNS integration (see Subsection 4.4).

Runtime configuration settings are organized in a two-tier structure applied during boot. First, a `base` configuration provides settings common to all nodes (e. g. monitoring agents, shared mount points, Slurm client configuration). Second, hardware- or service-specific configuration extend or override the base configuration for particular node types. Examples include GPU-specific services for different hardware generations, login-specific services for user-facing nodes, or specialized mount configurations. A node configuration file (Listing 1) maps hostname ranges to their specific configuration flavor.

```
# nodestart,[nodestop],configname
login1,login2,login
a3601,a3604,mi300a
g3605,g3612,l40s
g4401,g4402,h200
n3101,n3525,milan
n4101,n4626,genoa
```

Listing 1: Node-to-override configuration mapping (excerpt)

Each override directory (e. g., `genoa/`, `milan/`, `h200/`, `mi300a/`, `login/`) can contain systemd units, and mount and service configurations specific to that node type. The `SLX_LOCAL_CONFIG` variable (Subsection 5.2, Listing 4, line 4) controls which configuration flavor is applied during boot. Section 5 describes the boot process.

This separation allows changing mount points, updating SLURM prolog scripts, or reassigning nodes to different hardware profiles without rebuilding images. Configuration changes take minutes; full image rebuilds take about an hour.

4.4 Per-Node Boot Control

A central feature is controlling the node deployment by defining exactly which iPXE image is initially loaded. The configuration repository contains CSV files for boot file assignments (Listing 2) and a TOML file for deployment channel management (Listing 3).

```
# mac,hostname,bootfile,bootserver(optional)
00:11:22:33:44:01,n3101,rocky-9-x86_64-worker.efi,
00:11:22:33:44:02,n3102,rocky-9-x86_64-worker.efi,
00:11:22:33:44:03,n3103,rocky-9-x86_64-worker-test.efi,
...
00:11:22:aa:bb:01,g3601,rocky-9-x86_64-worker-latest.efi,
00:11:22:aa:bb:02,g4401,rocky-9-x86_64-worker-test.efi,
```

Listing 2: Example per-node boot file assignments

The CSV can optionally include a `bootserver` column to specify an alternate DHCP next-server (TFTP endpoint) for individual nodes. This enables failover scenarios where, if the primary server becomes unavailable, specific nodes can be updated to boot from an alternate server.

The naming convention <os>-<arch>-<flavor>[-<channel>].efi encodes the base image (`rocky-9`), architecture (`x86_64`), flavor (`worker`), and optionally a deployment channel (`latest`, `last`, `test`). Without a channel suffix, nodes boot the stable production image. The corresponding qcow2 images follow a similar pattern with revision suffixes (e.g., `rocky-9-x86_64-worker.qcow2.r9752`).

Deployment channels are managed through a TOML configuration file (Listing 3) that maps channel names to specific revision IDs. A Python script synchronizes this file with S3: The CI/CD pipeline writes the `latest` field after successful builds, and cluster operators promote revisions by manually updating channel pointers. The `[base]` section tracks base image revisions, while the `[worker]` section contains flavor-specific revisions including the previous stable revision for quick rollback. Rolling back production means changing the `stable` pointer to `last`; no images are copied.

```
[base]
latest = "9678"
stable = "9678"

[worker]
latest = "9752"
last   = "9061"
stable = "9752"
test   = "9752"
```

Listing 3: Excerpt from images.toml

The workflow supports both single-node and cluster-wide deployment channel changes. To reassign a single node, the boot assignment file (Listing 2) is updated with the desired deployment channel, committed to GitLab, and a script synchronizes the change to DHCP via the Infoblox API. Each boot file (`*.efi`) contains an embedded URL pointing to the corresponding deployment channel boot menu on S3 (see Section 6, Listing 5, lines 3–4), which in turn references a specific image revision. For cluster-wide changes, only the TOML file (Listing 3) needs to be updated and synchronized to S3. This gives us fine-grained control.

Testing on reserved nodes: Before cluster-wide deployment, we assign test nodes to the `test` boot file (see Section 6, Listing 5, line 15) and reserve them from Slurm scheduling. Once validated, these nodes are switched back to the default boot file.

Graceful cluster-wide rollout: After successful testing, the `stable` channel pointer in Listing 3 is updated to the newly validated revision and synchronized to S3. Then, all nodes are scheduled for reboot using `scontrol reboot ASAP`. Nodes stop accepting new jobs and reboot automatically when their running jobs complete. Since the maximum wall-clock time is four days, the entire cluster is updated within this period without any job termination.

Emergency rollback: If single nodes have problems with a new revision, they can be switched back to the previously validated revision using the `last` boot file (see Section 6, Listing 5, line 15). Alternatively, the `stable` channel pointer in Listing 3 can be updated to reference the `last` revision, rolling back all nodes on next reboot without changing individual boot file assignments.

New nodes are registered manually: hardware vendors provide MAC addresses during procurement. A Python script reads these MAC lists and generates the boot file assignment listing (Listing 2). An update script then reads this listing file and creates or updates the corresponding DNS and DHCP records (hostnames, IP addresses, boot file assignments) via the INFOBLOX API.

5 Network Boot

The network boot process is initiated by the PXE-ROM (Preboot Execution Environment) and its HTTP capable extension iPXE, which subsequently load the kernel and initramfs. The initramfs then loads the main system image and applies the node-specific configuration. The image delivery infrastructure is build upon on a two-tier DNBD3 server hierarchy. The system is supported by one primary server that is backed by S3 and two caching proxies. The DNBD3 servers are responsible for streaming system images to all diskless compute nodes.

5.1 Server Architecture

The primary server is a virtual machine (2 vCPUs, 4 GB RAM) that mounts S3 via `rclone` FUSE and runs both TFTP (`port 69/UDP` for the initial PXE boot) and the primary DNBD3 server (`port 5003/TCP` for image streaming). Two physical servers with local SSDs (1 TB each) act as the caching proxies. During boot the DNBD3 client receives an ordered server list: `proxy1`, `proxy2`, `primary`. It then connects to `proxy1` and starts requesting blocks. If the block is not yet cached on `proxy1`, `proxy1` requests the missing block from the other DNBD3 servers and sends the block back to the client.

When the first node boots a new image, only the primary server has the blocks, served from the S3-mounted qcow2 file. DNBD3 servers operating in proxy mode query all known servers (including each other) for missing blocks, caching them on local SSDs for subsequent requests. As more nodes boot the same image, the proxies gradually accumulate all required blocks through demand-driven caching and peer exchange. Subsequent nodes then boot entirely from the proxies, reducing load on the primary server and S3. A background replication process proactively syncs complete images, ensuring full availability even before all blocks have been requested.

This architecture tolerates the failure of any two servers. If both proxies fail, clients fall back to the primary. If the primary fails after proxies have cached the image, nodes continue booting from proxies.

The previous cluster, NEMO1, successfully booted over 900 nodes simultaneously using a comparable DNBD3 infrastructure, demonstrating that the protocol scales well beyond our current cluster size.

5.2 Boot Sequence

Figure 2 shows the complete boot sequence. The process begins with the PXE firmware requesting the iPXE binary via TFTP. This binary contains an embedded iPXE script that chainloads to the configured boot menu stored in S3 via HTTPS. The menu is another iPXE script pointing to revision-specific kernel, initramfs, and boot parameters.

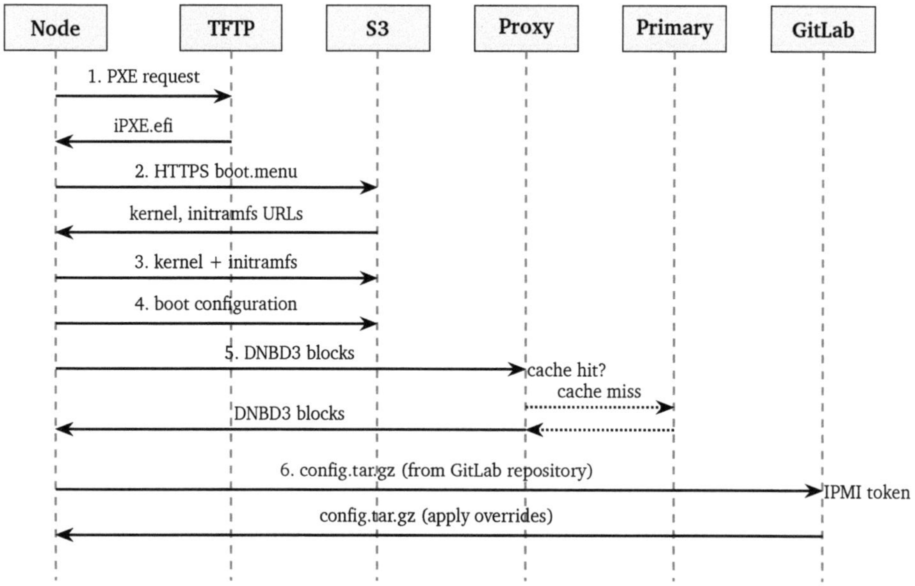

Figure 2: Boot sequence showing TFTP handoff to HTTPS, DNBD3 block streaming with proxy caching, and runtime configuration from GitLab. Dotted lines indicate cache misses that trigger upstream fetches.

During boot time the boot configuration file (Listing 4) is downloaded. This file specifies the DNBD3 server list (line 1: `proxy1`, `proxy2`, and `primary` server), the DNBD3 image path on servers (line 2), the revision ID that defines the image version (line 3), the flavor for the configuration overrides (line 4, see Subsection 4.3), and the API endpoint to fetch the `config.tar.gz` from, which contains the base and override configuration directories (line 5).

```
1 SLX_DNBD3_SERVERS='10.x.1.1 10.x.1.2 10.x.0.11'
2 SLX_DNBD3_IMAGE='rocky-9-x86_64/worker/rocky-9-x86_64-worker.qcow2'
3 SLX_DNBD3_RID='9752'
4 SLX_LOCAL_CONFIG='genoa'
5 GITLAB_API_PROJECT_PATH='https://gitlab.../api/v4/projects/...'
```

Listing 4: OpenSLX configuration retrieved from S3

Our custom DRACUT module scripts load the DNBD3 and `xloop` kernel modules, connects to the first available server, and mounts the qcow2 root filesystem read-only and configures the copy-on-write layer. The final step fetches and applies the runtime configuration from the GitLab API using a token stored in an IPMI Field Replaceable Unit (FRU) field (Intel Corporation et al., 2015). The IPMI FRU data areas provide non-volatile storage on the BMC for hardware inventory and custom data[18] (Dell EMC, 2017).

6 Artifact Management

All build artifacts are stored in S3, organized into four top-level directories (Listing 5). The `boot/` directory (lines 1–4) contains files served via HTTPS during early boot: kernel, initramfs, boot configuration file, and boot menus. A pre-configured, 20-character, random string in the path prevents accidental access without requiring authentication (see Section 7). The `dnbd3/` directory (lines 5–6) stores the final qcow2 images with CRC files, accessed only through the DNBD3 protocol. The `rocky-9-x86_64/` directory (lines 7–13) holds the build artifacts: base images (line 7), flavor-specific metadata (checksums, kernel versions), and deployment channel pointers. The `tftpboot/` directory (lines 14–15) contains the iPXE binaries that DHCP points to.

[18] GitHub repository of `fru-tool` for writing FRU information to the BMC: https://github.com/Xilinx/fru-tool, visited on 29.04.2025

```
boot/<secret>/rocky-9-x86_64/<flavor>/<rev>/{boot.menu,config}
boot/<secret>/rocky-9-x86_64/<flavor>/<rev>/{initramfs,vmlinuz}-<kernel>
boot/<secret>/rocky-9-x86_64/<flavor>/boot.menu
boot/<secret>/rocky-9-x86_64/<flavor>/boot-{last,latest,test}.menu
dnbd3/rocky-9-x86_64/<flavor>/rocky-9-x86_64-<flavor>.qcow2.r<rev>
dnbd3/rocky-9-x86_64/<flavor>/rocky-9-x86_64-<flavor>.qcow2.r<rev>.crc
rocky-9-x86_64/base/<rev>/{CHECKSUM,kernel,rocky-9-x86_64.qcow2}
rocky-9-x86_64/base/{last,latest,stable,test}
rocky-9-x86_64/base/kernel-{last,latest,stable,test}
rocky-9-x86_64/<flavor>/<rev>/{CHECKSUM,kernel}
rocky-9-x86_64/<flavor>/{last,latest,stable,test}
rocky-9-x86_64/<flavor>/base-{last,latest,stable,test}
rocky-9-x86_64/<flavor>/kernel-{last,latest,stable,test}
tftpboot/rocky-9-x86_64-<flavor>.efi
tftpboot/rocky-9-x86_64-<flavor>-{last,latest,test}.efi
```

Listing 5: S3 bucket path structure

7 Security

The main pillar of the security architecture is the network design: NEMO2 operates in a physically secured, ISO 27001:2022-certified datacenter with segregated network access. The boot infrastructure (DNBD3, TFTP) operates on a dedicated network protected by firewall rules that prevent access from outside of the cluster. Compute nodes receive images over this isolated network segment. Comprehensive network segmentation and authentication details are documented in Wiebelt et al. (2026). The second pillar is the diskless provisioning model, which significantly reduces the attack surface compared to local-disk systems, since nodes can be restored to their original state simply by rebooting, discarding any changes made during operation. Additional security considerations include ensuring artifact integrity, restricting privileged access, properly managing the secrets required for operation, and leveraging immutability for attack mitigation.

Artifact Integrity: Boot artifacts (kernel, initramfs, boot configuration files) are served from S3 via HTTPS with server certificate validation. While these boot artifacts are publicly available over HTTPS, the core system images delivered via DNBD3 are only accessible through the DNBD3 servers in the internal cluster network. The URLs for the boot artifacts stored in `boot/` contain a 20-character random path component, providing obscurity against enumeration attacks. The DNBD3 protocol employs CRC32 checksums for block integrity verification, protecting against corruption during transport. User credentials are managed centrally through federated login, eliminating the need for password distribution or storage on compute nodes (Wiebelt et al., 2026).

Secret Management: We distinguish between build-time, runtime, and API secrets. Build-time secrets are stored in Ansible playbooks encrypted with Ansible Vault[19]. The Vault passwords are stored as protected CI/CD variables in GitLab, accessible only to project administrators. These secrets are decrypted and used during image builds but are never embedded in the resulting images. The only runtime secret needed on compute nodes is the GitLab API token to fetch the runtime configuration. This token allows read-only access restricted to artifact downloads from the runtime configuration repository; it cannot modify repository contents. The token is stored in the IPMI FRU field of the node BMC, which is not readable by regular users. API write access for S3 and Infoblox DHCP/DNS require separate credentials. For S3, these are saved in CI/CD variables; for Infoblox DHCP/DNS authorized administrators apply these changes from their local workstation.

Immutability as Security: The diskless architecture provides image immutability. System images are mounted read-only at the block device level by design. Compute nodes have no write access to the shared DNBD3 image. Changes to the file system while the node is running are captured by the copy-on-write layer. Each node's copy-on-write layer is encrypted using `dm-crypt` with an independent, volatile encryption key generated at boot time, so that data at rest on the local drive is unreadable after a reboot or when a failed drive is disposed of. Both the copy-on-write layer and the scratch partition used for Slurm jobs are discarded on reboot, preventing persistent malware. An attacker gaining root access can only affect that single node's runtime state, not the shared image potentially affecting other nodes.

8 Conclusion and Future Work

The described diskless architecture provides reproducible builds from version-controlled sources and a rollback mechanism through deployment channel switching, while eliminating the management of local disk installations on compute nodes. By leveraging institutional services for S3, DHCP, and GitLab CI/CD, the only infrastructure we maintain is three DNBD3 servers.

[19] Ansible Vault encryption: https://docs.ansible.com/ansible/latest/vault_guide/, visited on 07.04.2025

We are considering several enhancements in the coming years. Image signing using GPG or sigstore[20] would enable cryptographic image verification. While DNBD3 CRC files protect against corruption during transfer, sigstore would detect tampering and verify images integrity through cryptographic verification. The DNBD3 server plans to support the iSCSI protocol as a transport mechanism, which would eliminate the need for custom kernel modules (DNBD3 and `xloop`). Image-level encryption remains a future goal to further enhance the security of our deployment architecture.

The node-specific runtime configuration newly support GPG encryption. If secrets need to be distributed to compute nodes, encrypted archive files can be fetched from S3 instead of the GitLab API and decrypted using a protected encryption key stored in the IPMI FRU. This would ensure that malicious actors who gain access to the runtime configuration files cannot exploit their contents.

The presented architecture demonstrates that modern CI/CD practices can be successfully integrated into HPC cluster management. By combining established technologies with Infrastructure as Code principles, we have created a flexible and scalable provisioning system. The modular design and reusable pipeline components enable other mid- to large-scale infrastructures to adopt this approach with minimal adaptation effort, resulting in more maintainable and reproducible system deployment architectures.

Acknowledgments

The authors would like to thank the state of Baden-Württemberg for its support of bwHPC and the German Research Foundation (DFG) for funding under »Project number 455622343« (bwForCluster NEMO 2).

Parts of the developments presented in this paper were made possible through the contributions provided by the projects bwLehrpool, bwCloud 3 and bwHPC-S5 that are supported by the Ministry of Science, Research and Arts Baden-Württemberg.

[20] Sigstore signing framework: https://www.sigstore.dev/, visited on 05.05.2025

Corresponding Author

Michael Janczyk: michael.janczyk@rz.uni-freiburg.de
eScience, Rechenzentrum, University of Freiburg,
Hermann-Herder-Str. 10, 79104 Freiburg, Germany

ORCID

Michael Janczyk https://orcid.org/0000-0003-4886-736X
Jonathan Bauer https://orcid.org/0000-0002-5624-2055

References

Allen, B. S. et al. (2020). »Modernizing the HPC System Software Stack«. In: SC20, Atlanta, GA. Zenodo. DOI: 10.5281/zenodo.4324415.

Bauer, J. et al. (2019). »A Sorting Hat For Clusters. Dynamic Provisioning of Compute Nodes for Colocated Large Scale Computational Research Infrastructures«. In: *Proceedings of the 5th bwHPC Symposium. HPC Activities in Baden-Württemberg*. Freiburg, September 2018. Ed. by M. Janczyk, D. von Suchodoletz and B. Wiebelt. TLP, Tübingen, pp. 217–229. DOI: 10.15496/publikation-29055.

Bruno, A. E., S. J. Guercio, D. Sajdak, T. Kew and M. D. Jones (2020). »Grendel: Bare Metal Provisioning System for High Performance Computing«. In: *Practice and Experience in Advanced Research Computing 2020: Catch the Wave*. PEARC '20. Portland, OR, USA: Association for Computing Machinery, pp. 13–18. ISBN: 9781450366892. DOI: 10.1145/3311790.3396637.

Dell EMC (2017). *OEM FRU Technical White Paper*. Tech. rep. Dell EMC. URL: https://dl.dell.com/manuals/all-products/esuprt_solutions_int/esuprt_solutions_int_solutions_resources/general-solution-resources_white-papers10_en-us.pdf (visited on 29. 04. 2025).

Intel Corporation, Hewlett-Packard Company, NEC Corporation and Dell Computer Corporation (2015). *IPMI: Platform Management FRU Information Storage Definition*. Tech. rep. v1.0, Document Revision 1.3. Intel Corporation. URL: https://www.intel.com/content/dam/www/public/us/en/documents/specification-updates/ipmi-platform-mgt-fru-info-storage-def-v1-0-rev-1-3-spec-update.pdf (visited on 29. 04. 2025).

Janczyk, M., D. von Suchodoletz and B. Wiebelt (2019). »bwForCluster NEMO. Forschungscluster für die Wissenschaft«. In: *Proceedings of the 5th bwHPC Symposium. HPC Activities in Baden-Württemberg*. Freiburg, September 2018. 5th bwHPC Symposium. Ed. by M. Janczyk, D. von Suchodoletz and B. Wiebelt. TLP, Tübingen, pp. 29–50. DOI: 10.15496/publikation-29041.

Kurtzer, G. M., V. Sochat and M. W. Bauer (2017). »Singularity: Scientific containers for mobility of compute«. In: *PLOS ONE* 12.5, pp. 1–20. DOI: 10.1371/journal.pone.0177459.

Morris, K. (2020). *Infrastructure as Code. Dynamic Systems for the Cloud Age*. 2nd ed. O'Reilly Media. ISBN: 9781098114664.

Rettberg, S., D. von Suchodoletz and J. Bauer (2019). »Feeding the Masses: DNBD3. Simple, efficient, redundant block device for large scale HPC, Cloud and PC pool installations«. In: *Proceedings of the 5th bwHPC Symposium. HPC Activities in Baden-Württemberg*. Freiburg, September 2018. 5th bwHPC Symposium. Ed. by M. Janczyk, D. von Suchodoletz and B. Wiebelt. TLP, Tübingen, pp. 231–243. DOI: 10.15496/publikation-29056.

Suchodoletz, D. von, J. Leendertse, B. Wiebelt, M. J. Messner and M. Janczyk (2021). »Stateless System Remote-Boot als Business-Continuity-Konzept«. In: *Sicherheit in Vernetzten Systemen 28. DFN-Konferenz*. Hamburg, F1–F21. ISBN: 978-3-7528-9805-7. DOI: 10.6094/UNIFR/218386.

Wiebelt, B., K. Meier, M. Janczyk and D. von Suchodoletz (2016). »Flexible HPC: bwForCluster NEMO«. In: *Proceedings of the 3rd bwHPC symposium*. Ed. by S. Richling, M. Baumann and V. Heuveline. Universitätsbibliothek Heidelberg, pp. 128–130. DOI: 10.11588/heibooks.308.418.

Wiebelt, B., D. von Suchodoletz and M. Janczyk (2026). »bwForCluster NEMO 2: Sustainable Tier-3 HPC Infrastructure. Finding DORIE: Diskless Architecture enabling Optimized, Reproducible, Integrated, and Efficient HPC Operations«. In: *Proceedings of the 10th bwHPC Symposium. HPC Activities in Baden-Württemberg*. Freiburg, September 2024. 10th bwHPC Symposium. Ed. by M. Janczyk, D. von Suchodoletz, B. Wiebelt and M. Frank. KIT Scientific Publishing, Karlsruhe, pp. 213–228. DOI: 10.58895/ksp/1000169488-14.

bwSFS – A Federated Storage Backbone for Research Data Management

A Foundational Infrastructure for RDM Services

Dirk von Suchodoletz[*], Markus Quandt[†], Ulrich Hahn[†], Kolja Glogowski[*], Mark Seifert[*], Jan Leendertse[*], Dorothea Iglezakis[‡]

[*]eScience, University of Freiburg, Freiburg, Germany
[†]Data Center (ZDV), Eberhard-Karls University, Tübingen, Germany
[‡]University Library, Stuttgart, Germany

Abstract

The federated Baden-Württemberg Storage-for-Science (bwSFS) provides efficient access to both generic base-level and specialized services for research data management of the state universities. It consolidates the various storage demands of the research communities utilizing the bwHPC clusters in Tübingen and Freiburg as well as extensions made by the Galaxy project through de.NBI. Beyond providing access to large data volumes the system places a strong emphasis on open standards and long-term usable software components to support RDM. It assists researchers throughout the entire research data lifecycle, particularly in data generation, data analysis, and data publication, including metadata enrichment, data citation, and long-term storage. The infrastructure already fosters beside domain specific support the collaboration with discipline-specific consortia of the NFDI. Shared operational models require close coordination among participating institutions. An additional extension to the system is being implemented through bwSFS-2 by the universities of Stuttgart and Hohenheim, adding both increased capacity and new redundancy options to the object storage federation. A careful balance must be struck between achieving synergies and redundancy, while managing the associated increase in coordination effort.

1 Introduction

For excellent science, well-developed and scalable IT research infrastructures are essential – ones that are embedded within the strategic vision of the respective research institutions.[1] These infrastructures provide efficient access to both generic base-level and specialized services for (domain specific) research data management (RDM). Consolidated and federated services help avoid the creation of redundant structures and prevent overprovisioning at decentralized units.[2] bwSFS (abbreviation for »Baden-Württemberg's Storage-for-Science«) is an infrastructure built on a coordinated statewide concept for LSDF.[3] The presented approach enables a focus on well-defined, securely operated systems with flexible redundancy levels.

Shared use of such services supports scientific work efficiently, while also addressing Green IT considerations through climate-conscious procurement and energy-efficient operation. At the same time, consolidating various needs must not constrain researchers' freedom to choose their own scientific methods. Since both the storage infrastructure and the associated RDM services are readily available, there is no need for extensive procurement, installation, or configuration processes. Individual researchers, research consortia, and clusters – as well as newly appointed faculty – benefit from a fast project start, allowing them to focus their limited resources on the domain-specific layers of the hardware and software stack. This significantly reduces the overall effort for all parties involved in tendering, procurement, and the operation of increasingly complex systems. Core topics such as research data management, including aspects like minimum data retention requirements, can be better supported and integrated into institutional processes such as new appointments, regular modernization efforts, and shifts in research focus. Storage infrastructures like bwSFS also simplify compliance with data protection, sustainability, and operational security requirements.

[1] See e.g. the Freiburg IT infrastructure concept of the FISK, https://uni-freiburg.de/frs/wp-content/uploads/sites/11/IT-Infrastrukturkonzept-fuer-die-Forschung.pdf, visited on 24.06.2025

[2] Due to procurement and funding logic, often based on the theoretical maximum demand at one time.

[3] Large Scale Data Facilities, phase III, (Schneider et al., 2020)

2 Focus and Concept of bwSFS

The focus of the implemented Storage-for-Science system lies in providing a distributed infrastructure.[4] It pools resources and creates specialized hubs by concentrating on specific scientific disciplines. At the Tübingen site, bwSFS supports the disciplines of bioinformatics, astrophysics, geosciences, and eHumanities; in Freiburg, it focuses on elementary particle physics, neuroscience, and microsystems engineering from all state higher education institutions. This selection is closely aligned with the scientific focus of the local bwHPC clusters – BinAC in Tübingen and NEMO in Freiburg – whose computing capacities are used by researchers for various computational workflows. (Suchodoletz et al., 2023)

To effectively support data-intensive research with diverse requirements, a coordinated, federated provision of storage infrastructure tailored to RDM needs is advantageous. However, meeting RDM requirements also implies a commitment to long-term service availability, which should be sustainably ensured through the cooperation of multiple institutions. bwSFS is conceived as a foundational infrastructure on which additional services are built. This approach enables support for various target groups using a shared hardware cluster. Differentiation is based on technical requirements, user needs, and integration into data workflows – whether through external storage systems or internal university networks. Operations follow a tiered responsibility model: base-level storage services are provided by the computing centers, while discipline- or application-specific RDM services are often managed by domain administrators, project teams, or consortia of the National Research Data Infrastructure (NFDI).

2.1 Primary Target Research Communities in Freiburg

Researchers from various disciplines, many of whom are already using scientific computing services (Janczyk et al., 2019; Wiebelt et al., 2016), have regularly approached the computing center for support in research data management or for recommendations on designing secure storage systems. These inquiries were used to gather requirements, which were then consolidated into a shared vision for a DFG grant proposal. At the Freiburg site, the following user groups are the primary focus:

[4] For technical details on the hardware and software stack, see Suchodoletz et al. (2026).

Bernstein Center Freiburg (BCF) – The BCF is the central scientific institution at the University of Freiburg for coordinating research in computational neuroscience and neurotechnology. It integrates a large number of externally funded research projects in both experimental and theoretical neuroscience, as well as their applications in biology, computer science, microsystems engineering, and medical research. The center brings together research groups from nine faculties, institutes, and research units into a multidisciplinary research hub. The brain is a complex, high-dimensional, and adaptive dynamic system. Understanding its function requires innovative concepts and effective methods, particularly for analyzing and interpreting the immense volumes of data generated by high-resolution imaging techniques or implanted multi-electrode systems. The associated simulations are computationally intensive and generate large datasets.

Signal Research – There are several working groups at the University of Freiburg including Electron Microscopy Facilities, Developmental Genetics of Pattern Formation and Differentiation research, Microscopy and Image Analysis Platforms (MIAP), Structural Biology, and the multidisciplinary Cluster of Excellence CIBSS.[5] They bundle a wide spectrum of scientific interests who utilize Electron Microscopy (EM) approaches in research with high-volume data generation. The University of Freiburg currently develops a Technology Platform concept that links the EM facilities across the campus. To guarantee efficient data handling and processing, this platform will bundle data analysis ranging from image analysis to 3D reconstruction and correlative microscopy approaches. A shared data repository helps to ensure data safety and fosters sufficient as well as efficient availability of storage capacities to the different laboratories across the university involved. The various handled data sets ranging from genetics to biochemistry generated by cryo-EM, light microscopy and high resolution camera recordings reaching into the terabyte scale per single run.

Materials and devices in microsystems engineering (IMTEK) – Microsystems engineering is the art of miniaturizing, building microscopic components that are 100 times finer than a human hair. These components can be used to create microsensors or microactuators, which can be combined with electronics to make intelligent microchips that can sense things, make decisions and perform actions. The reliability of miniaturized components that are driven electrically and operate under mechanical action and in physiological environments is crucial. Several groups at IMTEK work on issues of

[5] Centre for Integrative Biological Signaling Studies, https://www.cibss.uni-freiburg.de/, visited on 01.06.2025

reliability using experimental and simulation techniques. When assessing reliability of components, it is crucial to store and archive raw experimental data of material composition and structure, device function and electrical and mechanical qualification. Only the storage of large data sets enables a post-mortem analysis of the origins of failure. Since high resolution images are needed for detailed analysis of structures in the submicrometer to nanometer range, large amounts of data are acquired for each approach of the different research groups. They routinely carry out classical molecular dynamics simulations with 10-100 million atoms. In addition to positions, the researchers typically store velocities and other associated information, such as local potential energy, virial, strain etc., some of which is computed during post-processing. This means a single frame of the simulation requires 10–20 GByte of storage. When the typical molecular dynamics snapshots at intervals of 1 ps; for a 1 ns simulation are written, up to 10–20 TByte of are easily reached.

ATLAS – Elementary particle physics and astroparticle physics investigate the fundamental building blocks of matter, their interactions, and the underlying symmetry structure of the physical laws governing the microcosm. These fields also aim to understand the composition of matter and energy in the universe, addressing questions such as the matter-antimatter asymmetry, dark matter, and dark energy. Following the landmark discovery of the Higgs boson in 2012, fundamental questions remain – such as the detailed structure of the Higgs sector, the mechanism of electroweak symmetry breaking, and whether there are additional particles, forces, or symmetries beyond the Standard Model of particle physics. The nature of dark matter and dark energy also remains largely unknown. The experimental particle physics groups are primarily involved in the ATLAS experiment at the LHC, the direct search for dark matter in the XENON experiment, and the search for axions in the CAST experiment. In addition, they conduct R&D for upgrades to current experiments and for the development of future experiments in these research areas. They also contribute to generic developments in innovative detector and information technologies. Theoretical groups provide precision predictions for a wide range of processes within the Standard Model and its extensions. A central focus is on studying the phenomenology of particle theories at the LHC to address the unresolved fundamental questions.

Galaxy – The analysis platform is used by a wide range of scientific communities, each with distinct storage requirements and data management practices. Researchers in genomics may work with raw sequencing reads and aligned genomes, biodiversity scientists may analyze geospatial species distribution datasets, while climate scientists might process multi-terabyte simulation results. In cheminformatics or NLP, highly structured compound databases or large-scale corpora need to be queried, annotated, and analyzed reproducibly. These diverse use-cases result in a broad spectrum of data sizes, formats, and access patterns – from tens of megabytes to tens of terabytes per project. At present, the European Galaxy server alone manages over three petabytes of active user data, reflecting the scale of its cross-domain user base. This includes raw data, processed results, shared workflows, training materials, and metadata critical for reproducibility. The platform's ability to preserve complete analysis histories, tool versions, and parameters across such vast datasets ensures that insights remain traceable and verifiable, regardless of domain. The project was not part of the initial proposal but instead, as part of the extension funding concept, (Wesner et al., 2016) integrated its own requirements into the system by effectively »buying in.«

Further disciplines housed at the university have been allocated storage space for »cold data« primarily for archival purposes, extending beyond the focus on active data management to a larger number of research groups. These include research groups and projects at the Hilde Mangold House, developmental biology, electron microscopy at the central facility of the Faculty of Biology, and research groups in biology, nephrology, and pharmacology that make use of these resources. In addition, the Microscopy and Image Analysis Platform (MIAP) – a joint network for scientific imaging and image analysis infrastructure – as well as several groups in structural biology are represented. Other groups and institutes include anthropology, geobotany, the Cluster of Excellence BrainLinks-BrainTools, and additional groups at IMTEK.

2.2 Primary Target Research Communities in Tübingen

At the Tübingen site, there has long been a growing need for secure, long-term storage of scientific data. In addition to astrophysics and geophysics from the Tübingen HPC cluster BinAC (Krüger et al., 2017), the main focus lies in bioinformatics and life sciences, where increasing volumes of data are processed via the de.NBI platform. Demand for secure and efficient data storage and transfer is already high and expected to grow further with the launch of the refreshed cluster and the expansion of de.NBI. A key focus of bwSFS in Tübingen is also on storage and transport encryption, as well as secure data transfer, due to the highly sensitive nature of much of the stored material, primarily human genome data. The main research groups served by bwSFS at the Tübingen site include:

Quantitative Biology Center (QBIC) – The QBiC in Tübingen provides RDM, project consulting, bioinformatics analyses, and method development for the University of Tübingen and the Faculty of Medicine, providing a central service point for high-throughput life science data. QBiC employs bwSFS as the main storage stack for the entire data management, which comprises raw data from high throughput technologies, imaging and bioinformatics analyses. Data stored and processed at QBiC is expected to grow considerably in the future, and so is the demand for a large-scale enterprise storage system such as bwSFS, which can combine high performance with secure storage and transport security. Geo-redundancy an the possibility to restore data quickly from regular snapshots are also a key requirement in QBiC's storage stack.

Applied Bioinformatics group (ABI) – The Kohlbacher Lab at the University of Tübingen specializes in the analysis of omics data (genomics, proteomics, metabolomics), structural bioinformatics, and computational immunomics. It is lead by Oliver Kohlbacher and has strong ties with QBiC and experimental labs to develop and apply innovative methods and algorithms to tackle complex challenges in the life sciences. It has a well-earned reputation for its contributions to the field, particularly in the development of high-quality research software. A second focus is the Translational Bioinformatics unit (TBI), which operates at the intersection of medical informatics and bioinformatics. As a vital member of the DIFUTURE consortium, the group is dedicated to developing and establishing Data Integration Centers as part of the German Medical Informatics Initiative.

Centre for Genetic Epidemiology (CGE) – The CGE is a newly created core facility by the Medical Faculty of the University of Tubingen, which aims to bridge the gap between clinical, epidemiological and basic research. Among its main objectives are the identification of genes and risk factors for various complex diseases such as Parkinson disease, cancer and diabetes, the CGE also tries to identify enriched cohorts for therapeutic intervention to provide better health care, and aims to develop software tools to analyze next generation data to understand the disease mechanism. To meet these goals, the CGE applies state-of-the-art genomic, bioinformatic and genetic- epidemiological approaches to pursue an individualized medicine (iMed) program to understand the molecular underpinnings of various complex diseases. The data collected in these studies comprise whole exome and genome sequencing in familial and sporadic patients, and is thus of quite sensitive nature. The CGE employs bwSFS as a secure and performant storage backend to process the data at the de.NBI platform.

Computational Astrophysics – A key research area of the Department of Computational Physics led by Christoph Schäfer at the Institute for Astronomy and Astrophysics are numerical particle methods, which focus on meshfree particle methods such as Smoothed Particle Hydrodynamics, Molecular Dynamics and Tree algorithms and their applications on astrophysical processes such as protoplanetary discs and embedded protoplanet evolution, circumbinary discs, planetesimal and planetary embryo formation processes, impacts and collisions. Most of the simulation data is stored on bwSFS, with particular emphasis on high performance and throughput as well as data security and reliability, which allows to run large-scale simulations and store large amounts of data with high availability for fast postprocessing, e.g., visualisation.

Center for Plant Molecular Biology (ZMBP) – The ZMBP researches the molecular processes of plants and their interactions with the living and non-living environment. Modern technologies such as light and electron microscopy, genomics, and metabolomics are routinely used in this context, producing large data sets. Their evaluation from a variety of perspectives and their long-term, reliable storage are therefore essential, especially since different experiments/data sets must be compared with each other over several years. This essential infrastructure is extremely important not only for the ZMBP, with its current 10 professorships, but also for its Collaborative Research Center (SFB 1101) and the Cluster of Excellence »Green Robust.«

Several **other research groups** in Tübingen employ bwSFS as one of their primary tool for research data storage, reflecting diversity of research at the University of Tübingen. For instance, the Digital Humanities Center relies heavily on bwSFS's object store backend for the InvenioRDM data management platform, which is used as an infrastructure for the archiving and publication of research data from all humanities and cultural studies. Other examples include the Computational Psychiatry group headed by Tobias Hauser which employs modern cognitive neuroscience and computational modeling methods to understand the neurocognitive mechanisms underlying mental illnesses, and stores some of its research data on bwSFS.

2.3 bwSFS-2

As an extension of the federated storage system between Tübingen and Freiburg, bwSFS-2 is designed to complement these existing infrastructures. It primarily aims to facilitate the acquisition and availability of high-quality, large-scale experimental data from the two Stuttgart based universities, as well as huge quantities of simulation and HPC data. In addition, it provides mechanisms for targeted data sharing (including with external collaborators, such as industry partners), enables data publication, and prepares for sustainable long-term archiving. bwSFS-2 is therefore intended not only to host active research data (»hot data«) but also to accompany data throughout its lifecycle up to publication. The synergies created by the expansion of bwSFS through bwSFS-2 will have a lasting impact, as a closely coordinated and jointly developed evolution of the »bwSFS-x infrastructures« is planned between the partner universities of Tübingen, Freiburg, Stuttgart, and Hohenheim, with the possibility for further institutions to join in the future.

Various working groups and communities from the engineering sciences (fluid mechanics, thermodynamics, mechanics, visualization, production engineering, aerospace), natural sciences ((computational) physics, meteorology), and life sciences (food chemistry and medicine, animal and plant sciences, biochemistry, land use, physiology) are planning to use bwSFS-2 for the management and annotation of their large-scale data sets.

2.4 Integration into Research Data Management

Beyond providing large data volumes – resulting from the immense storage needs of increasingly digitized scientific disciplines and emerging data-driven methods bwSFS places a strong emphasis on open standards and long-term usable software components to support RDM. It assists researchers throughout the entire research data lifecycle, particularly in data generation, data analysis, and data publication, including metadata enrichment, data citation, and long-term storage. By building discipline-specific data management services on top of bwSFS, the groundwork is laid for simplifying researchers' everyday handling of their data and integrating these processes into their daily workflows.

A future-oriented approach to RDM therefore operates in federations and also considers existing services, third-party offerings, and the use of appropriate interfaces for data and metadata exchange. Modern RDM infrastructures must align with the established standards of their respective scientific communities to remain attractive and relevant in the long term. The collaborative nature of scientific research – across institutional boundaries – and the core RDM principle of reusability of research data at national and international stages must be supported technically by bundling measures and fostering cooperation among the infrastructure facilities of as many universities as possible. This explicitly includes collaboration with discipline-specific consortia of the NFDI at the national level, and the European Open Science Cloud (EOSC) at the international level.

2.5 System Sizing

The sizing of the proposed major research instrument followed a phased process. Initially, individual research groups with significant storage needs approached the applicants for support. The team then drew on data collected during the state-funded bwFDM-Info project[6] and conducted a targeted survey of known research groups in the relevant focus areas – coordinated with the university Vice Presidents for Research – to determine current storage needs.

The system was co-funded by the German Research Foundation (DFG) and the state of Baden-Württemberg, and has been gradually expanded through further support from additional grant providers such as the Federal Ministry of Education and Research. bwSFS and the services built on top of it are designed to meet RDM requirements in a way that is as transparent as possible for the relevant scientific disciplines. The necessary technical components, development work, and training are provided by the bwHPC-S5 support project, funded by the state of Baden-Württemberg. (Bartel et al., 2022)

The design of bwSFS ensures that the storage requirements of the applicants for their data-intensive research and workflows are met. Since a time-limited funding program is insufficient to support sustainable RDM, accompanying measures were implemented to address both the issue of long-term data accessibility and the necessary human and technical resources. This includes the division of the system into a research-focused and an infrastructure-focused component, as well as the support provided through the

[6] The state initiative on RDM, https://bwfdm.de/en/, visited on 12.06.2025

bwHPC-S5 project for data- and compute-intensive research. Thanks to these measures, the participating infrastructure institutions are able to support researchers in using the system, connect to existing infrastructures, and maintain the long-term operation of the RDM infrastructure well beyond the initial funding period. The universities of Freiburg and Tübingen, represented by their computing centers, have developed a comprehensive concept for establishing an RDM infrastructure that, in line with recommendations from the German Science and Humanities Council (Wissenschaftsrat, 2020) and the Council for Information Infrastructures (Informationsinfrastrukturen, 2017), can be integrated into larger national and international structures, such as those required by the NFDI consortia.

3 Operational and Funding Model

As with HPC systems, an attractive infrastructure can serve as a »crystallization core,« particularly when participating projects are only charged for actual incremental costs.[7] This is feasible when certain hardware components – such as storage heads for connecting additional enclosures – are already available. Especially in the case of storage systems, bundling demand leads to significant cost savings. This is illustrated by the following example: If a storage system is procured with a final capacity of 100 TByte and a depreciation period of five years, it accounts for 500 TByte-years. However, assuming a linear fill rate from zero to full capacity over that period, only 250 TByte-years are actually needed. Since not all projects and research groups start simultaneously or immediately write large volumes of data, this supports a staggered procurement model, in which system expansion is carried out in phases. This approach, however, is only efficient when dealing with sufficiently large volumes.

Unlike compute infrastructures for AI or scientific computing, replacing a storage system is far less trivial. First, data does not simply »disappear« at the end of a project – minimum retention periods must be observed, and the data may be important for follow-up research. Second, migrating data from an old to a new storage system might cause high loads, which can significantly impact system performance from the user's perspective over an extended period. To enable structured and long-term storage system development, a funding model aligned with the entire institution is recommended. Such

[7] This is a proven concept introduced with the bwForCluster NEMO, see Wesner et al. (2016).

a model allows for more efficient procurement compared to uncoordinated purchases of small independent systems. The strategic goal is to shift toward »buying shares« in larger infrastructure systems.[8] Depending on the type of scientific institution, funding should come from the following sources:

- Base institutional funding: The operating institution should be equipped with independent baseline funding to ensure availability of the necessary staff for planning, setup, and ongoing administration of the storage systems. This ensures operational capability, including financial management and infrastructure renewal.
- Central funds: Used to supplement baseline storage capacity and make strategic investments, enabling allocation of storage to different users within an institution (e.g., faculties, departments, projects, individual researchers). Typically, storage systems are renewed in larger blocks and redistributed in metered units based on demand. This guarantees near-immediate resource availability and allows the system to be treated as a general-purpose resource within funding proposals. Depending on institutional practice, this model may also include centrally guaranteed resources for faculty appointments.
- Internal contributions: From the respective entities like institutes, research groups, or individual professorships that cover their needs through participation in shared systems, rather than procuring and managing their own infrastructure.
- Third-party funding: Acts as either initial or expansion financing, especially for large-scale systems like bwSFS, which are jointly operated across institutions.

Storage infrastructures should be integrated into the overall institutional funding model. This is made possible by associating shares either with participation in the project (via co-applicant researchers) or through follow-up expansion funding from project grants. Given that renewal cycles for many storage systems range from six to ten years – with formal depreciation often shorter, but systems typically expanded over time – anticipated storage needs should be consolidated with strategic reserves. This ensures a unified and transparent process for all stakeholders, whether covering standard requirements, newly approved collaborative research centers (CRCs), excellence clusters, or freshly appointed professors.

[8] There is an increasingly positive attitude towards such measures by the DFG and other funding agencies.

Basic and small-scale needs should be met through central institutional funding, allowing aggregation of a critical mass while keeping accounting efforts manageable. These contributions can be documented as institutional co-funding in grant applications. Any needs beyond that should be assigned to specific projects or professorships and funded decentrally, so as not to overburden the shared core infrastructure.

Sharing large storage resources across many users, federating storage systems, and ensuring fair cost distribution require accounting of allocated resources over time. Differences in storage types – protocols, data layout, distribution, and redundancy levels must be taken into account, as they result in varying operational overhead. Monitoring of the resources is conducted via dedicated state-of-the-art instances, which aggregates provisioning and usage data from the various storage systems. This data forms the basis for detailed analysis of storage utilization, data throughput, and overall system performance.

4 Support Concept

Because the storage system serves a wide range of user groups and needs, it requires broad and multifaceted support. This support must cover both domain-specific expertise and general technical assistance. It spans everything from basic administrative-level provisioning of storage access – such as NFS, SMB, or Object Storage shares – and technical consultation, to assistance with implementing higher-level services and workflows. For file share provisioning, support often involves quota management and assignment of access rights. The Object Storage system offers a comprehensive tenant environment that allows user groups to independently manage their S3 buckets and access policies. Additional users include operators of higher-level RDM services, who typically provide direct support to end users for their specific applications.

In Freiburg, the Research Data Management Group, and now the Central Data Facility (CDF),[9] provide case-specific consulting – ranging from planning research projects and selecting suitable storage infrastructures, to using the associated RDM services. The CDF also serves as a key liaison to faculty-level support structures, including data stewards and IT administrators based in departments or collaborative projects. It plays an

[9] The RDM facility at Freiburg university, https://uni-freiburg.de/cdf/, visited on 01.06.2025

increasingly important coordinating and mediating role, aligning with the state-wide FDM initiative and coordinating with the AK FDM, while organizing access to national, regional, and local resources. It also fosters cooperation with faculties and supports the integration of local data stewards.

At the Tübingen site, a Central Registration Platform (ZAS) was developed as a self-service portal for user and project management.[10] Users can register with a dedicated service password and gain access to comprehensive information about their storage projects. Metadata such as project descriptions and publications can be recorded there, and the platform offers secure communication for technical details, access credentials, and operational information. For each storage project, groups are automatically created to manage granular access rights. The PI of the storage project can manage group memberships independently using an automatically generated access key. ZAS synchronizes its database with the the Tübingen HPC cluster BinAC (Krüger et al., 2017) where possible, ensuring consistent user and group IDs to facilitate the export of storage resources into the cluster. In addition, user information, access credentials, and permission groups are synchronized with the domain controllers of the bwSFS SMB/AD server, enabling authorized users to mount the storage resources directly as network shares using their service credentials.

From the administrator's perspective, ZAS significantly simplifies the management of bwSFS resources by associating not only users and resources, but also permissions, metadata, and publications directly with the storage projects. All steps of project management, including database synchronization, are automated – only the final step, actual storage provisioning, currently requires manual input. An automated provisioning solution based on AWX/Ansible in a high-availability Kubernetes environment has been developed and is currently in its final testing phase.

5 Conclusion and Future Developments

Over the course of its planning and operation, the system has provided valuable experience in various technical and organizational aspects (Suchodoletz et al., 2019; Wehrle et al., 2017). Providing a dedicated system for RDM has helped many research groups

[10] The user interface, https://zas.bwsfs.uni-tuebingen.de, visited on 21.06.2025

actively engage with the topic. The consolidation of multiple groups onto a shared storage system reduces inefficiencies and makes it easy to onboard additional users through incremental expansion. The availability of different storage options – ranging from traditional network shares to object storage – enables researchers to optimize data storage according to their specific needs. The base system for object storage is currently being expanded to include two additional university sites in the state: Stuttgart and Hohenheim. The bwSFS-2 framework, currently under development, consists of a hardware layer for central storage, a hardware layer for long-term storage, and a dedicated software layer responsible for resource and access management, metadata assignment, quality assurance, interfaces to publication repositories and archival systems, as well as for data offloading and provisioning. Of particular importance is the metadata system – often realized through specialized or domain specific services, which enables discipline-specific enrichment of the data through individual yet standards-oriented metadata schemas creating the ideal conditions for FAIR publication or archiving of the data. The ongoing activities involve a step-by-step transformation of the original S3 storage configuration on the hardware layer into a secure, multi-site research data storage system spanning the four locations.

Thanks to its close integration with resources for the scientific computing such as BinAC and de.NBI cloud in Tübingen as well as NEMO and bwCloud-OS in Freiburg, the bwSFS system is already being used by several NFDI consortia as a central component for research data management in a variety of roles. For example, Galaxy is used by several research groups, as are DataPLANT's DataHUB for *omics and OMERO for the storage of microscopy data. The design of the system and its associated services could thus serve as a blueprint for other research domains and NFDI consortia, enabling more efficient data exchange between different RDM platforms and communities within the NFDI in the medium term.

Acknowledgments

bwSFS is funded by the Deutsche Forschungsgemeinschaft (DFG, German Research Foundation) – 405998531, 405999126. The de.NBI/Galaxy extension and bwSFS-2 extension are made possible through BMBF grant 031 A538A and INST 41/1183-1 (LAGG) respectively. The authors further thank the Baden-Württemberg state for the continuous support of the bwHPC-S5 project and the recent support of de.NBI.

Corresponding Author

Dirk von Suchodoletz: dirk.von.suchodoletz@rz.uni-freiburg.de
eScience Abteilung, Rechenzentrum Albert-Ludwigs-Universität Freiburg,
Hermann-Herder-Str. 10, 79104 Freiburg, Deutschland

ORCID

Dirk von Suchodoletz https://orcid.org/0000-0002-4382-5104
Markus Quandt https://orcid.org/0000-0002-2090-4782
Ulrich Hahn https://orcid.org/0000-0003-4471-9263
Kolja Glogowski https://orcid.org/0000-0002-1361-5712
Mark Seifert https://orcid.org/0000-0002-1042-6107
Jan Leendertse https://orcid.org/0000-0001-5676-493X
Dorothea Iglezakis https://orcid.org/0000-0002-8524-0569

References

Bartel, R. and J. Salk (2022). »bwHPC-S5 - Scientific Simulation and Storage Support Services«. In: *Proceedings of the 7th bwHPC Symposium. HPC Activities in Baden-Württemberg*. DOI: 10.18725/OPARU-46056.

Informationsinfrastrukturen, R. .-. R. für (2017). *Enhancing Research Data Management: Performance through Diversity. Recommendations regarding structures, processes, and financing for research data management in Germany*. URL: https://rfii.de/?p=2075.

Janczyk, M., D. von Suchodoletz and B. Wiebelt (2019). »bwForCluster NEMO. Forschungscluster für die Wissenschaft«. In: *Proceedings of the 5th bwHPC Symposium. HPC Activities in Baden-Württemberg*. Freiburg, September 2018. 5th bwHPC Symposium. Ed. by M. Janczyk, D. von Suchodoletz and B. Wiebelt. TLP, Tübingen, pp. 29–50. DOI: 10.15496/publikation-29041.

Krüger, J. et al. (2017). »Bioinformatics and astrophysics cluster (BinAC)«. In: *Proceedings of the 3rd bwHPC Symposium. HPC Activities in Baden-Württemberg*, pp. 91–95.

Schneider, G. et al. (2020). *Rahmenkonzept der Hochschulen des Landes Baden-Württemberg für datenintensive Dienste – bwDATA Phase III (2020-2024)*. DOI: 10.15496/publikation-55923.

Suchodoletz, D. von, K. Glogowski, M. Seifert, M. Quandt and U. Hahn (2026). »Technical Foundations and Service Integration in the bwSFS Storage Infrastructure. Research Data Management Practice«. In: *Proceedings of the 10th bwHPC Symposium. HPC Activities in Baden-Württemberg*. Freiburg, September 2024. 10th bwHPC Symposium. Ed. by M. Janczyk, D. von Suchodoletz, B. Wiebelt and M. Frank. KIT Scientific Publishing, Karlsruhe, pp. 265–282. DOI: 10.58895/ksp/1000169488-17.

Suchodoletz, D. von, U. Hahn, B. Wiebelt, K. Glogowski and M. Seifert (2019). »Storage infrastructures to support advanced scientific workflows. Towards research data management aware storage infrastructures«. In: *Proceedings of the 5th bwHPC Symposium. HPC Activities in Baden-Württemberg*. Freiburg, September 2018. 5th bwHPC Symposium. Ed. by M. Janczyk, D. von Suchodoletz and B. Wiebelt. TLP, Tübingen, pp. 263–279. DOI: 10.15496/publikation-29058.

Suchodoletz, D. von et al. (2023). *Rahmenkonzept der Universitäten des Landes Baden-Württemberg für das High-Performance Computing (HPC) und Data-Intensive Computing (DIC) für den Zeitraum 2025 bis 2032*. DOI: 10.15496/publikation-90185.

Wehrle, D., B. Wiebelt and D. von Suchodoletz (2017). »Design eines FDM-fähigen Speichersystems«. In: *10. DFN-Forum Kommunikationstechnologien, 30.-31. Mai 2017, Berlin, Gesellschaft für Informatik eV (GI)*, pp. 145–154. URL: https://dl.gi.de/bitstream/handle/20.500.12116/470/paper10.pdf.

Wesner, S., D. von Suchodoletz and G. Schneider (2016). »Überlegungen zu laufenden Cluster-Erweiterungen in bwHPC«. In: *Kooperation von Rechenzentren, Governance und Steuerung - Organisation, Rechtsgrundlagen, Politik*. Ed. by D. von Suchodoletz, J. C. Schulz, J. Leendertse, H. Hotzel and M. Wimmer. Berlin, Boston: De Gruyter Oldenbourg, pp. 331–342. DOI: 10.1515/9783110459753-028.

Wiebelt, B., K. Meier, M. Janczyk and D. von Suchodoletz (2016). »Flexible HPC: bwForCluster NEMO«. In: *Proceedings of the 3rd bwHPC symposium*. Ed. by S. Richling, M. Baumann and V. Heuveline. heiBOOKS, pp. 128–130. DOI: 10.11588/heibooks.308.c3729.

Wissenschaftsrat (2020). *Zum Wandel in den Wissenschaften durch datenintensive Forschung*. URL: https://www.wissenschaftsrat.de/download/2020/8667-20.html.

Technical Foundations and Service Integration in the bwSFS Storage Infrastructure

Research Data Management Practice

Dirk von Suchodoletz[*], Kolja Glogowski[*] Mark Seifert[*] Markus Quandt[†]
Ulrich Hahn[†]

[*]eScience, University of Freiburg, Freiburg, Germany
[†]Data Center (ZDV), Eberhard-Karls University, Tübingen, Germany

Abstract

Modern RDM requires storage infrastructures that support a wide range of technical and disciplinary demands across the data lifecycle. The bwSFS storage infrastructure addresses these needs by providing a robust and extensible platform composed of traditional file-based storage (via NFS/SMB) and scalable object storage accessed through HTTPS REST APIs. Designed for integration into complex service ecosystems, bwSFS enables domain-specific RDM services, including those developed within the NFDI context, to build upon a stable technical foundation. To support sustainable RDM practices, bwSFS is complemented by a suite of interoperable services that facilitate data versioning, sharing, publication, and the assignment of persistent identifiers. Its proximity to high-performance computing (HPC), cloud platforms, and analysis frameworks such as Galaxy further enhances its utility for data-intensive research workflows. A key feature of the infrastructure is its geo-distributed erasure coding across four federated sites, ensuring high availability and geographic redundancy. This paper outlines the technical design of bwSFS, its integration with higher-level RDM services, and its role in enabling collaborative, FAIR-aligned data practices across scientific disciplines.

1 Introduction

Modern storage systems for research data management (RDM) are typically embedded within complex and heterogeneous service ecosystems. The various phases of the data lifecycle impose different requirements on storage technologies, necessitating a differentiated provisioning approach. At the foundation lie scalable base-level storage services, which provide a flexible platform for domain-specific and community-oriented RDM services to build upon. For Baden-Württemberg Storage-for-Science (bwSFS) the operations group responsible for the base-level storage services acts as the interface to the administrators of higher-level RDM services. Their role includes providing service support through storage operation and configuration, closely coordinated with the administrators of the dependent services. This group often also serves as the point of contact for the respective NFDI subject consortia and their specific requirements.

Effective RDM additionally often requires integration with computing resources such as high-performance computing (HPC) systems, cloud infrastructures, or data analysis platforms like Galaxy. These interdependencies can influence both the physical location and the type of storage required for research data. The underlying technical infrastructure for sustainable RDM must therefore be designed for growth, scalability, and long-term operation. A central goal is to avoid time-consuming data migrations during system transitions while simultaneously providing durable services for data publication and long-term archiving, often with time horizons of ten years or more. This document extends upon the organizational concepts developed in the context of bwSFS (Suchodoletz et al., 2019, 2026), elaborating them at the technical level and highlighting the interconnections with ongoing RDM services.

2 Fundamental Storage Services

To address the diverse storage requirements of RDM, the bwSFS infrastructure primarily relies on two complementary technologies: traditional file storage, provided via NFS or SMB shares within the local campus network, and a more recently adopted object storage system, which is accessed via an HTTPS REST API. These technologies differ significantly in their usage patterns but complement the needs of research communities and the tools and services they employ.

2.1 File Storage: NetApp ONTAP

A core component of the system, particularly for supporting classical demands such as data ingestion and processing, is a file storage environment based on NetApp FAS8200 systems. These systems export network file systems using NFSv3, NFSv4, and SMBv3 protocols. In addition to the performance-optimized primary systems at the main site, mirrored storage systems are available at a secondary site to enable geo-redundant replication of primary data (see Subsections 2.3 and 2.4). These secondary systems, based on NetApp AFF-A300 all-flash arrays, support transparent cold data offloading to the object storage system using FabricPool (S3 tiering). This configuration provides failover from the primary to the secondary system in the event of a disaster, minimizing downtime.

As part of infrastructure expansion funded through capacity growth initiatives, a NetApp AFF-A400 all-flash system has been deployed in Freiburg to support high-performance backend requirements for the de.NBI cloud and Galaxy analysis platform (Suchodoletz et al., 2026). Given the substantial storage capacity demands of several Petabytes, this system also leverages S3 tiering (FabricPool), whereby cold or infrequently accessed data is transparently offloaded to object storage and recalled as needed to the high-performance flash layer. This tiering process remains completely transparent to NFS clients.

To reduce latency for remote access to the FAS8200 systems in Tübingen, FlexCache instances have been deployed at the Stuttgart and Konstanz sites. These components are described in detail in Subsection 3.8.

2.2 Object Storage: NetApp StorageGRID

In addition to network-based file storage, bwSFS utilizes a geographically distributed object storage system based on NetApp StorageGRID. Traditional file storage systems are engineered for block-level access to files organized within hierarchical directory structures, with a focus on high-performance in-place modifications and low-latency read/write operations. In contrast, object storage systems are optimized for scalable, efficient, and (optionally) geographically distributed data storage, with an emphasis on durability and resilience. Rather than mutable files, these systems store immutable objects that can be replaced or deleted but not modified in place. Internally, objects are managed using a key-value database without a hierarchical file structure,[1] allowing for the efficient storage of very large numbers of objects.

Access to StorageGRID is provided via the S3 protocol,[2] and fine-grained access control can be implemented using flexible access policy definitions. Object storage is not a direct replacement for file storage, but there are numerous use cases such as repositories, data archives (see Subsections 3.2 and 3.5), or the storage of raw and processed research data, where in-place modifications are unnecessary or even undesirable.

The initial bwSFS object storage setup was distributed across four locations: two in Freiburg (FR1 and FR2) and two in Tübingen (TU1 and TU2). StorageGRID enables flexible configuration of data placement across sites and storage nodes through the use of Information Lifecycle Management (ILM) rules,[3] allowing various redundancy levels and giving control over the distribution of objects between storage nodes and sites. As part of the ongoing bwSFS-2 initiative, a new distributed StorageGRID deployment is currently being established in cooperation with the Universities of Stuttgart and Hohenheim (Suchodoletz et al., 2026). This instance will integrate storage nodes from Freiburg and Tübingen with additional nodes in Stuttgart and Hohenheim, forming a geographically distributed system spanning all four sites. It will employ an erasure coding scheme (EC 6+2) capable of tolerating the complete failure of any single site without incurring data loss.

2.3 Configuration of Storage Systems in Freiburg

The configuration of the bwSFS storage systems in Freiburg is distributed across two primary data center locations of the university computing center,[4] as illustrated in Figure 1. Detailed configuration parameters of the respective systems are listed in Table 1.

1 For client access, a hierarchical structure can be emulated if required.
2 NetApp StorageGRID supports an API that is largely compatible with Amazon S3.
3 Information Lifecycle Management (ILM) rules define placement, erasure coding configuration, and lifecycle operations for stored objects.
4 Hermann-Herder-Straße 10 (FR1) and Platz der Alten Synagoge 1 (FR2)

Table 1: Storage system capacities and details for Freiburg site (FR1 and FR2)

Storage System	Location	Nodes	Type	Disks	Raw Capacity
FAS8200	FR1	2	HDD	480 × 10 TB	4.8 PB
AFF A300	FR2	2	SSD	36 × 7.68 TB	276 TB
AFF A400	FR1	2	SSD	72 × 7.68 TB	552 TB
StorageGRID	FR1	25	HDD	1500 × 12 TB	18.0 PB
StorageGRID	FR2	15	HDD	900 × 12 TB	10.8 PB

The central file storage system at the primary site (FR1) consists of a NetApp FAS8200 cluster with a usable capacity of approximately 3.5 PB. This system hosts several Storage Virtual Machines (SVMs), which provide dedicated access endpoints (NFS or SMB) across various networks. Some SVMs are also connected to distinct Active Directory (AD) domains, allowing for flexible integration into heterogeneous IT environments.

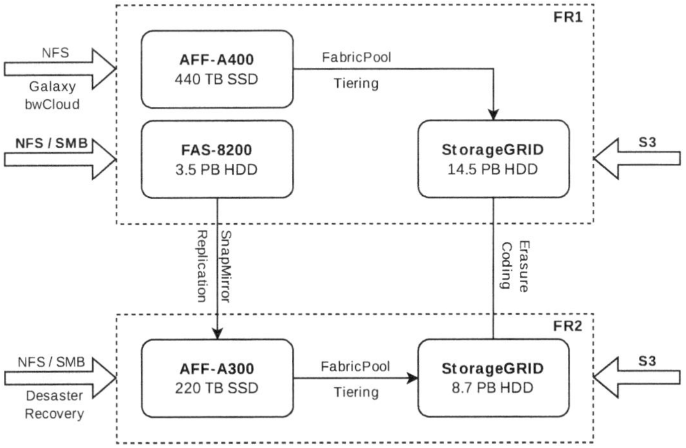

Figure 1: bwSFS storage Freiburg (FR1 and FR2)

To ensure disaster resilience, parts of the primary file storage are replicated hourly via SnapMirror to a NetApp AFF-A300 system located at the secondary site (FR2). In the event of a complete failure of the primary system, access can be redirected to the secondary system, allowing timely restoration of data availability. The AFF-A300 is a full-flash system with a net usable capacity of 220 TB in the SSD tier. To meet extended capacity demands, cold data is transparently offloaded to an S3 tier using FabricPool, with the StorageGRID system at FR2 serving as the object storage backend.

Additionally, an independent full-flash file storage system based on a NetApp AFF-A400 is operated at FR1. This system provides a net usable capacity of 440 TB in the SSD tier and also uses an S3 tier (FabricPool), offloading cold data to the StorageGRID instance at the same location (FR1). Access to this system is exclusively via NFS. Data tiering operations (both offloading and recall) are fully transparent to end users.

The object storage infrastructure comprises a NetApp StorageGRID system with a total of 40 storage nodes (25 located in FR1 and 15 in FR2). Each node provides a net usable capacity of approximately 580 TB, resulting in a total system capacity of just over 23 PB before considering the reductions introduced by further node-based redundancy mechanisms.

For data stored exclusively at one of the Freiburg sites – such as tiered data from the AFF-A300 and AFF-A400 systems – the »EC 8+2« erasure coding scheme is employed. This scheme offers high storage efficiency (25% overhead) and can tolerate the failure of up to two nodes at a given site without data loss. For data that is to be redundantly distributed across both Freiburg sites, a dual-site replication setup is used. In this case, each site stores data with »EC 6+1« erasure coding, and data is additionally replicated across the two sites. While this configuration results in a higher storage overhead (133%), it enables the system to withstand the failure of a node at each site as well as the complete outage of one site, without compromising data integrity.

Looking into potential future developments, the addition of a third StorageGRID location within Freiburg is planned. This expansion would significantly improve the efficiency of cross-site data distribution. For example, a scheme such as »EC 4+2« could be employed, which offers robust fault tolerance with a moderate storage overhead of 50 %.

2.4 Configuration of Storage Systems in Tübingen

The system configuration in Tübingen differs in scale due to the varying requirements of the participating user groups (Suchodoletz et al., 2026), but follows the same fundamental architectural principles as the Freiburg deployment. A geo-redundant setup has been implemented across two independent data center facilities – TU1 located at Wächterstraße 76 and TU2 at Morgenstelle 24/3. These sites are interconnected via high-speed bidirectional fiber links with a capacity of 40 Gbps. The overall architecture is illustrated in Figure 2. Detailed configuration parameters of the respective systems are listed in Table 2.

Table 2: Storage system capacities and details for Tübingen site (TU1 and TU2)

Storage System	Location	Nodes	Type	Disks	Raw Capacity
FAS8200	TU1	4	HDD	960 × 10 TB	9.6 PB
AFF A300	TU2	2	SSD	48 × 7.68 TB	368 TB
StorageGRID	TU1	6	HDD	360 × 12 TB	4.32 PB
StorageGRID	TU2	18	HDD	1080 × 12 TB	12.96 PB

The file storage component at TU1 is realized using two NetApp FAS8200 HA pairs. Individual volumes can be distributed transparently and efficiently across storage aggregates on both systems, forming a logically unified storage pool with a raw capacity of 960 × 10 TB (approximately 7 PB of usable capacity). To safeguard against data loss, regular snapshots are taken and, together with the active filesystem, are mirrored to a NetApp AFF-A300 all-flash system located at TU2. This secondary system provides 293 TB of SSD storage and utilizes SnapMirror technology to maintain synchronized copies.

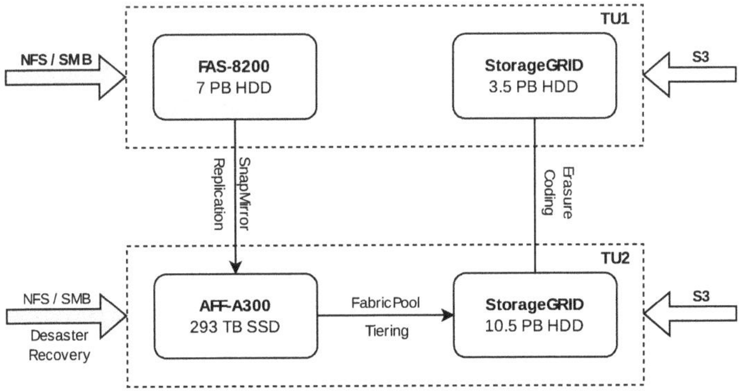

Figure 2: bwSFS storage Tübingen (TU1 and TU2)

Data is retained at TU2 for a maximum of 30 days. Subsequently, the coldest data blocks are automatically offloaded to object storage for long-term preservation via FabricPool tiering. Approximately 10.5 PB of object storage in Tübingen is designated for this long-term archive tier. In the event of a disaster, hot data blocks are automatically replicated from the object store into the AFF-A300 flash cache to restore fast access.

The original design envisioned a unified object storage infrastructure spanning both sites and four operational rooms, integrating FabricPool tiering with the federated object storage into a single large system. However, the highly asymmetric expansion of object storage components led to technical challenges, particularly with the metadata database, which would have imposed severe limits on usable capacity without additional complex interventions.

To resolve these issues, both project partners agreed to segment the object storage system into multiple components, each tailored for specific use cases. As a result, the Tübingen site now operates three distinct object storage components:

- 10.5 PB FabricPool tiering for long-term storage, located locally within a single operations room (TU2).
- 2 × 2.1 PB geo-redundant object storage (replicated) across both data center rooms (TU1 and TU2), serving as a local object storage solution for the Tübingen site.
- 2.1 PB object storage component at TU1, allocated for federated use as part of the bwSFS-2 infrastructure.

This multi-component design enables the desired combination of long-term archival, local performance-optimized access, and federated sharing capabilities. It was achieved without incurring mutual technical limitations among the storage layers.

3 Research Data Management Services

To support sustainable research data management (RDM) with the bwSFS storage infrastructure, a set of complementary services has been developed to address the diverse use cases and requirements of participating projects. These use cases frequently include data deposit with version control, data sharing and publication, and the assignment of persistent identifiers to researchers, publications, institutions, and funded projects.

To ensure scalability and long-term sustainability, the software components built atop bwSFS should ideally leverage open-source technologies, open standards, and standardized interfaces. This approach increases abstraction from the underlying storage layer and fosters vendor independence. In addition to offering economic benefits, it simplifies long-term system maintenance by allowing individual hardware components to be replaced at the end of their lifecycle with minimal disruption.

While domain scientists typically define how data is stored and annotated with metadata, it is advisable to work with well-structured datasets referenced via inventories and protected using checksums. This is particularly important in the final stages of the data lifecycle, such as publication or archiving. Unless specific community standards dictate otherwise, using formats such as BagIt (Kunze et al., 2018) or OCFL (Jefferies et al., 2024) is recommended.

3.1 Galaxy Analysis Platform, de.NBI Cloud, and bwCloud-OS

The processing and analysis of data constitute a substantial portion of the research data lifecycle. The Galaxy analysis platform benefits from access to two types of storage. Combining both – augmented by intelligent tiering and caching – enables efficient use of infrastructure while maintaining high throughput. During active data processing, Galaxy primarily uses the A400 system of bwSFS (mounted via NFS and equipped with S3 tiering).

The de.NBI Cloud – Galaxy's compute backend – relies on a high-performance All-Flash AFF-A400 storage system to host NFS-mounted VM images and volumes. These virtual machines execute discrete analysis steps, which can be composed into complex workflows within Galaxy. The underlying storage serves mainly as a high-speed, temporary scratch space.

For delivering analysis results to users, Galaxy utilizes S3 object storage, currently via NetApp's FabricPool feature. In comparison to the scratch storage, this offers a higher degree of data protection through the use of erasure coding (EC 8+2). Long-term archiving and direct publication of datasets from within Galaxy also occur via this object storage layer. Target repositories for published datasets include systems like Invenio and Dataverse.

The high-performance POSIX-compliant storage infrastructure provided through additional funding is also utilized by bwCloud-OS to supply powerful virtual machines within an OpenStack-based cloud environment. Among the services built on this infrastructure are virtual machines operated by the NFDI consortium DataPLANT (Martins Rodrigues et al., 2021). These host services like the PLANT DataHUB (see Figure 3) and other tools supporting research data management in plant sciences. Large research datasets are likewise stored in the S3 object storage layer.

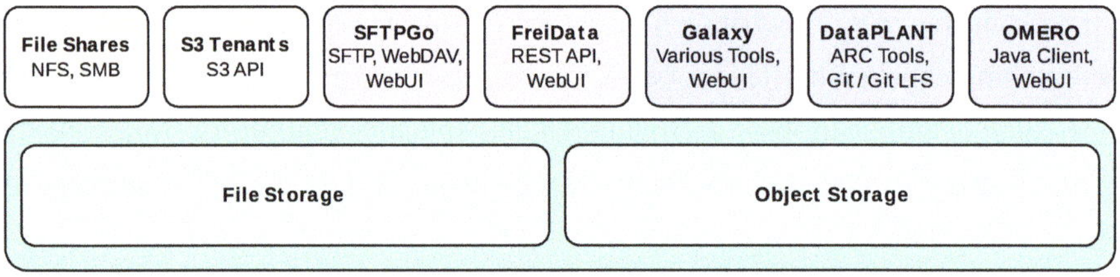

Figure 3: Higher level RDM Services ontop of bwSFS in Freiburg

3.2 Data Publication

Prominent services supporting the publication of research data include InvenioRDM, built on the Zenodo software stack. It is deployed in Tübingen[5] and in Freiburg under the name FreiData.[6] (Suchodoletz et al., 2022) InvenioRDM was selected as part of a statewide evaluation of data publication platforms conducted by the Science Data Centers of Baden-Württemberg (Axtmann et al., 2024).

InvenioRDM offers a user-friendly and customizable interface, supports the creation of domain-specific communities, and provides an OAI-PMH interface for harvesting. For DOI assignment, the system integrates with the DOI services of the respective university libraries. InvenioRDM natively supports the S3 protocol as its storage backend and leverages the geographically distributed S3 infrastructure of bwSFS. Pre-signed URLs are used to enable direct communication between clients and object storage, maximizing availability and performance. The extensive REST API of InvenioRDM enables seamless integration with third-party systems, such as a data publication workflow implemented for DataPLANT (Weil et al., 2023). Researchers can finalize and optionally

[5] FDAT data repository for the digital humanities, see https://fdat.uni-tuebingen.de, visited on 18.06.2025
[6] University data repository FreiData, https://freidata.uni-freiburg.de, visited on 18.06.2025

publish data packages generated by these workflows via the InvenioRDM web interface. These publication systems are not intended to replace existing repositories, but rather to complement them, offering local second copies or filling gaps in the current landscape.

Another widely used publication platform is Dataverse,[7] which underpins the DaRUS repository at the University of Stuttgart[8] and HeiDATA at Heidelberg University.[9] Like InvenioRDM, Dataverse offers an intuitive user interface, an OAI-PMH interface, and comprehensive APIs for automating processes. Datasets are organized into »Dataverse containers,« which can be individually configured with specific metadata fields and backend storage systems. Both S3-based and filesystem-based backends are supported. Direct upload and download features allow seamless integration with the bwSFS infrastructure for managing large datasets.[10] This capability enables research communities to utilize domain-specific metadata configurations alongside suitable backend storage systems.

As part of bwSFS-2, a direct interface to Dataverse-based systems such as DaRUS and Zenodo is under development. Through metadata schema mapping between bwSFS-2 and these repositories, low-barrier data publication with automated metadata ingestion will be supported.

3.3 Repository for High-Resolution Image Data

Additional research data management use cases driven by domain communities include the handling of large-scale image collections, such as those produced by high-resolution microscopy. The open-source image data management system OMERO provides user-friendly interfaces for accessing, visualizing, and interacting with microscopy image data. OMERO places a strong emphasis on preserving and enriching metadata associated with the images.

Through OMERO, researchers at participating universities gain the ability to manage the ever-increasing volume of microscopy data on top of the bwSFS storage infrastructure. Depending on the specific needs of research groups, OMERO instances can serve various purposes: as internal repositories for sensitive data, as collaborative platforms, or as

[7] See https://dataverse.org/, visited on 18.06.2025
[8] See https://darus.uni-stuttgart.de, visited on 18.06.2025
[9] See https://heidata.uni-heidelberg.de, visited on 18.06.2025
[10] See https://www.izus.uni-stuttgart.de/fokus/darus/bigdata, visited on 18.06.2025

publishing tools for presenting datasets publicly on websites or in scientific publications. Several instances are already in operation, maintained by the Signalling Campus, using NFS-based storage and potentially expanding to S3-based storage in the future.

3.4 Cross-Institutional Data Exchange

Many collaborations involving researchers using bwSFS require data exchange across institutional boundaries. While such exchange is technically feasible via the S3 object storage interface of bwSFS, it often demands deeper technical expertise in handling related tools and workflows.

To simplify this process, a service has been introduced that abstracts access to the object storage via SFTP and a web-based interface. The software SFTPGo enables efficient file exchange within a research group or with external collaborators at other institutions. At the time of writing, ten active SFTPGo instances are in operation at the Freiburg site.

3.5 S3-Based Data Archiving

To meet the requirements for data backup and secure long-term storage – particularly for unpublished data that must be retained in accordance with DFG guidelines but fall outside the scope of established repositories – S3-based archival services have now been implemented. This S3-based backup service introduces a »media discontinuity« by not being mounted as a standard filesystem, providing faster recovery times compared to local tape systems. It also forms the foundation for disaster recovery strategies, enabling the preparation of emergency infrastructures at remote alternative sites.

This service addresses the increasing demand for long-term retention and preservation of research data, typically for a minimum of ten years, and often with undefined retention periods pending transfer to formal archives. On the backend, this is handled by a federated object storage system, currently comprising two sites, and soon expanding to four.

3.6 Dedicated Storage Tenants in S3

To support the development of novel and specialized applications within scientific domains, bwSFS offers the flexibility of dedicated StorageGRID tenants for specific projects and research groups. At the IMTEK Simulation Lab, a research group led by Lars Pastewka, one of the main stakeholders of bwSFS, has developed a dtool-based data management framework. This framework implements the FAIR principles from an early stage in the data lifecycle, minimizing administrative overhead. (Hörmann et al., 2022, 2024) By providing an access layer on top of bwSFS S3, the framework enables data to be accessible, interoperable, and reusable by packaging data and descriptive metadata into self-contained dtool datasets. The dtool lookup server further enhances data discoverability by making data on a group-wide S3 object storage repository findable.

The dtool ecosystem has demonstrated its versatility in supporting both manual research data management and the rapid generation of thousands of datasets in automated workflows. Its key strengths, including simplicity, modularity, accessibility, and standardization via API, set it apart from other solutions and make it an ideal common denominator for cross-disciplinary research data management. Ultimately, the dtool ecosystem bridges the gap between unstructured data management approaches used by individuals and rigid FAIR platform solutions with strict metadata requirements, offering a flexible and efficient solution for research data management.

The IMTEK Simulation Lab also operates a public infrastructure for the surface topography community,[11] whose storage backend is the S3 object store of bwSFS. This cloud service incorporates management of topography (or surface roughness) data, including the publication of datasets and assignment of DOIs through DataCite. In addition to storing data, it is also possible to analyze topography data through bespoke workflows for statistical analysis and simulation tools, such as the boundary element method for contact mechanics. The cloud service currently hosts more than 23,000 individual surface topography measurements and over 200,000 workflow results.

[11] Public interface available at: https://contact.engineering, visited on 01.06.2025

3.7 Versioning and Sharing Data

At the University of Freiburg, a GitLab instance is used for versioning, collaboration, and sharing data and code of ongoing projects (Suchodoletz et al., 2023; Weil et al., 2023). In the context of DataPLANT, local extensions have been evaluated to handle large datasets and to enable their direct storage in the object storage system of bwSFS. As the service is integrated with the university's identity management system, as well as external providers like Elixir AAI and ORCID, a significant part of the complexity in managing users is already addressed – unlike in decentralized setups. This enables straightforward cooperative data access and supports horizontal collaboration across research groups.

3.8 Remote Access to NFS Storage Systems

To provide access to a broader user base, additional cache systems (NetApp HCI + FAS 2720) have been deployed at the Stuttgart and Konstanz sites and are connected to the main storage system via GRE tunnels. This addresses the challenge of increased latency due to the physical distance from the central storage – commonly known as the WAN problem. Using NetApp's FlexCache technology, frequently accessed data blocks are cached locally and asynchronously synchronized with the central system. Access conflicts are automatically resolved. As a result, users experience fast, low-latency access – even when NFS mounts point to remote volumes at the primary site. The cache systems have proven functional in practice, with performance measurements showing average latencies of less than 10 ms. This allows local data processing even from distant sites. However, an alternate workflow proved more common: scientific data are frequently processed not on local systems, but on remote platforms at major sites (e.g., de.NBI). In these cases, data transfers are executed directly on the main systems, resulting in low actual demand for the cache infrastructure.

3.9 Data Management in NEMO

As part of the bwHPC-S5 support project, the state of Baden-Württemberg funds a dedicated data management role associated with HPC systems, with a focus on supporting the interface between scientific computing and data handling. This includes managing so-called *workspaces* on NEMO. Workspaces serve as storage areas for research groups to manage data generated during HPC computations. By default, each group is assigned a 5 TB quota and an expiration date, along with certain requirements for the underlying storage system. In this case, the S3 object storage provided by bwSFS is used. The combination of the NetApp REST API and its S3 API allows workspaces to be automatically created, managed, and deleted after their expiration. Additionally, bwSFS provides high-performance transfer paths between storage and the HPC system. Its multi-tenant architecture allows individual research groups to fine-tune access control to their data using personal API keys and access control lists.

4 Summary and Outlook

After more than five years of planning and operation, bwSFS has fostered a broad landscape of research data management services built upon a robust and extensible technical base platform. This includes a range of services provided by NFDI domain consortia, such as DataPLANT and NFDI4BIOIMAGE. Researchers benefit from the proximity to HPC systems like BinAC and NEMO, as well as to infrastructures like bwCloud-OS, de.NBI, and Galaxy.

One area still lacking in user-friendly implementation is the provision of *dark archive* solutions – services that ensure secure data retention over a period of ten years without necessarily publishing the data. Additional challenges arise from the increasing adoption of AI methodologies, which rely on well-curated and technically accessible data corpora for training. Upcoming technical capabilities, such as Object Locks, will help meet the need for data immutability more effectively.

From its initial implementation as a joint effort between two universities, the system has now expanded to include four partners through the bwSFS-2 extension (Figure 4). This federated setup requires suitable organizational structures for coordinated governance, which are being established in early 2025 under the bwIT-AW.[12]

[12] bwIT-Allianz für die Wissenschaft (coordination office), https://uni-tuebingen.de/it/einrichtungen/zentrum-fuer-datenverarbeitung/bwit-aw/, visited on 18.06.2025

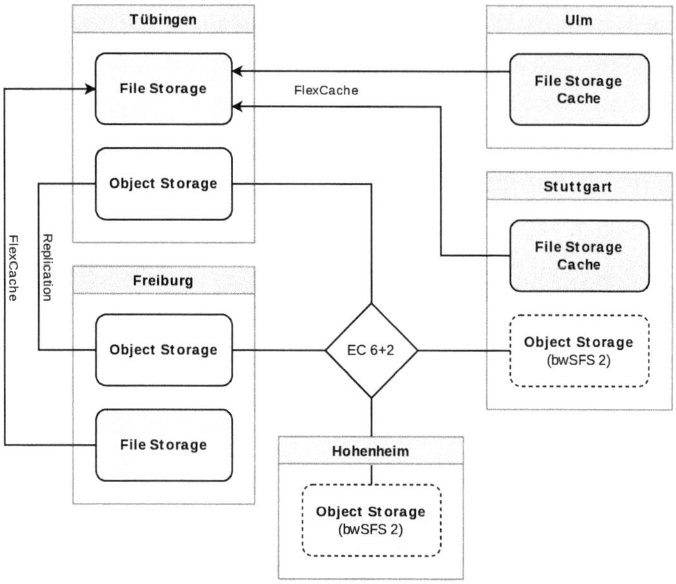

Figure 4: The bwSFS extended and improved architecture of bwSFS-2

Large-scale federated storage systems often depend, at least at some levels of integration, on vendor-specific solutions. While these provide certain technical advantages, they can also lead to long-term vendor lock-in or face discontinuation risks. Another challenge is aligning hardware lifecycle timelines, since many components now come with fixed-duration hardware support and software licensing. Nevertheless, a collaborative approach proves worthwhile, as it enables efficient storage with high geographic redundancy. This is achieved through geo-distributed erasure coding across the four participating sites, implemented within a jointly administered StorageGRID instance. Even in the event of a site failure or outage, data access remains unaffected – provided that the higher-level RDM services are equipped with appropriate failover and recovery mechanisms.

Acknowledgments

bwSFS is funded by the Deutsche Forschungsgemeinschaft (DFG, German Research Foundation) – 405998531, 405999126. The de.NBI/Galaxy extension and bwSFS-2 extension are made possible through BMBF grant 031 A538A and INST 41/1183-1 (LAGG) respectively. We further like to thank Baden-Württemberg state for the support of the bwHPC-S5 project.

Corresponding Author

Kolja Glogowski: kolja.glogowski@rz.uni-freiburg.de
eScience Abteilung, Rechenzentrum Albert-Ludwigs-Universität Freiburg,
Hermann-Herder-Str. 10, 79104 Freiburg, Deutschland

ORCID

Dirk von Suchodoletz https://orcid.org/0000-0002-4382-5104
Ulrich Hahn https://orcid.org/0000-0003-4471-9263
Markus Quandt https://orcid.org/0000-0002-2090-4782
Kolja Glogowski https://orcid.org/0000-0002-1361-5712
Mark Seifert https://orcid.org/0000-0002-1042-6107

References

Axtmann, A. et al. (2024). »Aufbau eines serviceorientierten und nachhaltigen Forschungsdatenmanagements - Aktuelle Überlegungen zur Strukturbildung im Bereich Forschungsunterstützung an den baden-württembergischen Universitäten«. In: *Bausteine Forschungsdatenmanagement* 1, pp. 1–20. DOI: 10.17192/bfdm.2024.1.8597.

Hörmann, J. L. and L. Pastewka (2022). »Lightweight research data management with dtool: A use case«. In: *Proceedings of the 7th bwHPC Symposium*. OPARU – Universitätsbibliothek Ulm. DOI: 10.18725/OPARU-46062.

Hörmann, J. L. et al. (2024). »dtool and dserver: A flexible ecosystem for findable data«. In: *PLOS ONE* 19.6. Ed. by S. R. Piccolo, e0306100. DOI: 10.1371/journal.pone.0306100.

Jefferies, N., R. Metz, J. Morley, S. Warner and A. Woods (2024). *Oxford Common File Layout - Specification*. Version 1.1.1. DOI: 10.5281/zenodo.14204936.

Kunze, J. A., J. Littman, L. Madden, J. Scancella and C. Adams (2018). *The BagIt File Packaging Format (V1.0)*. RFC 8493. DOI: 10.17487/RFC8493.

Martins Rodrigues, C., D. von Suchodoletz, T. Mühlhaus, J. Krüger and B. Usadel (2021). »DataPLANT – Ein NFDI-Konsortium der Pflanzen-Grundlagenforschung«. In: *Bausteine Forschungsdatenmanagement* (2). DOI: 10.17192/BFDM.2021.2.8335.

Suchodoletz, D. von, D. Brilhaus, M. Tschöpe and J. Bauer (2023). *GitLab as a tool for Research Data Management.* 1st Conference on Research Data Infrastructure (1st CoRDI), Karlsruhe, 12-14 September 2023. DOI: 10.5281/zenodo.10021180.

Suchodoletz, D. von, U. Hahn, J. Bauer, K. Glogowski and M. Seifert (2022). »Storage for Science - Aktueller Stand und anstehende Entwicklungen eines verteilten FDM-Systems«. In: *E-Science-Tage 2021: Share Your Research Data*. Ed. by V. Heuveline and N. Bisheh. Heidelberg: heiBOOKS, pp. 298–305. DOI: 10.11588/heibooks.979.c13741.

Suchodoletz, D. von, U. Hahn, B. Wiebelt, K. Glogowski and M. Seifert (2019). »Storage infrastructures to support advanced scientific workflows. Towards research data management aware storage infrastructures«. In: *Proceedings of the 5th bwHPC Symposium. HPC Activities in Baden-Württemberg*. Freiburg, September 2018. 5th bwHPC Symposium. Ed. by M. Janczyk, D. von Suchodoletz and B. Wiebelt. TLP, Tübingen, pp. 263–279. DOI: 10.15496/publikation-29058.

Suchodoletz, D. von et al. (2026). »bwSFS – A Federated Storage Backbone for Research Data Management. A Foundational Infrastructure for RDM Services«. In: *Proceedings of the 10th bwHPC Symposium. HPC Activities in Baden-Württemberg*. Freiburg, September 2024. 10th bwHPC Symposium. Ed. by M. Janczyk, D. von Suchodoletz, B. Wiebelt and M. Frank. KIT Scientific Publishing, Karlsruhe, pp. 247–263. DOI: 10.58895/ksp/1000169488-16.

Weil, H. L. et al. (2023). »PLANTdataHUB: a collaborative platform for continuous FAIR data sharing in plant research«. In: *The Plant Journal*, pp. 1–15. DOI: 10.1111/tpj.16474.